After the Fall

Other Works by Josephine Donovan:

Feminist Theory: The Intellectual Traditions of American Feminism
New England Local Color Literature: A Women's Tradition
Sarah Orne Jewett
Feminist Literary Criticism: Explorations in Theory (edited)

After the Fall

The Demeter-Persephone Myth in Wharton, Cather, and Glasgow

Josephine Donovan

THE PENNSYLVANIA STATE UNIVERSITY PRESS
University Park and London

Library of Congress Cataloging-in-Publication Data

Donovan, Josephine, 1941–
After the fall : the Demeter-Persephone myth in
Wharton, Cather, and Glasgow.

p.   cm.
Bibliography: p.
Includes index.
ISBN 0-271-00649-8
1. American fiction—20th century—History and criticism.
2. Women in literature.   3. Mothers and daughters in literature.
4. Demeter (Greek deity) in literature.   5. Persephone (Greek deity)
in literature.   6. Myth in literature.   7. Wharton, Edith,
1862–1937—Characters—Women.   8. Cather, Willa, 1873–1947—
Characters—Women.   9. Glasgow, Ellen Anderson Gholson, 1873–1945—
Characters—Women. I. Title.
PS374.W6D66 1989
813'.52'09352042—dc19   88–19490
                                                                      CIP

To
Ann Devigne Donovan

Contents

Acknowledgments

I would like to take this opportunity to thank the American Council of Learned Societies for providing me with a grant that enabled the completion of the book; and to acknowledge the contribution the following made to this study: Anne Barrett, Lucy Freibert, Barbara White, Philip Winsor, Eileen MacDonald, Nancy Sahli, the Reference/Interlibrary Loan staff of the University of New Hampshire (especially Jane Russell), Elizabeth Ammons, Marilyn Emerick, Kathleen Roos, my brother, sister, and parents, and my dogs, Rooney and Jessie.

Introduction

But golden-haired Demeter sat there apart from all the blessed gods and stayed, wasting with yearning for her deep-bosomed daughter. Then she caused a most dreadful and cruel year . . . over the all-nourishing earth: the ground would not make the seed sprout.

—Homeric hymn, "To Demeter," 7th century B.C.

The oldest and most complete extant version of the ancient Demeter-Persephone myth is the Homeric hymn "To Demeter," which is believed to date from the seventh century B.C. The Eleusinian mystery religion, of which this myth is the central text, dates back to the Early Mycenaean period (1580–1500 B.C.).

The hymn opens with Persephone playing in a flower-filled meadow apart from her mother, Demeter.[1] As she reached for a particularly "radiant" flower, the "earth yawned" and swallowed her up; thus she was "rapt away" by Aïdoneus [Hades], god of the underworld, also known as Pluto. Demeter frantically searched for her daughter; she "sped, like a wild-bird, over the firm land and yielding sea, seeking her child." Finally, on the tenth day Hecate told her that she suspected where Persephone was. Shortly thereafter Helios informed Demeter that "Hades seized her and took her loudly crying in his chariot down to his realm of mist and gloom." "[G]rief yet more terrible and savage came into the heart of Demeter." Her bitter sorrow cannot be assuaged; implacable, she cast a barren pall upon the earth. To end this plague Hades agreed with Zeus's request to release Persephone to her mother, but not before "secretly" giving her "sweet pomegranate seed to eat, taking care for himself that she might not remain continually with grave, dark-robed Demeter." Thus Persephone returned to Demeter. "And when Demeter saw them, she rushed forth as does a Maenad down some thick-wooded mountain, while Persephone . . . when she saw her mother's sweet eyes . . . leaped down to run to her, and falling upon her neck, embraced her." But Demeter suspected foul play; "her heart suddenly misgave her for some snare, so that she . . . asked [Persephone] at once: 'My child, tell me, surely you have not tasted any food while you were below?' " For if she has, she must forever spend a third of the year beneath the earth with Hades and two-thirds with Demeter.

Persephone answered that yes, Hades "secretly put in my mouth sweet food, a pomegranate seed, and forced me to taste against my will." She further related how the original abduction occurred: while gathering flowers with several other young women (one of whom was Artemis), she plucked a golden narcissus, whereupon the earth parted and Hades "bore [her] away, all unwilling, beneath the earth."

"So did they then with hearts at one, greatly cheer each the other's soul and spirit with many an embrace." Thereafter, Hecate became companion to Persephone, and Demeter allowed the "idle and utterly leafless" plain to put forth grain. "[A]s springtime waxed, it was soon to be waving with long ears of corn, and its rich furrows to be loaded with grain."

The Demeter-Persephone myth is singularly relevant to the historical transition that occurred in middle-class women's culture in the late nineteenth century in the Western world. It allegorizes the transformation from a matricentric preindustrial culture—Demeter's realm— to a male-dominated capitalist-industrialist ethos, characterized by growing professionalism and bureaucracy: the realm of patriarchal captivity.

Demeter represents the world of the mothers. It is a green world, "a ploughed field, a garden."[2] In the nineteenth century the goddess Diana was often used to represent her green-world arena. Indeed, Robert Graves theorizes in *The White Goddess* that early in their history the figures of Diana, the woodland goddess, and Demeter, the grain goddess, merged.[3] Both are aspects of the Great Goddess, also known as the "Lady of Wild Things,"[4] who expresses herself in different aspects at different times and places. In the Homeric hymn Artemis/ Diana was present in the meadow when Persephone was abducted but remained with her mother. Arcadian myth considered Artemis a sister of Persephone.[5] And C. G. Jung remarks that the Great Mother figure "also expresses itself as Cybele-Artemis."[6]

The Demeter-Diana-Persephone script is preeminent in United States women's literature of the late nineteenth and early twentieth centuries. Persephone represents the daughters who leave the sphere of the mothers and enter a period of patriarchal captivity, sealed by the eating of the pomegranate seed—which emblematizes the betrayal of the mothers.

In her pioneering analysis of the nineteenth-century "female world of love and ritual," Carroll Smith-Rosenberg remarks that "at the heart of this [female] world lay intense devotion and identification between mothers and daughters."[7] Numerous theorists have observed the "essential identity" between Demeter and Persephone in the ancient myth. As James Frazer notes in *The Golden Bough,* "the substantial unity of mother and daughter is born out by their portraits in Greek art, which are often so alike as to be indistinguishable."[8] C. Kerényi also sees the two as aspects of one godhead.[9] The women's identity is integral because the nonoedipal condition of women's traditional life is one of repetition and stasis: the daughter is mother of the daughter. There is no change, no progress, no development. "Thus," as Smith-Rosenberg points out, "daughters walked in their mothers' footsteps and mothers strove to impart their domestic skills and lore" (33).

But, in the late nineteenth century, for a variety of reasons—some of which are discussed in chapter 1—daughters were becoming restless. When "economic and intellectual change offered bourgeois daughters . . . viable alternatives to their mothers' domestic roles . . . generational conflict and criticism [began to] mar this unself-conscious intimacy. Then, however, daughters began to experience their mothers' lives as oppressive. . . . Harsh generational conflict broke forth as psychological factors compounded institutional change" (Smith-Rosenberg, 33).

A patriarchal pall is thus cast in the late nineteenth century, ensnaring daughters in ideologies of male supremacy that condemn the matricentric world of female bonding. During the last decades of the century,

> male politicians, aided by male physicians, sex reformers, and educators, launched a concerted political attack condemning female friendships as lesbian and separate female institutions— whether educational or political—as breeding places for "unnatural" sexual impulses. . . . They transformed women's private emotions into a public issue. . . . It is . . . [a] moment of male invasion and politicization. (Smith-Rosenberg, 35)

The moment is expressed allegorically in Hades's abduction of Persephone from the green world of her mother.

To the extent that middle-class daughters of the late nineteenth and early twentieth centuries willingly embraced the ideologies of the sexologists and scientists, to the extent that they identified with the male-supremacist dogma of the era, the "new women" willingly ate the pomegranate seed. Indeed, in Edith Wharton's version of the myth, a playlet entitled "Pomegranate Seed" (1912), Persephone is at least a half-willing victim, lured by promises of wider knowledge, of expanding horizons beyond the limited domestic sphere of the mothers.

The transition from the world of the mothers—Demeter's realm— to the world of the fathers—patriarchal captivity—is the central text of the major women realists of the early twentieth century: Edith Wharton, Willa Cather, and Ellen Glasgow. Indeed, it is a central preoccupation of their literary foremothers of the New England local-color school, especially Sarah Orne Jewett and Mary E. Wilkins Freeman, as I point out in my earlier study *New England Local Color Literature: A Women's Tradition* (1983).

This work, therefore, may be seen as a continuation of that study, the final chapters of which, "Sarah Orne Jewett and the World of the Mothers" and "Mary E. Wilkins Freeman and the Tree of Knowledge," point in the directions followed here.

A word on the organization of the book. In chapter 1 I examine the ideologies that contributed to the "fall" discussed in this study and propose some theories to explain the phenomenon; I also consider some of the works of such transitional women writers as Mary E. Wilkins Freeman and Charlotte Perkins Gilman. In chapter 2 I examine a "prelapsarian" novel, *A Country Doctor* by Sarah Orne Jewett, considering it as in part a response to the theories most destructive of nineteenth-century women's culture, those of Krafft-Ebing. Chapters 3 to 5 are devoted to each of the three writers—Wharton, Cather, and

Glasgow—treated in this study. I elected to devote a chapter to each (rather than synthesizing collective phases in their work) and to pro-ceed more or less chronologically through their works, principally because I wanted to operate as inductively as possible without impos-ing a prefabricated pattern upon them and to show the development of each writer's treatment of the myth; but also because I thought it would be more convenient for readers who are interested primarily in only one of the writers. Unfortunately, this structure may mean that readers will find the reidentification of the same issues in the three writers tedious. If so, I apologize but feel that other considerations outweigh whatever inconcinnity this organization may entail.

Also, while I believe it is clear that I am focusing mainly on white, middle-class women's culture in chapter 1, for reasons of stylistic econ-omy I do not always append qualifiers with each use of the term *women*.

While the central assumption of this study is that a writer's ideologi-cal moment is a paramount determinant of her thematics, it is appar-ent that personal, biographical factors do impinge. These three women had in common that they were childless; otherwise, their per-sonal situations varied. Wharton was married and divorced and had heterosexual affairs; Glasgow never married, had at least one major liaison with a man, but also had intense ties with other women. Cather was, it is now known, lesbian; she had several intense relationships with women. The extent to which such factors affect a writer's work is a complex matter, which I shall not dwell upon here. I do, however, offer occasional speculations in the course of this study about such influences; for example, I follow Cynthia Griffin Wolff's thesis that Wharton had a difficult relationship with her mother, but I contend, against Wolff, that Wharton's thematics are best explained by her ideological, not her personal, context (see page 47 below).

Because they shared the same gender, class, race, and intellectual milieu, these writers lived in the same ideological environment. I main-tain that it is largely this historical context that explains why each writer dwelt so centrally upon the Demeter-Persephone myth. In other words, while their relationships with their own mothers may have been problematic,[10] it is their historical relationship with their mothers' generation (especially of women writers) that determined their interest in the issues the myth entails.

One other biographical factor seems relevant and that is their rela-tionship to rural and urban cultures. Of the three, Wharton was almost wholly immersed in an urban environment, and therefore her vision of Demeter tends to be less agriculturally rooted than either Cather's or Glasgow's—though in certain works Wharton did evince a sympathy for the green world envisaged in women's utopian imagination. Both Cather and Glasgow moved to an urban center, New York, to further their careers, but for both the roots of creativity remained rural. Glasgow in fact returned to Virginia, and while Cather remained in New York, she spent much time in rural New England and in the Canadian Maritimes. Their visions of the Demeter-Persephone myth tend to be more authentically agricultural than Wharton's. The underlying mythic patterns are nevertheless the same in the works of all three writers, because, I contend, they reflect and refract the ideological transitions that occurred during the historical moment they shared.

Each writer focused on different phases of the myth at different times (a point explored in the text). All three writers came to maturity during a period when a male-supremacist ideology was in the ascendancy. Each writer, however, eventually returned to a feminocentric or matriarchal vision. The forms that this vision took and the timing of its expression varied in the three writers, reflecting perhaps the influence of personal experience, as well as the political events of their later careers: the two world wars and the depression. Nevertheless, each came to a realization of the inadequacy, indeed the destructiveness, of male-supremacist ideology, embracing in its stead a healing, matriarchal vision. Unlike that of their predecessors in the nineteenth century, however, theirs remained problematic.

Finally, I emphasize the local-color generation of American women writers as influences on Wharton, Cather, and Glasgow because they were their immediate generational predecessors in women's literary history and as realists they were taken more seriously by the twentieth-century writers than were the sentimentalists, who comprised the other major nineteenth-century women's school. This is not to suggest that no other literary influences operated on Wharton, Cather, and Glasgow; however, in terms of the thematics traced in this study—the Demeter-Persephone myth—the local colorists, especially Jewett and Freeman, were of paramount importance. Their version of the myth and its contrast to the twentieth-century women's treatment illustrates dramatically the historical cultural change between the generations.

Similarly, I have chosen to make my case by dwelling in detail on three prominent women writers rather than attempting to do a comprehensive survey of all the women writers of the period. These three women fall logically together as a group, I believe, because they are closely linked by gender, generation, class, race, nationality, literary tradition, and period, and by the not inconsequential fact that they were writers of genius.

1

Demeter's Garden Destroyed

And at dawn the garden lay in ruin, for all the tender plants she had torn up by the roots and trampled down, and all the stronger-rooted shrubs she had striven to kill with boiling water and salt.

—*Mary E. Wilkins Freeman, "Evelina's Garden" (1896)*

What Evelina destroyed that night, metaphorically, was the green-world bower of the nineteenth-century women's community. Marginal, segregated, male-less, a Demeter-Diana world of romantic friendship, it sustained a women's culture and provided the social basis for the primary female literary traditions of the time, domestic sentimentalism and local-color realism.

By the latter quarter of the century that community, with its diachronic (mother-daughter) and synchronic (woman-woman) women's traditions, had begun to disintegrate. Women writers who began their careers in the 1890s and whose major production came in the early twentieth century—Edith Wharton, Willa Cather, and Ellen Glasgow—came of age in a context radically different from that of their predecessors. They wrote in and about a world where the women's community no longer cohered, where the "mothers' gardens" had been destroyed, where women's cultural traditions—including the literary—were problematic, where, in short, an ideology of male supremacy had gained hegemony. The scorched-earth gesture of Evelina had left the next generation of women writers on "barren ground," the title of one of Glasgow's major works. This study approaches the fiction of these three writers from the thesis that their writings centrally concern the exodus of women from their mothers' gardens and their "fall" into the world of the fathers, the capitalist patriarchy of early twentieth-century America.

On January 8, 1840, Sarah Edgarton wrote to Luella J. B. Case, a woman with whom she was intimately and romantically involved, "I would be one of Diana's maids of honor."[1] Diana/Artemis, the Roman-Greek goddess of the woods, protector of wildlife and the young, was unmarried, uninterested in men, and accompanied by a coterie of female companions.[2] She symbolizes a dominant and ideal-ized life-style among nineteenth-century women. In the women's lit-erature of the period the Diana figure is recurrent: she prefers the company of women, rejects men, is often at home in nature and solitude, and chooses independence, or a career, over marriage. In-deed, in numerous works the intrusion of men into the Dianic bower is seen as poisonous.[3]

The treatment of the Diana theme by Wharton, Cather, and Glasgow illustrates how, by their time, attitudes had changed. In *The Age of Innocence* (1920) Wharton presents the Diana figure (May Welland) negatively as a victim of a forced and stultifying ignorance. "The realm of Diana" was for Wharton "chaste and rule-bound," the traditional sphere to which women had historically been restricted. Moreover, Wharton saw the Dianic realm as existing apart from the world of art, which was a male sphere, she felt, to which women were still denied entrance.[4] Cather and Glasgow also present important Diana-Demeter figures, Alexandra Bergson in *O Pioneers!* (1912) and Dorinda Oakley in *Barren Ground* (1925), but, while more positive than Wharton's, they nevertheless operate in isolation, without a consoling female commu-nity, and in a world that is alien and fallen.

Although the transition from the myth of an Edenic/Dianic women's community to that of a lapsarian, male-dominated world may be seen in a number of late nineteenth-century women's writings, it is most appar-ent in the works of New England local colorist Mary E. Wilkins Free-man.[5] "Evelina's Garden," for example, embodies the transition in two characters, who are cousins, each named Evelina. The older Evelina is a Diana-Demeter figure. She lives alone, rejects men (having herself ex-perienced a brief, failed romantic encounter), and devotes herself to her extraordinary garden. As Alice Walker suggested of her own mother's garden, it is Evelina's art.[6] Significantly, she is able to create it only in seclusion, only on the margins, in the wild zone, only in a sanctuary free from patriarchal intrusion.

The younger Evelina, representing a new generation of women, the daughter's generation, is a Persephone. She is attracted to a man but bound by the older woman's will, which stipulates that she never marry and that she continue to care for the garden. In the end the younger woman breaks the terms of the will, destroys the garden, and marries. The will demonstrates the effort made by the older generation—the "mothers"—to guard their daughters within the traditional sphere of Demeter and to keep a women's culture alive.

But the younger women were being lured away, primarily, as in the traditional myth of the fall, by the attraction of wider knowledge. For the first time in history, the late nineteenth-century generation of middle-class daughters had the opportunity of entering the world of public, patriarchal discourse. Institutions such as universities, to which women had previously been denied entrance, were gradually opening their doors. Women were adjusting their vistas, looking to broader horizons; the rural matricentral community was beginning to seem too restrictive, too limiting. And yet there was the fear (voiced by the traditional women, the mothers) that the new knowledge the younger women were winning would obliterate older feminine traditions.

As one observer noted in 1891:

> It is no new discovery that the eating of the fruit of the Tree of Knowledge produces disillusion, or that a whole range of instinctive perceptions disappears through the formal education of the brain. . . . If reason can only reign by the obliteration of primitive instincts, how can the learned woman think to retain her intuitions as well as her newly won education?[7]

The tension here is between "reason," or Apollonian, patriarchal discourse, and "primitive instincts" or "intuition," which we may appropriate to women's holistic epistemological traditions, the knowledge of Demeter. The fear is that the latter will give way to the former.

This concern reflects a minority group's worry that its customs will be lost through assimilation. By the early 1900s assimilation, or indoctrination to dominant white, patriarchal ways, was being accomplished primarily in the public schools. Native American women of the time hid their children from officials seeking to capture them and place them in federal boarding schools. An Indian mother explained: "It is not the Hopi way of caring for children, this tearing them from their homes and their mothers."[8] For, as a scholar of Indian women's writings points out, "American schooling disrupted the traditional pattern of Native American education, by interrupting mothers' training of their daughters, and by encouraging daughters to scorn the lessons their mothers could teach."[9] A similar concern existed among other mothers of the late nineteenth century.

Modern education has been primarily a "paternal project," designed "to claim the child, to teach him or her to master the language, the rules, the games and the names of the fathers."[10] As Nel Noddings argues in her excellent study of education, the "traditional curriculum" is "a masculine project, designed to detach the child from the world of relation" and propel her or him "into a thoroughly objectified world." The result is "the systematic dehumanization of both female and male children through the loss of the feminine" (193). Noddings states that the modes of "manipulative striving" (164) taught in the schools are those appropriate for the masculine (oedipal) project of detachment from the mother; relational, receptive, intuitive responses—those more appropriate to mother-daughter contiguity (on the model proposed by Nancy Chodorow)[11]—are scorned. The "voice of the mother," according to Noddings, is therefore missing in the public schools.

In the late nineteenth century daughters were being pulled away from mothers into a world dominated by "the language of the father" (Noddings, 1). Carroll Smith-Rosenberg remarks in a recent article, "The New Woman as Androgyne" (1985), that "college education" in the late 1800s "functioned to draw young women out of their mothers' and grandmothers' domestic mindset" (*Disorderly Conduct*, 253). They were trained "to think and feel 'as a man'" (252). Since public discourse at the turn of the century was becoming increasingly male supremacist, new women-daughters were being indoctrinated in misogynist ideologies.

The transformation being discussed here is part of the larger postmedieval shift away from local, folk, and craft-oriented practices and epistemologies toward the scientific, rationalist discourse of the Enlightenment. The women's resistance to this discourse, seen in the works of the justly named *local* colorists, reflects to an extent the voice of the anomalous particular refusing to be erased by the imperialist imperative of the scientific paradigm. For the pretensions to universality of scientific knowledge and its generalizing "mathematizing" character meant that differences and particularities were erased, subdued, dominated. As two modern critics remark, "in the impartiality of scientific language, that which is powerless has wholly lost any means of expression."[12] Or, as Sandra Harding notes in her recent feminist critique of science, "it is the scientific subject's voice that speaks with general and abstract authority; the objects of inquiry 'speak' only in response to what scientists ask them, and they speak in the particular voice of their historically specific conditions and location."[13]

Michel Foucault has argued that the growth of scientific and quasi-scientific disciplines and the practices of bureaucratic institutions is part of a larger extension of power, an ideological imperialism that has filled the vacuum left by the "death of the king," the autocratic institutions overthrown in the bourgeois revolutions of the eighteenth century. A process that Husserl identified as the "mathematisation of the world,"[14] it ended in what Foucault calls "the medicalization of the anomalous" (*la médicalisation de l'insolite*)[15]—"the great nineteenth-century effort in discipline and normalisation" (*Power/Knowledge*, 61). The primary vehicles for the imposition of this ideological dominance were the new breed of professionals, teachers, bureaucratic "experts," physicians, and sexologists. The latter "entomologized," to use Foucault's term (*Histoire de la sexualité*, 60), women's anomalous "world of love and ritual" into species and subspecies of deviance (see further discussion of sexologists' theories below and in chapter 2).

Thus, while women's domestic space had been more or less immune to the disciplines imposed upon public institutional space theretofore, by the late nineteenth century their world had been invaded and degraded by male professional authorities, particularly sexologists.

A classic story by Sarah Orne Jewett symbolizes the tension between the rural sanctuary of Demeter-Diana and the encroaching world of patriarchal hegemony. In "A White Heron" (1886) the Diana figure is a young girl, appropriately named "Sylvia" (the Latin word for woods). She lives comfortably in the green, preliterate world of the mothers. An urban ornithologist comes to her farm, seeking information about a rare white heron he hopes to kill and stuff for his collection. Sylvia knows (in a preverbal, preoedipal sense) where the bird is, and in the end refuses to reveal its whereabouts. Her decision is to remain silent.

She is nevertheless attracted by the intruder. She is intrigued by his scientific knowledge, his urban sophistication, and, to a lesser extent, his sexuality. He, on the other hand, represents patriarchal civilization: the world of literacy, scientific (as opposed to holistic, intuitive, nonanalytic) knowledge, industrialism, and imperialistic militarism (symbolized by his gun). He is interested in the young girl only for exploitative reasons: he wants to use her knowledge of the woods in order to kill the bird for "scientific" purposes. His intent is to colonize nature and ultimately the female sanctuary where Sylvia flourishes.

"A White Heron" is a reverse fairy tale in which "Cinderella" rejects the handsome prince in order to preserve her woodland sanctuary.[16] Significantly, in Grimm's version of the story, with which Jewett would have been familiar, the Cinderella figure had planted twigs on her mother's grave, out of which, "nourished by her tears of lamentation," grew a tree from which emerged "a white bird that [was] her mother's spirit."[17] The heron in Jewett's story is a similar representation. That the ornithologist wishes to kill it, to colonize it, is a symbolic expression of the confrontation that is occurring during this historical period between patriarchal civilization and the preliterate world of the "mothers."

The confrontation is further illuminated when regarded through the perspective provided by recent French feminists who follow French Freudian theorist Jacques Lacan. Lacan interpreted Freud's stages of childhood development, in particular the transition from the preoedipal to the oedipal state, as a "fall" from a blissful state of oneness with the Mother—an intransitive state of preliterate silence—into the transitive state of patriarchal language, which he calls "the Symbolic."[18] Hélène Cixous, one of the French feminists influenced by Lacan, notes, "as soon as we exist, we are born into language and language speaks (to) us, dictates its law, a law of death."[19]

Women—writers especially—in this perspective are faced with a dilemma: either they may remain in the prepatriarchal world of the Mother (the world of nature), which means they remain silent, or they enter the patriarchal world of language (culture) and are forced to submit to its misogynist exigencies. As Xavière Gauthier explains, women can "find 'their' place within the linear, grammatical, linguistic system that orders the symbolic, the superego, the law . . . a system based entirely upon the fundamental signifier: the phallus." Or, they can refuse to engage in the realm of the Symbolic, of patriarchal systems. This means, however, that they remain silent. And, "as long as women remain silent, they will be outside the historical process. But if they begin to speak and write *as. men do,* they will enter history subdued and alienated."[20]

At no point in women's history was this dilemma more acute than at the turn of the century, because it was then that bourgeois women genuinely had the option of entering patriarchal civilization, the realm of the Symbolic. Before that they had remained segregated in woman-centered communities that sustained separate nonoedipal cultural traditions.

Sylvia in "A White Heron" faces the dilemma. Either she can remain in a realm of preoedipal silence and preserve her maternal sanctuary, or she can speak, reveal the bird's location to the ornithologist, and thereby end its life. To save the bird (symbolically the "mother") means to sacrifice a relation with the ornithologist. But such a connection has already been presented in the story as one of submission. When Sylvia and the stranger search the woods for the bird, "she did not lead the guest, she only followed, and there was no such thing as speaking first."[21] The price of patriarchal knowledge is submission to male direction. That Sylvia learns implicitly.

In the end Sylvia remains silent.

> No, she must keep silence! What is it that suddenly forbids her and makes her dumb? . . . The murmur of the pine's green branches is in her ears, she remembers how the white heron came flying through the golden air and how they watched the sea and the morning together, and Sylvia cannot speak; she cannot tell the heron's secret and give its life away.[22]

Sylvia prefers to remain in the wild zone, in the prelapsarian, preliterate, preoedipal world of the mothers, which by her gesture, a decade before Evelina, she saves.

Other aspects of this historical tension are illuminated in stories by Freeman. "Old Woman Magoun" (1905) brings out the Demeter-Persephone dimension of the mother-daughter connection during this period. In this tragic story the mother figure is actually a grandmother, old woman Magoun, who has brought up her granddaughter, Lily, from infancy. The old woman detests men and will not allow them in her home. When the girl's father comes to claim her, in order, the old woman thinks, to sell her into prostitution, the grandmother is faced with the problem of how to keep the girl in the mothers' world, to prevent her abduction to the world of the fathers, which she per-

ceives as worse than death. The old woman, like Demeter, is in competition with a patriarchal figure analogous to Hades, god of the underworld and death, over Lily-Persephone. The old woman uses her
women's herbal knowledge perversely to retain the girl; she allows her
to eat the poisonous berries of the deadly nightshade plant, which
causes her death. The old woman projects that the girl will meet her
mother in heaven, "a beautiful place, where the flowers grow tall,"
another image of Demeter's garden.[23] Persephone's fate had also been
sealed by eating, in her case the seeds of the pomegranate.

Another Greek myth relevant here is that of Daphne, a follower of
Artemis, who was turned into a laurel by (in some accounts) her
mother, Earth, in order to help her escape a rape attempt by—
significantly—Apollo (Rose, 141). Lily may be appropriated to
Daphne, the old woman to Mother Earth, and the father to Apollo.
Once again the mythical figures allegorize the "rape" by Apollonian
discourse of the women's realm.

Elizabeth Ammons and Sarah W. Sherman have recently suggested
that the central characters of Sarah Orne Jewett's *Country of the Pointed
Firs* (1896), Almira Todd and the unnamed narrator, who is a younger woman writer, may be seen also as (less grim) examples of
Demeter-Persephone. Ammons notes, "Jewett's modern-day earth
mother, a supernaturally attuned and yet ultra-earthbound Demeter,
makes the world bloom for her disinterred 'daughter' up from the
city." Significantly, one of the herbs associated with Demeter was pennyroyal, Mrs. Todd's favorite plant, which suggests that Jewett may
have consciously intended the Demeter identification.[24]

Since the younger urban woman in *Pointed Firs* is a writer, her situation is particularly relevant. The "plotless" plot[25] of the work involves
the writer's return one summer to the world of the mothers for
reinspiration, to reconnect with its ancient feminine rituals enacted by
herbalist-witch Almira Todd. But the author only visits the preliterate,
prepatriarchal rural area of Mrs. Todd. She cannot stay. She can only
attempt to give voice to its culture. Jewett herself was able to do so, but
her generation was the last so empowered. Wharton, Cather, and Glasgow are much more ambivalent toward the gardens of Demeter.

Other "mothers" in Freeman stories attempt like old woman Magoun
and the older Evelina to keep their daughters home. In "The Long
Arm" (1895) an older motherly partner in a lesbian-couple relationship
murders a man who courts her younger lover/daughter. "A New England Nun" (1887), Freeman's most celebrated story, presents a classic

Diana-Demeter whose housework, as Marjorie Pryse has pointed out,[26] has become a form of art, and who preserves her home as a sanctuary against a male intruder/suitor. As in all Freeman stories her gesture is presented ambivalently; the perspective of the daughter is present: Louisa Ellis's life is seen as painfully restricted, like the dog chained in the backyard or the bird she keeps caged.

Two poignant stories further illustrate Freeman's handling of the issue. One is "Arethusa" (1900) and the other "A Poetess" (1891). The classical Arethusa myth is similar to that of Daphne. Arethusa was "a follower of Artemis," "would have nothing to do with men," and loved "the freedom of the forest."[27] Trying to escape from Alpheus, the river god, she prays to Artemis to save her. The goddess obligingly changes her into a spring. In Freeman's story Arethusa is shy and reclusive, wants to remain with her mother and not marry. "I don't like men," she claims, "I am afraid of them. I want to stay with you."[28] She spends much time in communion with the arethusa flower, which grows only in a sheltered, hidden area of a nearby swamp, another image of the female sanctuary.

Arethusa finally agrees reluctantly to marry, but on the day of her wedding she is missing. They find her on one last visit to the swamp flower. She goes through the motions of marriage; she even bears children, but her heart remains in that secluded bower, to which every spring she makes a ritual pilgrimage. Her husband indulges this as a whim, never "dreaming that it had its root in the very depths of her nature, and that she perhaps sought this fair neutral ground of the flower kingdom as a refuge from the exigency of life."[29] This story shows how marginal the Dianic green world had become: it can only be entered periodically; much of Arethusa's year is spent like Persephone's, in patriarchal captivity.

An even more moving story is "A Poetess." This work opens with an image of a secluded garden, "all a gay spangle with sweet-peas and red-flowering beans, and flanked with feathery asparagus."[30] It is the green-world bower of Betsey Dole, an impoverished, half-starved spinster whose calling is writing poetry. The art she creates is occasional mourning verse, written primarily for neighbor women whose children have died. Her reward is the consolation it brings her friends. Their praise is to her "as if her poem had been approved and accepted by one of the great magazines. She had the pride and self-wonderment of recognized genius" (150). After Mrs. Caxton enthuses over a poem Betsey had written to commemorate her dead son,

Betsey returns home "buoyantly . . . there was no one to whom she could tell her triumph, but the hot spicy breath of the evergreen hedge and the fervent sweetness of the sweet-peas seemed to greet her like the voice of friends" (150). Betsey's art does not enter the mainstream of patriarchal discourse, but rather, privately printed and circulated among a circle of women, it remains within the Dianic enclave, which nourished and enabled it.

This idyll is destroyed, however, when a local minister, a patriarchal authority, condemns Betsey's work as sentimentalist trash. Unfortunately, she accepts his judgment and burns all her work. "Betsey had never had any lover, but she was burning all the love-letters that had passed between her and life" (155). Comparing herself to her pet canary, she asks "if it's fair": "Had I ought to have been born with the wantin' to write poetry if I couldn't write it—had I? . . . Would it be fair if that canary-bird there, that ain't never done anything but sing, should turn out not to be singin'? . . . S'pose them sweet-peas shouldn't be smellin' the right way?" (155).

Broken by the weight of patriarchal opprobrium, Betsey dies, asking that the ashes of her poetry be buried with her, and worse, that the minister, himself a would-be poet, write a "good" commemorative poem about her. Significantly, the final image in the story is of the bird who "began to chirp. He chirped faster and faster until he trilled into a triumphant song" (159). As Ann Romines remarks in a perceptive analysis of this story, "the canary's song is a triumph of nature— his own nature, which has never been questioned or violated. But Betsey Dole's finally triumphant *silence* is a product of . . . culture."[31]

The complex relationship between the woman artist and patriarchal culture is fully raised in this story. Unlike Sylvia, for whom silence is a choice, Betsey has it forced upon her by an intruding patriarchal aesthetic. Where earlier women figures were able to live contentedly inviolate in the green-world bower, and to create art within its confines (both the sentimentalist and the local-color traditions of the nineteenth century were largely female, both in authorship and readership), Betsey cannot. This story, published at the turn of the nineteenth century, illustrates the increasingly problematic relationship between women artists and the world of public discourse, now dominated by New York rather than feminized Boston. (Freeman herself was the first of the local colorists to deal primarily with a New York–based publisher, Harper; Wharton, Cather, and Glasgow all lived in and published through New York firms.)

On the other hand, Betsey Dole could have chosen to write "good" poetry; she could have chosen to write material that was acceptable by patriarchal standards. But that, too, would have meant a silencing of her own authentic feelings, of the emotions she shared with her neighbor women, emotions that were put down by the minister-patriarch as sentimental. As Mary Jacobus has noted, "access to a male-dominated culture may equally be felt to bring with it alienation, repression, division—a silencing of the 'feminine,' a loss of women's inheritance."[32] Wharton, Cather, Glasgow—all engaged in "a silencing of the 'feminine,'" at least in their early works. They did so because "women's access to discourse involves submission to phallocentricity, to the masculine and the Symbolic: refusal, on the other hand, risks re-inscribing the feminine as a yet more marginal madness or nonsense."[33] In the early twentieth century these women realists chose (not without ambivalence) the former course.

In order to understand fully the identity of Wharton, Cather, and Glasgow as *women* artists and their art as *women's* art, it is necessary to develop a theory of the female artist. Such a construction can only be adumbrated at this point in the development of feminist critical theory. But it seems that a vital element in the inspiration and articulation of women's art has been the role of the mother and the mother's garden. Jane Marcus notes that the young Virginia Woolf found "her mother's praise made her feel ecstatic." Woolf said it was "like being a violin and being played upon." Marcus finds "this metaphor, with its consciousness of the mother-daughter erotic and its conception of the unawakened artist as a stringed instrument that waits for the expert hand to lift the bow . . . perhaps the perfect figure to express the relationship between the woman artist and a mother/mentor."[34]

Betsey Dole was similarly animated by her friend's praise. The erotic connection is suggested by the "hot spicy breath of the evergreen hedge and the fervent sweetness of the sweet-peas" that greeted her on her return home. As Marcus notes elsewhere, "the discourse of Artemis is pure, savage, and antiurban, signifying both selfhood and sisterhood and a powerful sexuality in virginity. Artemisian discourse is directed against male desire."[35] A similar connection existed between the mother-mentor and the writer in *The Country of the Pointed Firs*. During this period Artemesian discourse was becoming increasingly difficult, however, and the identity of woman as artist increasingly problematic, as "A Poetess" indicates.

Women writers have always had to deal with the authority of patriarchal traditions in literature, as Sandra Gilbert and Susan Gubar, among others, have pointed out. Yet, they have always needed or sought to construct a female tradition of their own. They have sought out female antecedents. In some cases (notably in black women's literature, as Mary Helen Washington and Barbara Christian have remarked), the antecedents may be literally mothers and not really writers, though artists in their own way.[36] Mary Kelley has suggested that the sentimentalist women writers anxiously sought to find ancestor or relative women artists also to establish a female literary lineage.[37] The local colorists formed a ready female tradition whose ancestry is traced in my *New England Local Color Literature*.

As these examples show, the nature of and necessity for a female literary tradition have probably varied at different points in history. Yet, it appears that women's art is in some fundamental way linked with maternal inspiration, with maternal-lesbian passion. The muse remains female—even for women.

The terrible problem faced by early twentieth-century women writers was that the mother's domain was becoming increasingly seen as a restrictive, confining realm, one that cramped creativity rather than inspired it. Edith Wharton in particular railed against the mother-world, fearing confinement there, fearing maternal control, fearing the muteness it engendered. For Wharton the female Dianic realm was posed in opposition to the world of art, a patriarchal enterprise to which she demanded equal access.

At its worst the sphere of the mother had been ruled in the nineteenth century by the debilitating ideology of "true womanhood," which held that a proper woman is weak, passive, submissive, and domestic. Most of all she defers to others and is never so selfish as to take up a pen of her own. Clearly, twentieth-century women saw, this "angel" had to be "killed" before women could write. From the point of view of true womanhood, to be a woman and to be a writer was a contradiction in terms.

To the extent that late nineteenth-century "mothers" were governed by this ideology, they were fair game for the "daughters'" rebellions. But, unfortunately, the daughters also tended to reject as well an entire complex of feminine traditions, ways of seeing and being that could have been (and were in some nineteenth-century women's literature, particularly the local colorists') counterhegemonic. They rejected a tradition that was in effect what Foucault has labeled the *"insurrection of subjugated knowledges" (Power/Knowledge, 81)*.

While their repudiation of this tradition remained ambivalent (Ellen Moers points out that the "theme of maternal seduction" domi-
nates women's literature of the early twentieth century),[38] women
writers of the time came to identify with patriarchal literary traditions
as never before. They began to identify themselves as "male professionals," which meant rejecting the feminine models of their foremothers as vulnerable and weak, as inferior.

In a recent and insightful analysis of Charlotte Perkins Gilman's
archetypal story "The Yellow Wallpaper" (1892), Paula A. Treichler
interprets it in terms of the dilemma of the woman writer of the time
who was caught between an inherited patriarchal discourse, on the
one hand, but unable to break through to the "visionary" style, on the
other, that would have enabled authentic expression of women's subjugated knowledge.

The story (which pits a cloistered woman against a male "scientific
expert," her husband, who is a physician) involves the woman's confinement to a room with wallpaper that eventually becomes the subject of her obsessive interest. In the end the protagonist is determined
to strip the wall of the paper in order to reveal the woman she believes
is trapped inside.

Treichler contends that "unveiled, the wallpaper is a metaphor for
women's discourse,"[39] which has been erased by the dominant patriarchal discourse imposed by scientific authority. The woman's effort is to
"escape the sentence"—the title of Treichler's article—imposed upon
her: both the scientific-disciplinary sentence of being confined to the
margins in a state of "madness" and the sentence received as appropriate literary style (*inventio*) in patriarchal poetics. Treichler writes:

> I interpret the wallpaper to be women's writing or women's
> discourse, and the woman in the wallpaper to be the representa-
> tion of women that becomes possible only after women obtain
> the right to speak. In this reading, the yellow wallpaper stands
> for a new vision of women—one which is constructed differ-
> ently from the representation of women in patriarchal lan-
> guage. The story is thus in part about the clash between two
> modes of discourse: one powerful, "ancestral," and dominant;
> the other new, "impertinent," and visionary. (64)

The ancestral "dominant" discourse is, I suggest, that of the scientific
disciplines imposing hegemony over women's worlds at the end of the

models of the norm, is an expression of the increasing valorization of the masculine (or what Ann Douglas called a "militant crusade for masculinity")[43] that occurred in the late nineteenth century. This reassertion of male supremacy was a response to both the liberal and cultural wings of feminism. Both were seen as threatening: the liberal because it challenged the notion of the separate spheres, promoting as it did the entrance of large numbers of women into traditionally masculine occupations; and the cultural because it promised a feminization of the public world. Basil Ransom articulated this fear in Henry James's novel *The Bostonians* (1886) when he lamented, "the whole generation is womanized; the masculine tone is passing out of the world."[44]

He need not have worried, however, for the "masculine tone" was reasserted with a vengeance in the latter quarter of the nineteenth century. Two ideological forces contributed to this development. One was what Jonathan Katz has called "the invention of heterosexuality," a whole complex of prescriptions introduced by late nineteenth-century sexologists, eventually codified by Freud and particularly his followers into what Charlotte Perkins Gilman labeled a "revival of phallic worship."

The second was the assertion of the superiority of the male and of masculine traits and activities, such as war, in the theories of Charles Darwin and the social Darwinists. The extremes that this unappealing philosophy reached in the years preceding World War I are illustrated in the Italian Futurist Manifesto of 1909:

> We are out to glorify war:
> The only health-giver of the world!
> Militarism! Patriotism!
> The Destructive Arm of the Anarchist!
> Ideas That Kill!
> Contempt for Women![45]

This artistic manifesto was put out by the Young Turk modernists who were in the early years of the century breaking away from what were seen as decadent, genteel, feminized traditions in the arts. Such a reassertion of artistic "manhood" required, as evidenced in the manifesto, a contempt for the feminine-maternal. This was the dominant cultural mood when Wharton, Cather, and Glasgow came of age as artists.

In Ellen Glasgow's *They Stooped to Folly* (1929) a character comments that her intense relationship with another woman had happily occurred "before the serpent of Freudian psychology had poisoned the sinless Eden of friendship."[46] This observation signifies the extent to which female friendship had by that time become suspect, and how an awareness of sexuality had cast an evil pall upon it.

The process of what Lillian Faderman has labeled "the morbidification of female friendship" occurred in the last decades of the nineteenth century.[47] In her now classic analysis "Smashing: Women's Relationships before the Fall" (1979) (which inspired the title and was the original impetus for this study), Nancy Sahli attributes the demise of "romantic" friendship between women to the advent of sexologists' notions that, as an expression of "inverted sexual instincts," such relationships were degenerate and deviant. Subsequent studies, such as Faderman's, have reinforced the Sahli thesis.[48]

While Carl von Westphal invented the idea of the "congenital female invert" in 1869, it was Richard von Krafft-Ebing's *Psychopathia Sexualis* that was the most influential in popularizing the idea of female deviancy in this country. His work, first published in Germany in 1882, appeared in an American edition in 1886. Krafft-Ebing labeled as deviant and degenerate a whole series of female behaviors that today we do not necessarily associate with sexual intimacy between women. The *Psychopathia* is indeed an antifeminist bible, characterizing as "unnatural" any female behavior that does not serve male needs: "In woman voluntary subjection to the opposite sex is a physiological phenomenon. Owing to her passive *rôle* in procreation and long-standing social conditions, ideas of subjection are, in woman, normally connected with the idea of sexual relations."[49] Leaving aside the astonishing assertion that women's role in procreation is passive, it should be noted that Krafft-Ebing's central point in the *Psychopathia* is that any woman who does not conform to the above stereotype exhibits "antipathic sexuality," which he further claims is usually a sign of hereditary degeneracy.

Particularly degenerate are women who love other women and women who are inclined toward traditional male roles (thus rebutting both cultural and liberal feminism). Case #130 illustrates his rather narrow notion of deviance. As a youth "Mrs. X" preferred boys' sports; as an adult, "when attending the first and only ball she felt interest only in intellectual conversation, but not in dancing or the dancers."[50]

While today most of Krafft-Ebing's ideas seem ludicrous, they then provided the rationale for an ideology that effectively destroyed the nineteenth-century Dianic world of female friendship. By the turn of the century Havelock Ellis's *Sexual Inversion* (1897), and later Freud's speculations on female sexuality, cemented the tomb. In 1900 Dr. William Lee Howard's fairly typical view shows the extent to which sexologist ideology was an antifeminist backlash: "The female possessed of masculine ideas of independence; the viragint who would sit in the public highways and lift up her pseudo-virile voice, proclaiming her sole right to decide questions of war or religion . . . and that disgusting antisocial being, the female sexual pervert, are simply degrees of the same class—degenerates."[51]

Havelock Ellis was particularly suspicious of feminists and career women, whose lives in the work world, independent of husbands and households, left them exposed to lesbianism, by then perceived as a monstrosity against nature. "[H]aving been taught independence of men and disdain for the old theory which placed women in the moated grange of the home to sigh for a man who never comes, a tendency develops for women to carry this independence still further and to find love where they find work."[52] As Nancy Sahli summarized, however, because there was such "pressure against the intense, emotional, sensual, even sexual commitment between women that had existed without censure during the earlier part of the century . . . we can reasonably expect that many women adjusted their behavior to conform to the new standards" (25).

A novel, appropriately entitled *We Sing Diana* (1928), by Wanda Fraiken Neff conveniently illustrates the change in attitudes toward friendships between women that occurred in the pre–World War I years. In 1913 the protagonist was a student at a women's college where romantic friendships and crushes between women were the norm. When she returns in 1920 to the same school as a teacher, she finds that students are fully conversant with the new sexologist—particularly Freudian—discourse, and fully aware of sexuality. As a result "intimacies between two girls were watched with keen, distrustful eyes . . . one ridiculed their devotions."[53]

Thus, while the sexologists "resexualized" women in the early years of the twentieth century, that process required a denigration of lesbian relationship and a promotion of heterosexuality as the norm. As such, the sexologist contribution in effect recolonized women as dependents of men. George Chauncey, Jr., notes, "the increasing denigration of single sex institutions and relations and the new urgency attached to the development of women's relations with men in the 1910s and twenties constituted . . . a veritable 'Heterosexual Counterrevolution.' "[54] For "the new celebration of heterosexual bonding and the increasing hostility to homosexual relations between women evident in both the medical literature and the general culture were central to the general subversion of women's culture and solidarity" by the 1920s (144).

One result of the "Heterosexual Counterrevolution" was the flapper, "at once both sexually precocious and profoundly heterosexual" (144). Charlotte Perkins Gilman, still in the 1920s a powerful feminist voice, saw flapperism correctly as a new form of female subjugation. In 1923 she wrote, "it is sickening to see so many of the newly freed using their freedom in a mere imitation of masculine vices."[55] "No prisoned harem beauty, no victim of white-slavery, no dull-eyed kitchen drudge is so pitiful as these 'new women,' free, educated, independent, and just as much the slaves of fashion and the victims of license as they were before."[56]

Another result of the counterrevolution was the idea of the companionate marriage. This concept brought assimilationism into the bedroom. Men and women were declared similar and equal in sexual desire; marital sex was therefore perceived (in theory) as a partnership between equals. In reality, however, as Christina Simmons discovered, "despite the alleged equality of partnership in companionate marriage, male sexual leadership remained the norm."[57] Indeed, "exponents of companionate marriage" came to judge "women's sexuality acceptable only insofar as its energy was channeled into marriage and the service of men" (58). By 1929 a medical authority associated "lesbianism with a rejection of women's natural, subordinate role within heterosexual activity" (57).

By the 1920s therefore the ideology of the sexologists was firmly entrenched; love between women was seen as subversively deviant, and heterosexuality, with women in subordinate roles, had gained supremacy; the nineteenth-century women's culture, and with it the feminist movement, had been effectively destroyed.

The last gasp of cultural feminism was seen in the women's peace movement of the early twentieth century.[58] These feminists were responding to the growing endorsement of war as a healthy masculine activity and the concomitant growth in militarism that preceded World War I. As Jacques Barzun notes, "No one who has not waded

through some sizeable part of the literature of the period 1870–1914
has any conception of the extent to which it is one long call for
blood."[59]

A primary source of this pro-militarist ideology was social Darwinism, which managed to promote male supremacy, war, and capitalist
imperialism as necessary to the progress of the human species. Darwin's *Descent of Man*, which first appeared in 1871, does not explicitly
endorse war or capitalism, but it does enunciate a doctrine of male
superiority. Subtitled *Selection in Relation to Sex*, the work concentrates
on Darwin's theory of sexual selection, which worked, he believed, as
an adjunct to natural selection in effecting the evolutionary "descent
of man" from "some pre-existing form."[60]

The basic theory outlined in this work is that species progress
through the sexual selection of those males who are best equipped to
capture and retain females. (Darwin assumes a fundamental combat
among males for the female.) Those who win the fight win the female
and thus have more progeny. "Generally the less successful male . . .
fails to obtain a female, or obtains a retarded and less vigorous female . . . or, if polygamous, obtains fewer females; so that they leave
fewer, less vigorous, or no offspring" (242). Thus, "the law of battle
for the possession of the female appears to prevail throughout the
whole class of mammals" (575).

Two aspects of this theory deserve special attention. One is that the
advantages accrued by the victorious male descend only to male progeny. And, second, the entire process has meant that human males are
now superior to females.

On the first point Darwin gives as an example a male insect who has
developed superior sensory, locomotive, and prehensile organs. This
male has the advantage over his rivals. "[I]n such cases the males have
acquired their present structure not from being better fitted to survive in the struggle for existence, but from having gained advantage
over other males, and from having transmitted this advantage to their
male offspring alone" (225).

In humans advantageous characteristics include not just prehensile
organs but also intelligence, courage, and creativity. As a conse-
quence, these traits, descending through the male line, have made the
human male mentally superior to the female. In a section entitled
"Differences in the Mental Powers of the Two Sexes," Darwin makes
this quite clear. Men have developed "higher mental faculties, namely,
observation, reason, invention, or imagination," traits which have

been "transmitted chiefly to the male offspring" (587). "The higher powers of the imagination and reason," which "have been developed in man, partly through sexual selection—that is, through the contest of rival males, and partly through natural selection," "have been transmitted more fully to the male than the female offspring" (588). "Thus man has ultimately become superior to woman" (588).

It is not difficult to see how Darwin's theory became transcribed as social prescription. In social Darwinism the race was seen as furthered by the aggressive, competitive warrior activities of "superior" males. Herbert Spencer, one of its principal exponents, concluded that wars, however horrible, were a mechanism for social progress. "[W]e must . . . admit that without [war] the world would still have been inhabited only by men of feeble types sheltering in caves and living on wild food."[61] (Cultural feminists were quick to point out the obvious flaw in Spencer's logic; as Charlotte Perkins Gilman noted, even within Darwinian premises, it is clear that war "eliminates the fit, and leaves the unfit to perpetuate the race!")[62] American capitalists, such as J. D. Rockefeller and Andrew Carnegie, seized upon social Darwinism as ideological license to pursue their machinations ruthlessly.[63] David Parry's 1906 novel, *The Scarlet Empire*, even presented the view that democracy was an effeminate check on healthy imperialist exertions: "This damnable Democracy . . . is throttling the manhood of our entire race."[64]

Scholars have now identified the bully-boy, breast-beating rhetoric of social Darwinism as the sign of a severe "masculinity crisis" that occurred in Western culture around the turn of the century. Theodore Roszak, in reviewing the literature of the period, notes its "obsessive glorification of toughness" (93). Theodore Roosevelt's advocacy of the "strenuous life"; the growing naturalism in literature where "reality [is] held to be . . . crude, rapacious, and torn by bestial struggle" (90); the advent of a Bismarckian *realpolitik* in foreign affairs; and the apotheosis of figures like Roosevelt, Cecil Rhodes, and Houston Chamberlain, who saw themselves as "great predators . . . for whom the world is a jungle, a battleground, a gladiatorial arena" (91)—all were facets of the same promotion of pugnacious "manhood." This bellicose "blood and iron" worldview culminated not just in World War I but also in the "chauvinist metaphysics of Fascism and Nazism," which similarly attempted to "ennoble violence . . . [and] to cheapen compassion and tenderness" (93).

Like Roszak, Joe Dibbert sees this promotion of aggressive masculinity as a response to the threat of the nineteenth-century women's movement. In an article entitled "Progressivism and the Masculinity Crisis," Dibbert notes, "one of the by-products of the present . . . redis-covery . . . of the 'woman problem' is the simultaneous discovery of a crucial identity crisis for the American male during the period 1880–1920."[65] American men "by the late nineteenth century were becom-ing increasingly fearful of female moral, social, and cultural pre-eminence, to say nothing of growing female interest in politics" (445).

Progressivism was not just a reform movement. It paralleled aspects of modernism as an assertion of a supposedly healthy, vigorous man-hood against what was seen as a feminized, degenerate past. Dibbert also remarks that Theodore Roosevelt symbolized this spirit; he was seen as "successfully rescuing the American male from a threat of too much femininity" (452). Particularly interesting is Dibbert's discussion of male athletics, which became seen as the "only place where masculine supremacy is incontestible" (*Independent*, 1909). Feminist attempts to have boxing and football abolished were roundly rebuffed as examples of the corrupting feminine influence (446).

The feminists themselves launched a powerful counterattack on social Darwinism, beginning in 1875 with Antoinette Brown Black-well's *The Sexes throughout Nature*. In 1884 Sarah Orne Jewett at-tempted to subvert some of its tenets in her novel *A Country Doctor*. The most important articulations of the feminist position were, how-ever, Eliza Burt Gamble's *The Evolution of Woman, an Inquiry into the Dogma of Her Inferiority to Man* (1893) and Charlotte Perkins Gilman's *Women and Economics* (1898).[66] But theirs were voices lost in the wind. The ideological volume of social-Darwinist, male-supremacist rhetoric in the early years of the twentieth century easily drowned them out.

Writers of the time could hardly ignore its influence; Wharton, Cather, and Glasgow were no exception. Ellen Glasgow, for example, once claimed Darwin's *Origin of Species* was "the book that influenced [her] mind most profoundly" in her youth.[67] This is not to suggest that these writers absorbed social Darwinism uncritically; they ab-sorbed it nevertheless.

Wharton, Cather, and Glasgow dealt centrally in their fiction with the dilemma of women living in a fallen world, one dominated by the male-supremacist voice of the fathers and in which the mothers' gar-den had been destroyed. Willa Cather once stated, "the world broke in two in 1922 or thereabouts."[68] Her generation of women writers was on the far side of the divide.

2

Nan Prince
and the Golden Apples

Whether it were some favoring quality in that spot of soil or in the sturdy old native tree itself, the rich golden apples had grown there, year after year, in perfection, but nowhere else.

—*Sarah Orne Jewett*, A Country Doctor *(1884)*

On the Thacher homestead, where Adeline Thacher Prince and her infant daughter, Nan, arrive exhausted one November evening—the opening scene of Sarah Orne Jewett's novel *A Country Doctor* (1884)—there is a golden apple tree.[1] The apple tree is, of course, associated with the Garden of Eden in Judeo-Christian myth,[2] but the Tree of Life in Greek mythology is also a bearer of golden apples, guarded by the Hesperides, the Daughters of Evening. The golden apple tree in *A Country Doctor* symbolizes the paradisiacal women's community envisioned in the literature of the nineteenth-century women's local-color school.[3]

Jewett's novel opens in the evening when wayward daughter Adeline Prince returns defeated from her excursion into patriarchal territory, back to the rural female sanctuary where three women—Adeline's mother, Mrs. Thacher, and two sisters, Eliza and Jane Dyer—sit knitting, reminiscing, and eating golden apples and cake. It is yet another Jewett image of the consoling female community, the world of the mothers, of Demeter. It is evening, the moon is on the wane; Persephone is returning, dying, to the land of her mother's garden.

Nan Prince, the infant daughter, spends her formative years in this matriarchal sanctuary. An Artemis-Diana figure, she is nourished and empowered in the wild zone, in nature, in a female wilderness.

The motif of the golden apples provides us with a useful thread by which to reanalyze this important Jewett novel, which expresses so directly the central theme of late nineteenth-century women's literature: whether to leave the mother's garden, the "female world of love and ritual," for the new realms of patriarchal knowledge that are opening up to women, thanks largely to the gains made by the nineteenth-century women's rights movement.

Throughout the women's literature of the period, but especially in key stories by Jewett and Mary E. Wilkins Freeman, we note an intense ambivalence felt by women characters between the women's rural world on the one hand and, on the other, the beckoning world of wider knowledge and broader horizons offered by entrance into male-dominated institutions and professions such as medicine, hitherto barred to women. One Freeman story is indeed entitled "The Tree of Knowledge" (1900). Here as elsewhere in women's literature the fear is that the intrusion of men and/or patriarchal knowledge will destroy women's culture and epistemological traditions. In the Freeman story one character wonders "if it might not sometimes be better to guard the Tree of Knowledge with the flaming sword, instead of the gates of a lost Paradise."[4] Nan Prince's story is an early attempt by a woman writer to wrestle with this issue.

A figure from Greek mythology associated with the golden apples is Atalante, who one authority stipulates is a "by-form of Artemis."[5] Brought up in the wild, she could "outshoot and outrun and out-wrestle" all the men who opposed her.[6] Like other Dianas, "she had no liking for men except as companions . . . and she was determined never to marry."[7] She does, however, agree to wed the first man who can defeat her in a footrace, since she knows that none can. Finally, however, a suitor appears who carries three golden apples from the Hesperides' Tree of Life. At intervals through the race he throws them before Atalante, who stops to pick them up, thereby losing the race.

If in *A Country Doctor* these apples represent the paradisiacal women's community, then the message of Atalante is that Nan Prince must relinquish the apples if she is to win the race, if she is to succeed in patriarchal institutions, if she is to become a "male professional." That is, she must leave behind the women's world and its culture.

The golden apples are mentioned twice again in the novel. The first time is during one of the few moments when Nan reveals an inclination toward "romantic friendship" with other women, or, to put it in more modern terms, a lesbian tendency. That occurs during her school years when she develops a "smash" on one of her girlfriends. "[A]fter one of the elder girls had read a composition which fired our heroine's imagination, she worshiped this superior being from a suitable distance, and was her willing adorer and slave. The composition was upon The Moon" (82)—a repetition of the Diana motif. Nan gives this idol some of the "treasured" golden apples from the Thacher farm. In this context Nan fantasizes returning one day to the rural homestead, as "the reigning queen," and having as "the favored guest" "the author of the information about the moon" (83).

The final mention of the apple tree occurs in the concluding episode of the novel when Nan, now a physician, returns to the rural area where she grew up, visits her mother's grave, and thanks God for her future. In this important scene Nan reconnects to her matriarchal roots: the Dyer women accept her as a doctor; Nan considers that her mother's spirit had been "guiding her" all along; and she gathers a couple of golden apples. Now, however, it is daylight, a contrast to the dark night in which her mother, suicidal, had trod the same path years before. In Jewett's notes for *A Country Doctor*, which are in the Houghton Library, she outlines its conclusion as follows: "For end— goes down to the river shore and sees the old graves & everything by day that her mother passed by night and sits in the [word unclear] of juniper and looks across the river at her future!"[8]

It is clear from this and from the structure of the novel that Nan's relationship with her mother is pivotal. The death of the mother is the opening episode; the reconnection with the mother's spirit, the concluding scene. Nan's critical decision to become a doctor occurs epiphanally in the area associated with her mother near the Thacher homestead. In a period of despondence after graduation from secondary school, Nan realizes that traditional women's lives bore her, that like her mother she had a "longing for The Great Something Else" (171). "Of course, she could keep the house, but . . . any one with five senses . . . could . . . do any of the ordinary work of existence . . . she wanted something more" (164). With these reflections in mind Nan treks through the brush, "unconscious that she had been following her mother's footsteps, or that fate had again brought her here for a great decision" (165). In these critical moments of the novel's plot structure Nan is connected with her mother.

Adeline Thacher Prince represents the dark side of the rural nineteenth-century female world. We learn that she too had been ambitious, had had "dreadful high notions" (24), that she had become an alcoholic and returned "beggarly" (36), suicidal, and "worse than defeated, from the battlefield of life" (33). We also learn that she was somewhat frivolous and wasted her money on fancy clothes. She is hardly a model one would wish a daughter to emulate, and all are concerned lest Nan follow her mother's footsteps more than just literally.

But the premise of the novel is that Nan is able to reject and transcend the negative aspects of women's condition while retrieving and integrating the positive. Most of the other women in the novel are depicted as living boringly repetitive and limited existences. Like Adeline, several of them express dissatisfaction. Mrs. Graham, an Oldfields neighbor and friend of Dr. Leslie's (Nan's foster father), is immobilized; her only view of the world is through a window where she perennially sits. "I cannot see that the world changes much," she says. "I find my days piteously alike" (142). In Dunport, Eunice Fraley comments "sadly," "I so often feel as if I were not accomplishing anything. . . . It came over me today that here I am, really an old woman, and I am just about where I first started,—doing the same things over and over and no better than ever" (204). The other women— Grandmother Thacher, the Dyer sisters, Marilla, and Miss Prince, Nan's aunt—have similarly lived cyclical, nonprogressive lives. In later Jewett works, such as *The Country of the Pointed Firs* (1896), "Miss Tempy's Watchers" (1888), and "Martha's Lady" (1897), stasis and repetition are seen as a kind of *via negativa,* a redemptive experience, but here, as in other early works like "A Guest at Home" (1882), such a life is seen darkly as something to be escaped from, or transcended.

This then helps to explain one of the central questions raised by the novel: why does Nan decide to become a doctor, after Dr. Leslie, rather than an herbal-healer after the fashion of Eliza Dyer? At one point Nan lays aside a treatise on the nervous system and commences gathering herbs. Dr. Leslie remarks, "You will be the successor of Mrs. Martin Dyer, and the admiration of the neighborhood" (178). Yet Nan does not follow in the women's healing tradition; she does not elect to become a Mrs. Dyer or a Mrs. Todd but rather a professional "regular" physician. Why?

I suggest there are several reasons. First, as noted, she wants to move beyond the limitations of the rural women's world, especially its negative aspects, and in this sense move beyond her mother and the other women in the novel. Second, she knows that herbal healing does not have the authority of professional medicine. Mrs. Dyer is only "next to the doctor himself," the neighborhood "authority on all medical subjects" (29). And Nan clearly wants to be a leader, an authority: she holds the reins on her excursions with Dr. Leslie; she wants to pull the oars on her boating trips with suitor George Gerry. Nan wants to win Atalante's race.

The third and fourth reasons are more complex. Jewett herself said that medicine was simply a metaphor in the novel for any calling.[9] We may assume that the calling that she had preeminently in mind was writing. At several points in the novel Jewett makes allusions to literature, and in particular to the rural stories or oral histories that she feels are worthy of written transcription.

When the three women are reminiscing in the Thacher farmhouse early in the novel, as they eat the apples, they relate various family stories. The narrator compares the ritual of rural storytelling to urban theatergoing.

> The repetitions of the best stories are signal events, for ordinary circumstances do not inspire them. Affairs must rise to a certain level before a narration of some great crisis is suggested, and exactly as a city audience is well contented with hearing the plays of Shakespeare over and over again, so each man and woman of experience is permitted to deploy their well-known but always interesting stories upon the rustic stage. (16)

Later Mrs. Graham tells Dr. Leslie: "You doctors ought to be our historians, for you alone see the old country folks familiarly and can talk with them without restraint" (141). Dr. Leslie replies that active practitioners have no time for writing; only medical scholars write, and they lack the practical experience that would "make their advice reliable" (141)—a characteristic expression of Dr. Leslie's antiestablishmentarianism.

While in Dunport, Nan listens enthusiastically to Mrs. Fraley's narrative. "Really," she exclaims, "I think her stories of the old times are wonderfully interesting. I wish I had a gift for writing them down whenever I am listening to her" (276). As we all know, Sarah Orne Jewett had the gift, and if we consider *A Country Doctor* to be fictionalized autobiography, we can identify Jewett's process of becoming a writer with Nan's of becoming a physician, locating it within the antithesis specified above between women's culture and patriarchal systems. In other words, I suggest that Jewett herself faced the same question as Nan—of remaining within the women's world or of entering the mainstream of patriarchal production. Nan's decision to become a professional doctor and not an herbalist parallels Jewett's determination to become a professional author, a poet and not just a "poetess" like Betsey Dole. Similarly, Nan wished to have access to male-dominated culture because such entrance lent one authority and gave one power: it gave one a cultural voice. To avoid such entrance, to remain in the wild zone, in those matriarchal pockets of rural New England, meant to remain silent, meant that one's experience would never be inscribed in history. Sylvia in "A White Heron" exemplifies this choice: she remains silent and thereby preserves the female sanctuary, but she remains illiterate, outside the traditions of recorded history and literature.

This was not a choice that Jewett herself could make. Just as the writer-narrator in *The Country of the Pointed Firs* could not remain in Dunnet Landing and Nan could not remain in Oldfields, Jewett could not remain in South Berwick. They all chose to seek patriarchal status and to have cultural authority. Their passages were facilitated, however, by feminine or feminized mentors who had themselves access to patriarchal institutions: Annie Fields in the case of Jewett, Dr. Leslie in the case of Nan.

Dr. Leslie is worth a moment's consideration. It is true he is a man and something of a father figure (it is well known that he was modeled on Jewett's own father, himself a country doctor). However, he is as nontyrannical a patriarch as one could imagine, himself an outsider and a rebel, one who is skeptical of the received authority of medical scholarship, who reveres women's healing traditions and is something of an "irregular," to use the medical vernacular of the day. He practices a fully "feminized" philosophy of child-rearing, that of nonintervention (promoted by the Beecher sisters, among others); he fully allows Nan to grow as she will, to do as she pleases, often slipping into a passive role with her (as when she drives the carriage).

Jewett's third reason, therefore, for having Nan choose Dr. Leslie rather than the woman herbalist as her model was, I suggest, that she was justifying her own choice of writing as vocation, a choice that meant entrance into patriarchal institutions, which Jewett wished to use in order to preserve and serve the matriarchal world where her roots remained. Nan represents this attempt to "raid," as it were, patriarchal systems in order to promote, exalt, enhance matriarchy.

Finally, I believe Jewett wrote this novel in the spirit of a synthesized liberal/cultural feminism to argue that women could honorably engage in traditionally masculine careers such as authorship and medicine without forsaking their female identities; that where such vocations may entail a repudiation of traditional female roles, they do not mean that one has thereby become a man. And in this way Jewett engaged in the tricky dialogue about gender role identity that was heating up in the 1880s, thanks to the advent of the so-called sexologists.

The prevailing medical opinion in the nineteenth century had been that "motherhood was woman's natural destiny, and those females who thwarted . . . their body's design must expect to suffer."[10] In the early 1870s Dr. E. H. Clarke of the Harvard Medical School published his *Sex in Education,* which urged that women were "destroying their wombs and their childbearing potential by presuming to pursue a course of higher education intended by nature only for the male sex."[11] It was "unnatural" for women to pursue higher education, just as it was "unnatural" for them to be feminists. As early as 1837 the Pastoral Letter written against the Grimké sisters noted: "When she assumes the place and tone of a man as a public reformer . . . her character becomes unnatural."[12] And, of course, feminists like Mary Wollstonecraft (who, by the way, in 1792 advocated that women be physicians), Frances Wright, and others were condemned as "semi-women, mental hermaphrodites" in the literature of "true womanhood."[13]

But antifeminism received its greatest boost when the theories of the European sexologists, in particular those of German physician Richard von Krafft-Ebing, noted in chapter 1, appeared in the 1880s. I propose that *A Country Doctor* may have been one of the earliest feminist repudiations of Krafft-Ebing and other theorists who saw women's choices of masculine vocations as unnatural, indeed pathological.

As noted, in Krafft-Ebing's *Psychopathia Sexualis,* women who do not marry and bear children are not "real" women, and passivity is seen as women's natural style. Krafft-Ebing connected these tendencies with sexual attraction to women, or what later became labeled lesbianism, which he called "antipathic sexual instinct." This "type" of woman— that is, one who was childless, who aspired after a traditionally masculine occupation, who was attracted to other women, and who in some cases adopted a "mannish" style—was called a "viragint." Krafft-Ebing believed that such inclinations were in many cases congenital, the result of hereditary degeneration. Many of the parents of such freaks were alcoholics, for example.

Not only does Nan Prince in many ways resemble this type, it seems probable that the extensive discussions of what is natural and unnatural in the novel relate to this issue. Dr. Leslie early announces: "I see plainly that Nan is not the sort of girl who will be likely to marry. When a man or woman has that sort of self-dependence and unnatural self-reliance, it shows itself very early. I believe that it is a mistake for such a woman to marry" (137). The doctor notes further: "Nan's feeling toward her boy-playmates is exactly the same as toward the girls she knows" (137). In other words, Nan was not particularly interested in boys, an attitude that later dismays her suitor, George Gerry. Indeed, we have noted her crush on a girl schoolmate, and even during her courtship period she seems more interested in Mary Parrish, who is her "favorite among her new friends" (262). In fact, the main appeal of George is that he "did not trouble Nan with unnecessary attentions, as some young men had" (263). He does not insist "upon her remembering that he was a man and she a girl" (244). The roles are further dislodged in an episode where Nan quickly takes charge and deftly sets an injured man's dislocated shoulder when George stands helplessly by. Afterward George "felt weak and womanish, and somehow wished it had been he who could play the doctor" (266). Later we learn he feels "his manliness was at stake" (295). Curiously, in her notes for the novel, Jewett specifies George was "not a bit effeminate,"[14] which she excised from the final version, although she does stress that he was a "manly fellow" (246, 291). Nevertheless, Nan discovers that she cannot accept the passive role, she cannot play "yielding maiden" (319), and so she rejects George.

Earlier Nan's schoolmates had to reassure themselves that "their schoolmate showed no sign of being the sort of girl who tried to be mannish and to forsake her natural vocation for a profession" (160)— which seems to me a clear-cut response to the Krafft-Ebing theory of the "viragint." Nan did not even look "strong-minded" (160), and in her notes for the novel Jewett amplifies in another excised passage:

"[Nan] shrank from the conspicuous and by no means alluring example of some ~~professional~~ [*replaced with* so called strong-minded] women whom she ~~knew~~ [*replaced with* happened to meet]."[15] In the novel Jewett stresses how much "a little lady" (220) Nan was, how she was "anything but self-asserting," which of course is contradicted by her behavior throughout the novel; she nevertheless "had no noisy fashion of thrusting herself before the public gaze" (301). Medicine, Jewett urges, is a "most womanly and respectable calling" (193).

Nevertheless, as a child Nan had wished "over and over again that [she] was a boy" (180). And Dr. Leslie, noting her "unnatural" bent, early decides that she should devote herself to something other "than the business of housekeeping and what is called a woman's natural work" (137). For "it was not with her, as with many of her friends, that the natural instinct toward marriage, and the building and keeping of a sweet home-life, ruled all other plans and possibilities" (159).

Many of Krafft-Ebing's descriptions of women "tainted with antipathic sexual instinct"[16] bear a resemblance to Nan. Case #130, for example, describes a Mrs. X who "used to rove about the fields and woods in the freest manner, and climbed the most dangerous rocks and cliffs" (324). Nan Prince was "wild as a hawk" (60). "She won't go to bed till she's a mind to . . . she'd be'n up into . . . oaks, trying to catch a little screech owl. She belongs with the wild creatur's . . . just the same natur' " (61). "She'll run like a fox all day long" (62).

Mrs. X's insistence on carrying on "intellectual conversation" (325) at a ball is a reaction one could readily imagine of Nan. "She [Mrs. X] was startled . . . at the flight and novelty of her thoughts, at her quick and precise method of arriving at conclusions and forming opinions" (326), similarly applicable to Nan. Krafft-Ebing further notes, "the female urning [another term applied to the "congenital" female "invert"] may chiefly be found in the haunt of boys. She is their rival in play. . . . Love for art finds a substitute in the pursuits of the sciences" (399).

Other traits of the female "urning" Nan displays are that she exhibits a lack of "taste for female work" (Krafft-Ebing, 409), a "lack of skill and liking for female occupations" (419), a "bold and tomboyish" style (420). Case #162, held as an example of "viraginity," preferred boys' games as a child and "had always preferred masculine work, and has shown unusual skill in it" (421). Finally, Nan is clearly depicted as being in a line of congenital degeneracy. Her mother, as noted, was an alcoholic, had "a touch of insanity" (99), and was suicidal.

Many of Krafft-Ebing's "cases" are cross-dressers. Jewett does not deal with this issue in this novel (Nan is not interested in clothes) but does in two other stories of this period: "An Autumn Holiday" (1880) and "Hollowell's Pretty Sister" (1880). "Tom's Husband" (1882) and "Farmer Finch" (1885) also address the issue of gender role reversal.[17]

"[V]irtually every literate European household" had a copy of the *Psychopathia Sexualis* soon after its appearance in 1882, the year Jewett and Annie Fields made their first trip to Europe.[18] Fields had a reading knowledge of German, the language in which it was published. Sarah's father, Theodore Herman Jewett, was a specialist in "obstetrics and diseases of women and children."[19] While Dr. Jewett died in 1878, Krafft-Ebing and other sexologists (Ulrichs, Moll, Westphal) had been publishing their theories about female inverts since 1869. Carl von Westphal, for example, in 1869 "published a case study of a young woman who from childhood on preferred to dress as a boy and play boy's games, and had always been attracted to women. . . . She became a new type," and medical journals became flooded with papers on women like Westphal's.[20]

We know that Dr. Leslie, Dr. Jewett's analog, has an extensive medical library, subscribes to the latest medical journals (187), and rejects European medical opinion (at one point he lays aside a French volume in annoyance [129]). Nan herself occasionally reads these works but generally with similar disregard.

It seems likely that Dr. Jewett would have been aware of the sexologists' theories and that he and Sarah may have discussed them. Her own proclivities could have readily been identified with this "new type" of woman that European theorists were condemning as a pathological freak.[21] Naturally, she and her father would have rejected those theories. They did so by espousing a different concept of nature, one derived from the organicist Romantic theory promoted by Emerson and Margaret Fuller: that people, like plants, are born with inherited designs or entelechies and that the individual must be allowed to unfold as this predisposition dictates. Hence the numerous organic metaphors in the work. Dr. Leslie resolves, for example, to let Nan grow "as naturally as the plant grows, not having been clipped back or forced in any unnatural direction" (102). Nan is described as a flower that "has sprung up fearlessly under the great sky, with only the sunshine and the wind and summer rain to teach it" (303). Like Margaret Fuller's ideal feminist in *Woman in the Nineteenth Century,*

Nan was allowed to "learn [her] rule [not] from without, [but] to unfold it from within."[22]

In this sense Nan is an exemplar of liberal feminism with its emphasis on individualism, as epitomized in Elizabeth Cady Stanton's 1891 address, "Solitude of Self," and assimilationism, that women should enter into established masculine professions. But the novel goes beyond this liberal perspective. Rather, it is another of Jewett's attempts at synthesis. Unlike later writers for whom a return to the Dianic wilderness is an escape, a retreat from patriarchal oppression, or for whom, as in the case of the early Edith Wharton, the Dianic world is seen as one of suffocating limitation,[23] Jewett's protagonist was able to negotiate between patriarchal systems and Demeter's world, the land of the golden apples. Although discriminated against, Nan is not destroyed or subdued by her experience in medical school. Unlike her mother, a Persephone, and unlike later Dianic figures—such as Alexandra Bergson in Cather's *O Pioneers!* and Dorinda Oakley in Glasgow's *Barren Ground*—Nan returns from her other-world journey unscathed. Nor is she required to abandon or to silence feminine traditions. Rather, she is able to use patriarchal knowledge to preserve a matriarchal world. In this Nan resembled her creator, who in her writings, which after all were published (unlike those of Betsey Dole), preserved the matriarchal vision.

3

Edith Wharton
and the Pomegranate Seed

*[T]hey sang to me so bewitchingly that they almost lured me from the
wholesome noonday air of childhood into some strange supernatural
region where the normal pleasures of my age seemed as insipid as
the fruits of the Earth to Persephone after she had eaten of the
pomegranate seed.*

—*Edith Wharton, "Life and I"*

In her unpublished autobiographical fragment, "Life and I," probably written in the early 1920s, Edith Wharton compares her childhood
enthrallment with words to Persephone's consumption of the pomegranate seed.[1] In the ancient myth Persephone's eating of the forbidden fruit (symbolically, of knowledge) is an irrevocable, transformative act that seals her fate and certifies the permanence of her fall
from the paradisiacal garden of her mother into the patriarchal captivity of Hades's underworld. It is analogous to the consumption of the
fruit of knowledge in the Judeo-Christian myth of the fall. In the
Greek myth, as a result of her daughter's disappearance, Demeter
makes the earth barren and lifeless. Persephone's gesture may also be
analogized to that of Evelina in Freeman's 1895 story. In both cases
the green world of Demeter, the sanctuary of Diana, has been destroyed by the daughter's act.

The Persephone-Demeter myth allegorizes the historical mother-daughter transition that occurred toward the end of the nineteenth century in the Western world. Partly as a result of the nineteenth-century women's movement, young middle- to upper-class women were leaving their mothers' bowers in increasing numbers and entering such institutions of the male-dominated public sphere as universities and the professions. In the process these women were leaving behind the women's sphere of "love and ritual," which had its own traditions and values; they were assimilating into a world governed by a social-Darwinist ethic that espoused a doctrine of male supremacy and by a patriarchal ideology premised upon the exchange of women.

Like Demeter, late nineteenth-century mothers were struggling to keep their daughters "home," thereby sustaining women's culture, otherwise doomed by the daughters' abduction-betrayal. The daughters, on the other hand, were eager to expand their horizons, to engage in new systems of discourse, like Persephone, unaware that such involvement entailed patriarchal captivity.

In the epigraph Edith Wharton, who (unlike her local-color predecessor, Sarah Orne Jewett) usually takes the rebellious but male-identified daughter's point of view, celebrates Persephone's act as an expansive experience that yields wider knowledge. However, throughout her work she tacitly acknowledges that the world resulting from Persephone's abduction and Demeter's pall is barren and lifeless. Her major early novels, for example, *The House of Mirth, Ethan Frome,* and *Summer,* depict an irredeemably fallen world.

Persephone's act may be seen (like every myth of the fall) as an ontogenetic experience that occurs as every infant enters into culture. According to Lacanian-Freudian theory, that entrance is a "fall" from the preoedipal world of the mother into "the Symbolic." It is a fall from the intransitive, into consciousness, into language.

In "Life and I" Wharton, significantly, sees words as the magic tokens that allow entrance into the realm beyond childhood. In Lacanian theory words or language is the vehicle that assures entrance into the Symbolic, into patriarchal discourse. Significantly, it was Wharton's father who taught her the alphabet. And yet words for Wharton, as the seeds for Persephone, lead to captivity within patriarchal systems of discourse. Characteristically, Wharton contrasts the excitement of patriarchal realms with the "insipid" world of childhood, of the preoedipal mother's garden. Implicit in Wharton's contrast is the idea that real, important, serious experience lies in the realm of the father, while the unimportant, the silly, the trivial belong in the maternal world, women's sphere.

To be a serious author therefore for Wharton meant to be a patriarch. In numerous stories she puts down the silly, sentimentalist woman author.[2] Her own self-identification as masculine may be seen in her nearly universal use of the masculine I-narrator. In many cases the "old-boy" tone of the narrative style is overbearing: the setting usually a book-lined study—the fathers' library—the narrator smoking a cigar with an old Harvard schoolmate.[3]

In an early novella, *The Bunner Sisters* (written c. 1891), Wharton reveals her sensitivity to the problematic use of patriarchal style (or *inventio*) by women. Part of a distancing that occurs between two sisters is the epistolary use by one sister of inappropriately Johnsonian rhetoric. The other sister, Ann Eliza, wished "that Evelina had laid aside her swelling periods for a style more suited to the chronicling of homely incidents"; "after each reading she emerged impressed but unenlightened from the labyrinth of Evelina's eloquence."[4] The suggestion here, beyond question, is that women lose contact with one another, cease to communicate fully, as they engage in patriarchal stylistics. Significantly, in *Bunner Sisters* the principals are Persephone-Demeter figures and the epistles are sent during Evelina-Persephone's captivity (see discussion below). Interestingly, in her earliest work, which includes *Bunner Sisters,* Wharton's own style was much more in the tradition of her New England local-color "predecessors," Sarah Orne Jewett and Mary E. Wilkins Freeman, than her later style.

Percy Lubbock notes that Wharton "liked the company of men because 'she had . . . a very masculine mind . . . and she liked to be talked to as a man.' "[5] Louis Auchincloss recalls, "It was said of Edith Wharton that she and Theodore Roosevelt were self-made men, and the saying pleased her."[6] In *French Ways and Their Meaning* (1919) Wharton reveals her contempt for the traditional homebound woman and her acceptance of the superiority of the male experience and intellect. "The woman whose mind is attuned to men's minds has a much larger view of the world and attaches much less importance to trifles." "American women," she says, "are like children." Because of their separate existence, women have no "intellectual and social part in the lives of men" and therefore grow "without the checks, the stimulus, and the discipline that comes of contact with the stronger masculine individuality."[7]

In passages in "Life and I" that were not included in her published autobiography, *A Backward Glance,* Wharton further reveals an early contempt for her own sex. Her "only play-mates," she remarks, were "little boys. Dolls & little girls I frankly despised" (12).

In the same manuscript Wharton shows that she had fully accepted the sexologists' notion of "romantic friendships" among women as pathological. Wharton describes a young woman who "became passionately, morbidly attached to me" (29). She was "a queer, shy, invalid girl of twenty or so, in whom I suspect there were strong traces of degeneracy" (29). The terms *morbid* and *degenerate* were, as noted, stock sexologist jargon on the subject. R. W. B. Lewis also notes that Wharton saw lesbianism as a "degeneracy" and thought Nathalie Clifford Barney, a celebrated sapphist, "appalling."[8]

In a peculiar and rather sadistic anecdote in "Life and I," Wharton describes an episode that prefigures her late story "Roman Fever." She explains how, out of boredom, she lured a young man away from his fiancée, who was desperately in love with him. She notes, "it amused us both to keep his poor fiancée on the rack for a few weeks" (52). "I *did* make the other girl miserable!" (52). Even in retrospect Wharton seems to find this episode amusing and appears unaware of the shocking cruelty involved of one woman to another. This emphatic rejection of female bonding and of the "female world of love and ritual" runs throughout Wharton's work.

In an early set of story ideas, "The Valley of Childish Things, and Other Emblems" (1896), Wharton describes a plot pattern that archetypally reflects her own attitude toward the women's sphere, seeing it coalesced with that of children. "A girl leaves the valley of childish things," she writes, "goes out in the world, learns much; returns to find her old friends still childish and at their games and resistant to what she has learned."[9] Like Persephone (in Wharton's version), this girl comes to reject the maternal realm through her accession to patriarchal knowledge.

By contrast, in the works of the local colorists (particularly Jewett) who remain within a women's culture and write from that vantage, the characteristic plot pattern is similarly cyclical but involves not a rejection of the maternal/matriarchal but a reunion with it, a reinspiration by it. Jewett's great work, *The Country of the Pointed Firs* (1896), is in this respect representative; it concerns the reunion of daughter-author-Persephone with mother-Demeter. Such a plot, I argue elsewhere, is reflective of the traditional women's lives of sacred repetition, expressive of what Mircea Eliade called "the myth of the eternal return," of the seasonal agricultural cycle of nature.[10]

For Wharton, adopting a masculine perspective, the maternal realm represents a horrifying stasis, an engulfing petrification, silence and muteness. For in the characteristically oedipal plot of the masculine quest, stasis—entrapment by the feminine—is the worst of evils.[11]

In her excellent biography Cynthia Griffin Wolff interprets Wharton's relationship with her own mother in Freudian terms, seeing Edith as posed between perennial childish dependency on an overbearing and hostile mother, and independence and freedom, an adult self-sufficiency. Writing was, according to Wolff, the means by which Wharton escaped from her mother's clutches and her own feeling of helpless dependency. But she notes Wharton's ambivalence: on the one hand she wanted to feel "a happy oneness . . . if not with Mother, then with 'birds' and 'grasses.' " Yet she fears the muteness of the preliterate realm: nothing is "worse than to be 'mute.' To be 'mute'— either as animal or as . . . baby—is to be vulnerable to pain; and words . . . can offer the promise of an escape from loneliness and helplessness" (26).

I propose that Wharton's rebellion and fear were not so much directed against her own mother personally as against the historical position of the traditional woman and the historical silence and muteness of her preliterate, nonoedipal experience.

In many stories Wharton casts the mothers in the roles of tacit collaborators, whose silence allows masculine corruption to continue unimpeded. In this she was expressing a moral condemnation of the separate spheres that paralleled the critique developed by the cultural feminists of the turn of the century.[12] "A Cup of Cold Water" (1899) and "Quicksand" (1902), in particular, deal with this theme.

Because of her rejection of the mothers, Wharton rejects her feminine literary predecessors as well, imputing to them a similarly dishonest collusiveness. She says (of writing *Ethan Frome*), "For years I had wanted to draw life as it really was in the derelict mountain villages of New Hampshire, a life . . . utterly unlike that seen through the rose-coloured spectacles of my predecessors, Mary Wilkins and Sarah Orne Jewett." Later she refers disparagingly to the "rose-and-lavender pages of [the] favorite authoresses."[13] As I have pointed out elsewhere, Wharton's indictment of Jewett and Freeman is more a projection of her own needs than an accurate assessment of their vision. In certain stories Freeman, especially, presented a view every bit as grim as Wharton's.[14] But Wharton needed to distance herself from "authoresses" in order to establish herself as an "author," to reject their view as feminine and "unrealistic" in order to legitimate her masculine view as the serious, adult one. The rejection of the local colorists is part of her wholesale rejection of the feminine-maternal.

In her unpublished memoir Wharton evinces nevertheless a strong nostalgia for the preliterate realm of the mothers. In speaking of her lifelong love of dogs, she notes her own "sense of being somehow, myself, an intermediate creature between human beings & animals & nearer, on the whole, to the furry tribes than to homo sapiens" (22). In *A Backward Glance* she recalls a particular "fairy tale at which I always thrilled—the story of the boy who could talk with the birds and hear what the grasses said. . . . I must have felt myself to be of kin to that happy child."[15]

Yet unlike her local-color predecessors, Wharton seems compelled to repress and deny this marginal interspecies wilderness, this Dianic realm. Instead of strong matriarchs rooted in the green world of female "love and ritual," we find collaborative mothers, abandoned and alienated daughters—"new women" struggling alone without a consoling female support community—proud of their freedom, new knowledge, and independence, but nevertheless like Persephone in fundamental captivity and prey to patriarchal incest.

In the ancient feminine myth of the fall the Persephone-Demeter figure was in many versions joined by Hecate, the goddess of death. They formed a women's trinity that corresponds to the choices available to women in Wharton's fictional world: Demeter, nonoedipal, preliterate silence; Persephone, freedom from Demeter but patriarchal captivity and incest; Hecate, death.

Wharton published a little-noticed but highly significant playlet, entitled "Pomegranate Seed," in 1912. Here the Demeter-Persephone script is presented in concentrated form. It is concerned primarily with the mother-daughter reunion after the abduction, and with the resignation of Demeter and Persephone to their alienated fate. Upon seeing her daughter again, Demeter cries: "Pale art thou, daughter, and upon thy brow / Sits an estranging darkness like a crown."[16] She is shocked by the sight and realizes that Persephone's removal is permanent. "Thy voice is paler than the lips it leaves. / Thou wilt not stay with me! I know my doom" (288).

Persephone announces that by her experience she is irrevocably changed: "Think'st thou I am the same Persephone / They took from thee?" (289). Demeter responds: "Within thine eyes I see / Some dreadful thing—" (289). She realizes Persephone is a half-willing victim: "Loving thy doom, more dark thou mak'st it seem" (289). She pleads with her: "Stay with me on the dear and ample earth" (290). But Persephone, the daughter in quest of greater knowledge, insists, "the kingdom of the dead is wider still" (291). Demeter recognizes her daughter's accession to new realms of knowledge. "Stand off from me," she says, "Thou knowst more than I" (291). And after Persephone returns to patriarchal captivity, Demeter muses "(after a long silence): I hear the secret whisper of the wheat" (291). Thus, the mother remains on a level of silent communion with the vegetative world, a green-world matriarch abandoned by her new-world daughter.

This dialogue signifies the interchange that was occurring between mothers and daughters at this moment in Western history. It is a repetition of the fundamental transition described above, of the luring of the daughters out of their mothers' gardens into the patriarchal symbolic. This is the fundamental subtext in Wharton's major work.

The Bunner Sisters (written c. 1891), Wharton's first novella, depicts two women exiled from the rural matriarchy of the local colorists, confined to a small shop that doubles as their home on a shabby street in lower Manhattan. The work records the destruction of the nineteenth-century women's community and the rupture of the mother-daughter bond, and in this respect recalls several Freeman stories, most notably "Evelina's Garden" (1896) and "Old Woman Magoun" (1905). It repeats the Demeter-Persephone myth: an older woman, the "mother," Ann Eliza, loses her younger sister, the "daughter," Evelina, to patriarchal control.

The plot is that the two sisters have kept a dress shop for years. Their lives are depicted as "narrow"; they live on the edge of poverty (231). One day Herman Ramy, who runs a clock-repair shop nearby, enters their lives. A competition is set up between the two women, but Ann Eliza withdraws in favor of her sister. The women begin to accede to Ramy's authority; they "fell into the habit of . . . accepting his verdict . . . with a fatalistic readiness that relieved them of all responsibility" (249).

Herman and Evelina become engaged, after which Evelina begins to look down on Ann Eliza, who "already counted for nothing in her sister's scheme of life" (272). Ann Eliza accepts the ideological valoriza-

tion of the married woman and denigration of the spinster; she sees
Evelina's "exclusion [as] both natural and just," which Wharton characterizes as an "idolatrous acceptance of the cruelties of fate" (272).
Nevertheless, Evelina's rejection "caused her the most lively pain. She
could not divest her love for Evelina of its passionate motherliness; no
breath of reason could lower it to the cool temperature of sisterly
affection" (272).

Evelina's marriage is a descent into the underworld. She and Herman move to St. Louis, leaving Ann Eliza alone. For a while Evelina
communicates in the ambiguous, periodic style noted above, but soon
all letters cease. Ann Eliza becomes frantic over the disappearance/
abduction of her daughter-sister. In the process of her search she
learns that Herman was a drug addict. Eventually, Evelina returns
home, exhausted and wracked. Ann Eliza greets her as a returning
child: "Vague words poured from [the older sister] as she laid her
cheek against Evelina's . . . endearments caught from [a neighbor's]
long discourses to her baby" (296). Evelina declares: "I've been to hell
and back" (299).

She describes Herman's addiction, her being abandoned with a
child who died, having to beg in the streets—in short a modernized
version of the "heroine's text" of the sentimentalist literary tradition,[17]
itself a variation of the Persephone abduction script. "It was a tale of
misery and humiliation so remote from the elder sister's innocent
experiences that much of it was hardly intelligible to her." It is a story
of a fall from maternal-feminine innocence. Evelina's experience becomes an alienating factor between the women: she "seemed even
more alien and terrible than the actual tale she told" (300). But "Ann
Eliza leaned over her, and for a long time they held each other without speaking" (302).

Despite such momentary reconnections the women remain estranged; their peaceful sanctuary has been fractured. Ann Eliza's "familiar heaven was unpeopled. She felt she could no longer trust in the
goodness of God . . . and there was only a black abyss above the roof
of Bunner Sisters" (303).

Evelina never recovers. As she is dying, her sister learns that in St.
Louis she had become a Roman Catholic. Like the pomegranate seed,
this conversion symbolizes Evelina's final accession to an alien patriarchal system. Ann Eliza felt "herself shut out of Evelina's heart, an exile
from her closest affections" (307); Evelina is "dying as a stranger in her
arms" (308). The amulet that Evelina is wearing around her neck

seemed "sacrilegious . . . a diabolical instrument of their estrangement" (308).

When a priest comes to perform the last rites, Ann Eliza feels completely dispossessed: "it seemed . . . that the shop and the back room
no longer belonged to her" (311). An "unseen power" appeared to
have taken control. She knew that Evelina "was going, and going,
under this alien guidance, even farther from her than to the dark
places of death" (311). The destruction of the women's community is
complete. Even at the funeral Ann Eliza, "a passive spectator, beheld
with stony indifference this last negation of her past" (312). The final
scene is of Ann Eliza alone, wandering the streets of New York, seen
likewise as the ultimate symbol of exile in other Wharton works, notably *The House of Mirth.*

The Demeter-Persephone script is carried through in Wharton's
second novella, *The Touchstone* (1900). This work engages in what
became a central Wharton preoccupation, the maintenance of moral
and artistic integrity in the face of temptation to capitulate to commercial exploitation. Underneath this overt theme, however, we can sense
that the real issue, the subtext, is the question of translating women's
private artistic material into public patriarchal discourse, an act that is
construed, in this work at least, as a sell-out.

Wharton was at this stage in her development still at the threshold
between the women's sphere, the realm of her mother and a women's
cultural community, and entrance into the patriarchal world of public
artistic success. Wharton had herself undergone a nervous breakdown
in the preceding years and had sought treatment with the (in)famous
S. Weir Mitchell, who apparently had also ministered in the late nine-
ties to Charlotte Perkins Gilman and Mary E. Wilkins Freeman, the
former having bleakly depicted his "professional sentence" in "The
Yellow Wallpaper." Her embroilment with her mother continued, at
least until the latter's death in 1901; commercial success and fame did
not come until after the publication of *The House of Mirth* in 1905. *The
Touchstone* therefore expresses, I believe, Wharton's underlying ambivalence about her own transition from the women's sphere to the
public realm of patriarchal discourse; she is sensitive, this novella
reveals, to the possibility that such a transition could be considered a
betrayal of the women's sphere, a sell-out to patriarchal powers. Once
again the signifying token of betrayal/abandonment of the women's
realm is the pomegranate seed.

The plot is that the central male character, Glennard, has some love letters written to him earlier by a famous woman author, Mrs. Aubyn, now dead, known for her celebrated novel *Pomegranate Seed.* In order to marry his fiancée, Alexa Trent, Glennard needs money. He finally decides to sell the love letters in order to finance the wedding. Afterward he worries lest Alexa discover that their "crop of innocent blessedness [had] sprung from tainted soil."[18]

After the publication of the letters there is considerable discussion about the moral propriety of publishing such private material. Women tend to feel it an exploitation of a woman's private experience; men, that it is legitimate public property. One woman, for example, protests, "It's the woman's soul, absolutely torn up by the roots—her whole self laid bare; and to a man who evidently didn't care . . . it's too much like listening at a keyhole" (37). But a man responds, "A personality as big as Margaret Aubyn's belongs to the world. . . . Such a mind is part of the general fund of thought. It's a penalty of greatness—one becomes a *monument historique*" (38). Another man observes, "You women are too incurably subjective. I venture to say that most men would see in those letters merely their immense literary value, their significance as documents. The personal side doesn't count where there's so much else" (39). The underlying issue is clearly whether women's *own* experience should be translated into public patriarchal discourse.

In the meantime, while Alexa reads the letters unaware of her husband's complicity, Glennard becomes more and more aware of Margaret Aubyn's presence. One evening he feels an intense "sense of her nearness . . . her presence remained the one reality in a world of shadows" (61). Here, as in her later story "Pomegranate Seed" (1931), Wharton casts the Persephone figure as a male; Glennard is in a shadowy underworld; the sale of the letters is equivalent to the eating of the pomegranate seed, but Margaret-Demeter's presence is calling him back. Eventually, Alexa discovers the truth, forgives him, and through the purgative process Glennard emerges renewed. His wife points out that he has changed into the man Margaret loved: "She's made you into the man she loved[.] *That's* worth suffering for, worth dying for—to a woman" (82).

Margaret therefore is a redemptive mother figure who brings Glennard back from the underworld. She represents the intense emotionality of the preoedipal experience and the humane values of a personalist ethic. In this story that intensity remains redemptive; the characters are brought back from the alienation that betrayal of the mother's garden entails.

"The Angel at the Grave" (1901) shows Wharton still within the tradition carved by her New England local-color predecessors, but her modifications of the classic local-color script are quite apparent. The story is a negative version of Mary E. Wilkins Freeman's "New England Nun" (1887). Once again the Persephone motif is explicit.

Paulina Anson rejects a suitor in order to remain the caretaker of the Anson house, which has become a kind of shrine to her grand-father, Orestes Anson, a celebrated theosophist. In commenting upon Paulina's hesitation before the suitor's proposal, the narrator asks, "Did Persephone, snatched from the warm fields of Enna, peer half-consentingly down the abyss that opened at her feet?"[19] Here as else-where Wharton departs from her classical source in suggesting that Persephone was something of a willing captive; this, of course, conso-nant with the "new woman's" will to knowledge registered in so many turn-of-the-century women's writings.

However, in this instance Paulina-Persephone rejects her potential abductor, preferring to remain in her sanctuary, devoted to writing her grandfather's biography. When she has finished, she discovers that "it was not so much her grandfather's life as her own that she had written" (250). Paulina had rejected the suitor in order to devote herself to her art, much as Louisa Ellis had done in "A New England Nun." "All her youth, all her dreams, all her renunciations lay in that neat bundle on her knee" (250).

Like Betsey Dole's work in Freeman's "A Poetess" (1891), Paulina's book is rejected by patriarchal authorities. The Boston publisher to whom she submits the work turns it down. She returns home, deso-late, feeling her life has been wasted. The story ends, however, on a twist that the local colorists would never have entertained. One day a young scholar comes to the house, declaring that her grandfather was a great genius and that one of his works had been prophetic. They retrieve his book and publish it; Paulina feels vindicated and that her life has served its purpose. It should be pointed out, however (and Wharton does not), that in the end Paulina has served as a vehicle for the transmission of a patriarchal tradition; her own work remains unpublished and therefore on the margins, silent. That the grand-father's name is Orestes recalls the Greek matricide celebrated in *The Oresteia,* which ratified what Friedrich Engels called the "world-historic" defeat of matriarchy.

Thus, even though she rejects Persephone's fate at the beginning, Paulina in effect succumbs in the end—a sign of Wharton's own transition into the patriarchal sphere and growing acceptance of patriarchal ideological hegemony, a sign, one could say, of Wharton's own ambivalent capitulation.

Wharton's first full-length novel, while ostensibly about the political problems of a liberal eighteenth-century Italian ruler, further reveals Wharton's preoccupation with women's transition from the traditional marginal women's sphere into patriarchal mainstream reality. The central focus of the issue in *The Valley of Decision* (1902) is Fulvia Vivaldi, an educated free woman who, along with her father (significantly she has no mother), influences the ruler-protagonist to embrace the new Enlightenment "religion of humanity."[20] Fulvia represents the ideal of assimilationist feminism, the woman scholar who has fully inscribed herself in the traditions of patriarchal knowledge, leaving far behind the traditional world of women. At a civic festival proclaiming a new liberal constitution, Fulvia gives a speech in Latin, which she has mastered (always a sign of patriarchal assimilation).[21] "The wall behind her was covered by an ancient fresco . . . representing the patron scholars of the mediaeval world: the theologians, law-givers and logicians . . . Origen, Zeno, David, Lycurgus, Aristotle . . . the forbears of the long line of theorists of whom Fulvia was the last inconscient mouthpiece" (2:278). In other words, Fulvia is one of the old boys; she is squarely placed in the patriarchal tradition. Contrasted to her is the protagonist's wife, who remains the sheltered-child type despised by Wharton. "Freshly perfumed and powdered . . . she curiously recalled [an] arrogant child" (2:230).

Despite Wharton's obvious preference for Fulvia, she sees her as a fundamental exile, one who is doomed by the forces of darkness. At the civic festival the crowd grows angry; the people fear Fulvia and have come to see her as a witch. Finally someone in the throng shoots her through the heart (significantly), and she dies. Wharton presents this as the triumph of ignorance over enlightenment (the crowd is carrying images of the Mountain Virgin [Mary]), but on a deeper level it reflects the tensions Wharton herself was experiencing between the powers of the women's Dianic-Demeter world (the Mountain Virgin) and the entrance into the patriarchal world endorsed by assimilationist feminism. In a strange way Fulvia is a Persephone who has abandoned Demeter and the women's world of "love and ritual." That she is shot in the heart signifies this abandonment/betrayal. The act may be seen as Demeter's revenge, transformative, turning the world to barren ground, and turning her daughter to Hecate, to death. Most of the new women in Wharton's world, however noble, appear to be doomed before they start, victims of maternal Erinyes, predestined for imminent death; one has only to think of Lily Bart.

Sanctuary (1903), Wharton's third novella, is a complex work that continues the moral investigations begun in *The Touchstone*. Here, too, the underlying conflict is between the maternal sphere, with its inherently humane value system, and the public sphere, dominated by the amorality of capitalist Darwinism. The upholder of the matriarchal tradition and ethic in this work is Kate Orme.

Engaged to a man named Dennis Peyton, she learns shortly before their marriage that Dennis had betrayed his brother's wife by denying that she was in fact his wife, thereby inheriting his brother's fortune himself. As a result the woman had killed herself and her child. Kate's accession to the knowledge of this sordid episode constitutes her personal fall. She began "to perceive that the fair surface of life was honeycombed by a vast system of moral sewage."[22] She had come to a "recognition of evil" and felt "a great moral loneliness" (111). "[L]ife lay before her as it was: not brave, garlanded and victorious, but naked, grovelling and diseased, dragging on its maimed limbs through the mud" (111). It is the betrayal of the traditional woman—Demeter—that has effected this sense of a fall in Kate. She nearly breaks her engagement but in somewhat subtle reasoning decides to marry Dennis nevertheless in order to keep his children from being tainted by this familial evil, and to see that the money gleaned by evil means goes to some good.

The second part of the novella skips ahead a generation: her husband died when their son Dick was six years old; he has since grown up, is an artist, and Kate has used the money to finance his education as an architect. Here, as in "The Angel at the Grave," the line of descent is patrilineal; women are able only to facilitate the transmission of the "descent of man."

The world in which her son and his generation operate is one severed from a maternal personalist ethic; it is governed primarily by a social-Darwinist capitalist ethic of competition and success, the survival of the fittest. Clemence Verney, a "new woman," fully divorced from the realm of Demeter and its values, exemplifies this new breed, epitomized finally in Undine Spragg. Clemence becomes interested in Dick, but Kate fears that the interest is not in him as a person, only in his success.

In a conversation with Clemence, Kate wonders aloud whether Dick isn't becoming too ambitious. Clemence demurs: "Can one be? . . .

Ambition is so splendid! It must be so glorious to be a man and go crashing through the obstacles. . . . I'm afraid I don't care for people who are superior to success. I like marriage by capture!" (124)—an allusion to the Darwinian notion that the superior male captures the female to ensure the survival of the fittest, the thesis proposed in Darwin's *Descent of Man* (1871). Dick has also accepted social-Darwinist ideology. When Kate suggests that Clemence may lose interest in him if he loses an art competition, he says in that event, "why, I shall have to make way for someone else. . . . That's the law of life" (129).

The moral crisis of the work occurs when Dick's chief competitor dies, willing his blueprints, which are superior to Dick's, to him. Dick thus has the option of using the blueprints dishonestly, pretending they are his, thereby winning the competition and the girl. Clemence casuistically argues that he should use the blueprints because in caring for his friend he lost time in preparing his own work, and these should therefore be seen as recompense. Kate, of course, sees it as a moral issue parallel to her husband's.

Finally, Dick decides against the fraudulent use of his competitor's material and withdraws from the competition. The decision is presented as a return to the maternal world and its ethic. He tells his mother that in the process of making his decision "old things you'd said and done kept coming back to me . . . like old friends I'd gone back on" (162)—the projected dishonesty is seen as betrayal of the mother. But finally Dick overcomes his resistance to the maternal influence: "suddenly, I don't know how, you weren't an obstacle any longer, but a refuge—and I crawled into your arms as I used to when things went against me at school" (162). In this work, then, the maternal triumphs; its ethic prevails.

Collectively, the stories published in the 1904 volume, entitled *The Descent of Man* with intentional irony, further convey the sense seen in earlier works of a fallen but entrenched patriarchy with women reduced to ineffectual, marginal roles ("The Descent of Man" and the much-anthologized "The Other Two"), in transition from the maternal realm to the patriarchal ("The Mission of Jane"), or in the thrall of patriarchal captivity ("The Lady Maid's Bell" and "The House of the Dead Hand").

The title story portrays the moral fall of a scholar engaged in Darwinian theory who compromises his integrity for commercial success. His wife is an ineffectual, marginal woman who, unlike Kate Peyton, makes no effort to provide a moral check on his behavior.[23]

"The Mission of Jane" is a variation of the Demeter-Persephone script. After the adoption of a girl, Jane, Lethbury's wife's (it is told from his point of view) personality changes. "She was no longer herself alone: she was herself and Jane. Gradually, a monstrous fusion of identity, she became herself, himself and Jane . . . he found himself carelessly squeezed into the smallest compartment of the domestic economy."[24] Jung once explained: "Demeter-Kore exists on the plane of mother-daughter experience, which is alien to man and shuts him out. In fact, the psychology of the Demeter cult bears all the features of a matriarchal order of society, where the man is an indispensable but on the whole disturbing factor."[25]

In Wharton's story the mother-daughter bond continues until Jane's education begins. As in other works of this period, that education brings Jane closer to her father and estranges her from her mother. When Jane approaches the age of ten, her mother announces "it was he who was to educate Jane. In matters of the intellect, Mrs. Lethbury was the first to declare her deficiencies" (371). Jane rapidly absorbs the new knowledge. "To her foster mother she seemed a prodigy of wisdom; but Lethbury saw . . . how the aptitudes in which Mrs. Lethbury gloried were slowly estranging her from her child" (372). " 'She's getting too clever for me,' his wife said to him . . . 'but I am so glad that she will be a companion to you' " (372). While the story ends humorously (by the time she's an adult Jane is such an apostle of modernity that both parents are relieved to see her go), it nevertheless reflects the historical transition young women of the period are undergoing. "Quicksand" is the other mother-daughter transition story in this collection.

Perhaps the most ominous story in the volume is "The House of the Dead Hand," which sounds a key that Wharton was to play to great effect in her next major (or perhaps one could say her first major) work, *The House of Mirth* (1905), also a "house of the dead hand." The story, set in Siena, describes a young woman who is effectively kept captive by her father. They live in a house over the portal of which is a "strange emblem. The hand was a woman's . . . a dead drooping hand, which hung there convulsed and helpless, as though it had been thrust forth in denunciation of some evil mystery within the house, and had sunk struggling into death."[26] The symbolism is obvious; the dead hand is that of the mother, now moribund, whose effect in challenging the moral iniquities of the public world is negligible.

The plot of this strange story is that a young Englishman, Wyant, has come to visit the home of Dr. Lombard to see the renowned

"Bergamo Leonardo." Wyant learns that Lombard's daughter, Sybilla, actually owns the painting, having invested all her savings in it for her father. "Wyant was struck by the contrast between the fierce vitality of the doctor's age and the inanimateness of his daughter's youth" (510).

Wyant learns that the girl wishes to escape; she hates the painting and wishes to sell it to have money for a dowry. But even after the father dies, the girl remains under his spell and control. She finds she cannot sell it, so she lives her life out in "the house of the dead hand" with the painting and her ineffectual mother. Ironically, the painting depicts a Circe-like figure (512); but unlike the mythical Circe (connected with both Demeter and Persephone), who casts a spell on men, turning them into animals under her control, and unlike her classical namesake, described by Virgil as "awe-inspiring" (*Aeneid*, book 6, line 11), Sybilla is herself a captive in the patriarchal underworld—a Persephone without Demeter.

Elaine Showalter has characterized *The House of Mirth* (1905) as "a pivotal text in the historical transition . . . from the homosocial women's culture and literature of the nineteenth century to the heterosexual fiction of modernism."[27] Lily Bart is another Persephone without Demeter. Disconnected from the green-world bower of the matriarchs depicted by the local colorists, Lily is in a condition of fundamental exile, alone with no supportive women's community and no emotional connections. She wanders in a patriarchal underworld governed by the economic ethic of social Darwinism, unchecked by the humane personalist values of the mothers. An object among objects, she is assessed only for her market value, and she herself, imprinted with her society's ideology, is rarely able to move beyond aesthetic judgments.[28]

Wharton emphasizes Lily's disconnection from the natural world (her name suggests a hothouse plant). She is described as "a captured dryad subdued to the conventions of the drawing-room," who at the beginning of the novel still manifests a "streak of sylvan freedom."[29] But like the other characters, she has "no real intimacy with nature" (68). Significantly, the only scene placed in a natural setting is one of the few episodes that offers hope: that in which Lily and Selden discuss his notion of a "Republic of the Spirit" (chapter 6). But Lily remains a "waterplant in the flux of the tides" (57), "a stray uprooted growth" (331), "something rootless and ephemeral" (331). Her final estrangement from Selden is analogized to "a deep-rooted plant torn from its bed" (332).

By contrast, the novel is set in the postlapsarian world of New York City, whose streets are "dreary" (7), "dull and bare" (240), a "post-matriarchal city of sexual commerce."[30] The opening scene takes place in Grand Central Station, which symbolizes the imperialist world of industrial capitalism at the height of ascendancy in early twentieth-century America. It is a world governed by the economic ethic of social Darwinism and its doctrine of male supremacy.

Caught from the beginning in the mechanisms of this nether world, Lily's fate is irreversible. There is in the novel a relentless sense that it is just a matter of time before her doom is sealed. Her poignant question, "Was it her own fault or that of destiny" (32)—the classical tragic puzzle—must be answered: "destiny." For, while her experiences within the novel plot the pattern of a fall (see below), the novel really takes place after the fall, in a place of exile from Demeter's garden. And in that sense, while Lily occasionally wanders in quest of that garden, there is for her no return because the world of the novel is irreversibly patriarchal.

Thus, the improbable series of coincidences that occur in the work—such as her encounters with Selden at Grand Central Station, with the cleaning woman and Rosedale at the Benedick, and Selden's glimpse of her leaving Gus Trenor's—which might seem to be flaws if considered from a realistic point of view, are really on a mythic level manifestations of a subterranean fate that has Lily in its grip. She is part of a "carefully elaborated plan" (7), "the victim of the civilization which had produced her" (9), enclosed in a cage, like a fly in a bottle (59).

The plan, the cage, the mechanism, is the heterosexist imperative of patriarchal culture. As described by Claude Lévi-Strauss, Juliet Mitchell, and Gayle Rubin, it is a culture predicated upon the exchange of women. "The controlled exchange of women . . . defines human culture [and] is reproduced in . . . patriarchal ideology."[31] Women's identity is therefore determined by *"their cultural utilization as exchange-objects."*[32]

The transition from the preoedipal to the oedipal is therefore for women, according to Rubin, a "conscription" into a patriarchal ideological system that posits them as objects for exchange.[33] Lily Bart, perhaps because of her "streak of sylvan freedom," resists this conscription, but cut off from matriarchal sources of power and identity, her situation is hopeless.

Parenthetically, it is interesting to note that most women's fiction—beginning with their earliest novels and protonovels in the eighteenth century—that deals with mainstream (patriarchal) society, based as it is upon the exchange of women, provides a negative critique of the (marriage market) rituals of that society. This is the main theme of the novel of manners, a genre to which *House of Mirth* belongs. Only where women writers deal with marginal worlds, at the fringe of mainstream society, in the wild zone, do they construct positive nonoedipal visions. This was the case with the New England local colorists.

It is in this patriarchal context that we must plot Lily's inevitable fall. The pivotal event of the novel must therefore be seen, as Elizabeth Ammons points out, as Gus Trenor's attempted rape of Lily, an episode that manifests a "perfect coalescence of predatory economics and sexual politics."[34] While the rape is not physically successful, mythically it is, for like Hades's rape of Persephone, it precipitates Lily's long journey through the underworld. Her market value destroyed, her place in the exchange network eliminated, she no longer has even the option of patriarchal incest (a choice seen in other Wharton novels, such as *Summer*); her only recourse is death.

Significantly, after the episode with Gus, the Eumenides—the Furies of female vengeance, associated in ancient myth with underworld goddesses Persephone and Hecate—begin to appear to Lily. They are best known in classical literature as the avengers of mother murder (Klytemnestra's by Orestes), and at this fatal moment Lily recalls having read Euripides' *Eumenides* and applies the legend somewhat superficially to herself. She too feels hounded by Furies and "alone in a place of darkness and pollution" (156). Mythically, Lily is a victim of mother murder in that her exile is the result of the destruction of Demeter's garden effected by patriarchal ascendancy in late nineteenth-century culture. The avenging furies that hound her were loosed by that event.

In this dark hour Lily, pathetically, seeks to retrieve the maternal bower. "What Lily craved was the darkness made by enfolding arms, the silence which is not solitude but compassion holding its breath" (156). In this mood, she seeks out her one potential female friend, Gerty Farish. But, again in an ironic twist of circumstances, Gerty is angry with Lily because she feels she has stolen Selden from her. Unaware, Lily seeks Gerty's apartment, hoping to "feel the hold of Gerty's arms" (157).

The scene that ensues, with the two women together in Gerty's bed, is a painful rehearsal of the demise of the nineteenth-century female world of "love and ritual": "The light extinguished, they lay still in the darkness, Gerty shrinking to the outer edge of the narrow couch to avoid contact with her bedfellow . . . every fibre in her body shrank from Lily's nearness" (175).

Yet Gerty cannot repress an awareness of Lily's sensual presence. "Everything about [Lily] was warm and soft and scented. . . . But as Gerty lay with arms drawn down her side in the motionless narrowness of an effigy, she felt a stir of sobs. . . . Lily flung out her hand, groped for her friend's, and held it out" (175). Lily asks Gerty to hold her, and Gerty obliges; she "silently slipped an arm under her, pillowing her head in its hollow as a mother makes a nest for a tossing child" (176). This momentary lesbian-maternal refuge is short-lived, however. With the return of daybreak the two women resume their alienated stances. In a hasty departure the two kiss perfunctorily, "but without a trace of the previous night's emotion" (178).

The furies continue to plague Lily. One critic has seen her trip to Europe as a voyage to "the underworld";[35] Lily begins to sense "ominous cracks and vapours" (210); in a final dismal exchange she and Selden meet in "deserted gardens" (227). And by the time she is living in the Emporium she has taken on the aspects of an "underworld goddess."[36] She begins to see the people around her as "shades in limbo" (283). The final scenes of the novel involve Lily's progressive decline, relieved momentarily by the visit to Nettie Struther's apartment, where the mother-child connection is ironically evoked, sounding the Demeter-Persephone theme. Lily's instincts now are pushing her toward escape; she begins taking chloral to help her sleep, and a final overdose leads to her death. Her last moments entail a sense of utter alienation, a sense of being cut off from any human connection, or of having any rootedness in a nourishing bower (331). As she settles to sleep, she imagines herself cradling the Struther child in a gesture that recalls Gerty's nestling of her. The final image is therefore of the Demeter-Persephone reunion, but ironically the only mother Lily embraces is death.

The year following *The House of Mirth* Wharton published an odd and atypical story, which featured one of her few authentically Dianic women, entitled "The Hermit and the Wild Woman" (1906). This archetypal story takes place on the margins of society, in the wilderness. It concerns a hermit, who has chosen to live in a cave to escape the ravages of the wars between the Guelfs and the Ghibellines (it is set in Renaissance Italy), and a "wild woman," who has been excommunicated from the church for having escaped from a convent. Both peacefully tend their gardens in the forest and occasionally help one another.

The wild woman is clearly a refugee from patriarchy; she had left the convent because of its severe regime of self-mortification in which initiates are forbidden to bathe. Bathing becomes a symbol of sensual participation in the green world, forbidden by patriarchy. Water is of course the traditional symbol of rebirth of vegetation, of physical life. In the convent the woman becomes obsessed with bathing, with reimmersing herself in this sensuous vegetative-animal world. One night she sneaks off to bathe secretly. Nothing, she says, "could have surpassed in ecstasy that first touch of water on my limbs. . . . And the water . . . seemed to crave me as I craved it. Its ripples rose about me, first in furtive touches, then in a long embrace that clung and drew me down; till at length they lay like kisses on my lips."[37] After this sensuous reunion with the green world, while in captivity, the woman decides to escape from the convent. She lives her life out in the wilderness, tending her garden and eating as a vegetarian, "for she said that in her vagrant life the wild creatures of the wood had befriended her, and as she had slept in peace among them, so now she would never suffer them to be molested" (586). She is also adept at herbal medicine. She is, in short, a Diana figure, whose world contrasts shockingly with the barren ground of *The House of Mirth.*

Justine Brent in *The Fruit of the Tree* (1907) is another Diana figure, one of the few attractive women in Wharton's repertoire, but considerably more compromised than the "wild woman" of the previous story. A working woman (a nurse) who is socially conscious, she nevertheless manages to retain her green-world roots as a source of strength. She is also a "new woman" who can hold her own with men.

One revealing scene shows Justine reentering the green-world bower as a native. Accompanying her are Cicily, her charge, and John Amherst, Cicily's father and Justine's employer (he is a wealthy factory owner); they are in quest of a rare native orchid. "Justine's sylvan tastes had developed in the little girl a passion for such pillaging expeditions."[38] As they enter the swamp, "Amherst, as became his sex, went first" (299). But as they move deeper into the green recesses, "Justine, leading the way, guided them . . . as fearlessly as a kingfisher" (300). She "looked like a wood-spirit who had absorbed into herself the last golden juices of the year" (302).

Justine has also benefited from "a youth of confidential intimacy with [her] mother" (145), which was spent by "a tiny hearth-fire" "in the wilderness" (146). After years of solitude Justine "had created for herself an inner kingdom," a "secret precinct" (152)—in other words she has been able to retain within herself a matriarchal bower that is nourishing and sustaining.

Contrasted to Justine is Bessy Westmore, Amherst's frivolous, leisure-class wife, a character out of *The House of Mirth*; her only interests are materialistic, and her mode of being, complaisant collusion in the capitalist/patriarchal exploitations of her class. In other words, she is one of the parasitical maternal collaborates whom Wharton excoriates throughout her fiction.

The plot, therefore, while ostensibly a muckraking problem novel about factory conditions and the ethics of mercy killing, on a deeper, mythic level concerns a mother murder, matricide. The new woman, Justine Brent, kills the mother figure, Bessy Westmore. This event takes place on both a literal and a symbolic level.

On a literal level Justine has the task of nursing Bessy, who has been paralyzed in a fall from a horse. (The paralysis is, of course, symbolic of the traditional woman's condition.) Bessy is in terrible pain, and the prognosis for a complete recovery is poor. "Bessy's moaning began to wear on [Justine]. It was no longer the utterance of human pain, but the monotonous whimper of an animal—the kind of sound that a compassionate hand would instinctively crush into silence" (431). Justine comes to believe the doctors are mindlessly keeping her alive "as a . . . sort of scientific experiment" (548). And in this sense her mercy killing (she finally gives Bessy an overdose of morphia) may be seen as an expression of a feminine critique of a dominant patriarchal tradition—that of medicine and science—and therefore another instance of women's resistance to the encroachment of these disciplines. Justine's humane antiscientific bent is emphasized on various occasions; her "sympathy" is described as being "less logical . . . [but] warmer, more penetrating" (446; see also 457). In other words, her instincts are more holistic, and in this sense more in tune with traditional women's culture, than the (male) doctors.

On the other hand, Justine's justification for her act has come from reading patriarchal *sententiae* that Amherst has copied earlier. These Nietzschean aphorisms affirm that the great soul is above the herd and has the right and obligation to make decisions beyond herd morality. It is in this Faustian spirit that she commits her act. Since the

Faustian will to power is undercut in the final scene of the novel (see below), it seems likely that Wharton felt Justine guilty of hubris in committing her deed.

The underlying mythic pattern is, however, that of the new woman destroying the mother and marrying the father (Justine eventually marries Amherst), an obverse oedipal pattern. One wonders if, like Lily Bart, Justine had read *The Eumenides*, for the Oresteian drama is the only ancient text in which a daughter participates in mother murder (Electra does not actually murder her mother, Klytemnestra, but she acquiesces in the act).

In terms of the mythic patterns under discussion, Justine's gesture may be seen as a repetition of the ontogenetic crisis that occurs as women enter into patriarchal culture: the preoedipal mother must be destroyed. Bessy's "preoedipal" character is accentuated in her dying scenes when she is reduced to an "animal-like" condition of muteness and paralysis. Historically, for the new woman to inscribe herself, to assimilate herself into patriarchy, the old woman—the mother—must be destroyed. That Wharton sees the old woman not as the powerful matriarch depicted by the local colorists but as a paralyzed collaborator (just as she fails to recognize the matriarchal power in her local-color predecessors, dismissing them as "roses-and-lavender" "author-esses") is symptomatic of the extent to which she herself is of the "daughters' generation," cut off from a female source, literarily and personally, an alien under patriarchal ideological "captivity."

Like Nan Prince in *A Country Doctor*, Justine must relinquish the golden apples, "the fruit of the tree"—another allusion to the fall—if she is to engage successfully in patriarchal systems. And she is a successful Atalante; Amherst comes to see her as an equal; he comes to realize that "woman can think as well as feel" (559), a discovery that "had the effect of making him discard his former summary conception of woman as a bundle of inconsequent impulses, and admit her at a stroke to full mental equality with her lord" (560).

Nevertheless, the denouement of Wharton's novel is problematic. Justine discovers that she too is hounded by avenging furies (though they are not named such). "She remembered some old Greek saying . . . that the gods never forgave the mortal who presumes to love and suffer like a god. She had dared to do both, and the gods were bringing ruin" (555). Justine's ruin is not so complete as Lily's. Eventually she and Amherst reconcile (he had been unable to accept her "mercy killing" as such), and he uses Bessy's money to construct a brave new world, a socialist factory. The concluding episode, a ceremonial to open this model plant, parallels Faust's great engineering triumph at the end of that epic, which Wharton accentuates by having Amherst recall Faust's "moment" looking "out at last over the marsh [he] had drained" (633). But the price of this public triumph is dear, and Justine, knowing that it required the death of the mother and her own compromise, provides the concluding ironic viewpoint. In the end, unlike Nan Prince, her role—that of complaisant assistant to Amherst—is not far removed from that of Bessy Westmore.

In the four years between *The Fruit of the Tree* and her next great work, *Ethan Frome* (1911), Wharton wrote several stories that are of special interest. The first of these, "All Souls" (c. 1908), is one of Wharton's ghost stories in which dead figures, usually women, come back to haunt the living. The plot details of this story are not important. What is significant is Wharton's sensitivity to the claims of a women's community, though in this case it is a community of the dead, of witches—recalling once again that the fundamental mythic event of this period in women's history is the death of the witch-woman matriarch. In this story one of the servant women in a Connecticut home is believed to be inhabited by a witch and involved in a coven. "Anyone," the narrator remarks, "who has once felt the faintest curiosity to assist at a Coven apparently soon finds the curiosity increase to desire, the desire to an uncontrollable longing . . . those who have once taken part in a Coven will move heaven and earth to take part again."[39]

But the death of the wild woman is signified in a story published the following year, "The Daunt Diana" (1909), in which Diana is reduced to the frames of a painting, an objet d'art, a commodity whose worth is haggled over by patriarchal connoisseurs. This is one of those stories narrated from the point of view of a patriarchal "old boy" who has contempt for women's alleged lack of appreciation for "great" art.

Two stories published in 1910 further amplify Wharton's thematic development. "Afterward," also a ghost story, demonstrates the inefficacy of women's moral influence, locked as it is in a marginal garden world, to check the Darwinistic behavior that reigns in capitalist patriarchy. A subterranean power gets revenge, however. The plot is that Mary Boyne remains ignorant of her husband's unethical business practices, spending most of her time tending her garden. One day a stranger appears and Ned, her husband, disappears with him. Mary later learns that the mysterious stranger is the ghost of a man Ned had cheated in a business deal, who had committed suicide. In discussing Ned's immoral behavior Mary is told: "It's the kind of thing that happens everyday in business . . . it's what the scientists call the survival of the fittest."[40] Ned, however, never reappears; the avenging furies—the powers from the mother's ethical sphere—have punished him.

"The Letters" is somewhat reminiscent of *The Fruit of the Tree*. Here again a competition is cast between a new woman, a governess, and a traditional woman, an invalid who lives in a "drug-scented room, [and] lavished [her attention] on her dog-earred novels and on the 'society notes' of the morning paper."[41] This woman soon dies, however, allowing the governess, Lizzie West, to marry her husband, Vincent Deering, who had already kissed Lizzie while his wife was alive.

From this point on the plot takes on the pattern of *The Bunner Sisters*. Deering proves himself undependable; he disappears for several years, leaving Lizzie in near poverty, only reappearing when he learns she has inherited a fortune. Meanwhile, a one-sided romantic friendship has developed between Lizzie and Andora Macy; however, Lizzie, like Ann Eliza, develops a vicious contempt for Andora because she is a spinster and has not been sanctified by male attention.

After their marriage, when Lizzie discovers that Vincent had probably married her for her money, she momentarily considers leaving him. Andora encourages such a move: "My darling!" she says, "Remember you have your child—and me!" (205). However, Lizzie cannot overcome her feeling of contempt for Andora (reminiscent also of Lily's condescension toward Gerty); "a feeling of estrangement" comes between them, and Lizzie decides to stay with imperfect Vincent because there seem to be no other options. Thus, bonding between women gives way to heterosexual marriage, to which there are no alternatives: patriarchal hegemony is complete.

Wharton stated that her motivation in writing *Ethan Frome* (1911) was to repudiate what she saw as the sentimentalist vision of the local colorists, her literary foremothers. She could not have been more successful. The barren, frozen world of Starkfield, an obviously symbolic name, could not be farther from the green-world bower of the local-color matriarchs. To read *Ethan Frome* in tandem with Jewett's *Country of the Pointed Firs* (1896) is to realize a study in contrast. Both are set in the New England landscape, on the margins of society, but Wharton's world is a paralyzed wintry wasteland, lifeless and ultimately loveless, where Jewett's Dunnet Landing is a lush summer paradise animated by what Smith-Rosenberg labeled female "love and ritual." Where Jewett's work concerns a mother-daughter reunion, and reinspiration for a daughter-artist from the Demeter herbalist Almira Todd, Wharton's is about mother-daughter estrangement, demonic maternal tyranny, spiritual paralysis, and death.

Yet Wharton's work can also be seen as a continuation of local-color thematic concerns. As noted in chapter 1, several of Mary E. Wilkins Freeman's late works concern efforts by the controlling mother to keep the daughter in the maternal sanctuary, but she is lured away by possibilities of wider knowledge, of integration into patriarchal systems.

Ethan Frome follows a similar script. As R. W. B. Lewis notes, in this novel, "as she often did, Edith shifted the sexes in devising her . . . central characters."[42] In extending his suggestion I propose that Ethan represents the daughter-author in confrontation with the mother. As in other early Wharton stories the rebellion is posed in terms of an involvement with what Annis Pratt has called a "green-world lover,"[43] represented in this novel by Mattie Silver.

A comparison with Jewett's late story "Martha's Lady" (1897), which concerns a maternal-lesbian reunion, is also instructive. In this piece a vibrant young urban woman comes to visit a relatively placid New England town; a rural woman, Martha, falls in love with her, and remains devoted to her for decades, long after the first woman has departed. Eventually, however, the women are reunited. In this story Jewett celebrates stasis and the waiting mode as a *via negativa* toward redemptive experience, the women's reconnection.

In *Ethan Frome*, a zestful youth, Mattie Silver, brings life (momentarily) into the household of Zeena and Ethan Frome. But here the concern is not with mother-daughter reunion, nor with positive female connections. Rather a triangle is set up; a heterosexual relationship threatens to destroy the mother-daughter bond to which the mother tenaciously and in the end demonically adheres. Stasis and waiting are not seen positively from the point of view of the women's community, but negatively from the masculine viewpoint as paralytical and poisonous.[44] This "masculine" viewpoint is that of daughter-author Edith Wharton, in rebellion against the world of the mothers. (Cynthia Griffin Wolff interprets the novel primarily in psychobiographical terms as reflective of Wharton's fearful feeling that to "regress" toward the "preoedipal" maternal realm means to succumb to passivity, dependency, and muteness, which is what happens to Ethan, under Zeena's control [174]. A "chilling, immobilizing, regressive passivity and dependence on Mother . . . served as the basis for the horror in *Ethan Frome*" [307].)

The central theme of *Ethan Frome* is the revenge of Demeter, seen in her dark aspect as Hecate, trying to keep her daughter under her control. Significantly, Ethan (representing the rebellious daughter) had early been interested in science and had taken some courses at a technological college,[45] but that curiosity about the wider world and new knowledge had given way to "inertia" (16) as Ethan succumbed to the mother's snare, seeming in late years to be "a part of the mute melancholy landscape, an incarnation of its frozen woe" (14).

The "melancholy landscape" is the mothers' world, seen from the point of view of the rebellious daughter. It harbors a matrilineal tradition of silence and paralysis. Ethan's own mother had early fallen ill, and while she "had been a talker in her day . . . after her 'trouble' the sound of her voice was seldom heard, though she had not lost the power of speech" (69).

Zeena followed a similar path. Within a year of their marriage she developed a comparable illness. "Then she too fell silent. Perhaps it was the inevitable effect of life on the farm, or perhaps, . . . it was because Ethan 'never listened' " (72). Ethan begins to wonder if, like his mother, "Zeena were also turning 'queer.' Women did, he knew" (73). And the final image of the book is of a graveyard, where "women have got to hold their tongues" (181).

One of our first glimpses of Zeena is with her face reflected in snowbanks, "drawn and bloodless" (64). Images of death are associated with her; "a dead cucumber-vine dangled from the porch like the crape streamer tied to the door for a death" (51). She is a ghost figure from the underworld, a Hecate whose own repression has turned her energies into demonic powers.[46] Eventually Ethan realizes that she "was no longer the listless creature who had lived at his side in a state of sullen self-absorption, but a mysterious alien presence, an evil energy secreted from the long years of silent brooding. . . . Now she had mastered him and he abhorred her" (117–18).

Zeena is another figuration of the "madwoman in the attic" seen in so many works of women's literature, but rather than interpreting Zeena ahistorically as the repressed side of a complaisant author,[47] I view this madwoman historically as the avenging matriarch, seen as demonic by the daughter-author willfully consuming the pomegranate seed in her quest for wider knowledge.

The famous sled ride may be seen as a descent into the underworld;

Ethan takes on the aspects of a "night-bird" as he pulls the sled out; "the spruces swathed them in blackness and silence. They might have been in their coffins underground" (167). The huge elm tree, an ironic inversion of the matriarchal tree of life, looms as a "black projecting mass" (170), finally merging in Ethan's mind with "his wife's face [and its] twisted monstrous lineaments" (170).[48]

After the accident Mattie cheeps like an animal (like Bessy in *The Fruit of the Tree*); she and Ethan are reduced to the world of stasis and muteness, which Wharton ascribes to the maternal realm. Their attempted escape has proved futile; theirs remains a death-in-life, perpetual confinement to the fallen world of an unplacated Demeter, who refuses to lift the barren lifeless pall she cast at the flight/betrayal of the daughter.

The same year as *Ethan Frome* Wharton published "Xingu," a somewhat tiresome satire of clubwomen bent on acquiring culture, which nevertheless includes intimations of a deeper mythic theme. Osric Dane, a woman writer, meets with members of a ladies book club to discuss her bleakly pessimistic novel *The Wings of Death* (*Ethan Frome?*). One of the women comments that the significance of the work is veiled in the way Agamemnon's face is disguised by another artist at the sacrifice of Iphigenia.[49] In alluding once again to the Oresteia myth, Wharton repeats the theme of patriarchal destruction of the Dianic daughter. Later the clubwomen outdo one another to show their knowledge of "Xingu," a nonsense word which one conjectures refers to "rites" performed at the "Eleusinian mysteries" (224)—the matriarchal religion whose ritual celebrated the story of Demeter and her reunion with Persephone. The befuddlement of the women and their complete disconnection from this ancient feminine culture further reflect the fundamental female alienation Wharton treats during this period.

The oedipal situation implicit in *The Fruit of the Tree* (where Justine, the new woman, murders a mother figure and marries the father-husband) and *Ethan Frome* (with its mother and daughter competition) is overtly evident in *The Reef*. Here the young woman, Sophy Viner, a new woman of sorts and a Diana figure, competes with a traditional woman, Anna Leath, for the attention of George Darrow, the father-husband. There is also an element of father-son rivalry between George and a son figure, Owen (actually he is Anna's stepson), over Sophy. While this theme is overt, what is unstated but assumed in the novel is that romantic/sexual involvement with a patriarch is redemptive for women—an ideology that assures that the patriarchal cultural imperative, exchange of women, will continue unchallenged.

Like Lizzie West in "The Letters," Sophy Viner is a young governess-orphan, a stock sentimentalist figure,[50] who encounters George Darrow on a boat crossing the English Channel. George is on his way to Paris, where he hopes to reconcile with a recently widowed old flame, Anna Leath. From the beginning Sophy is contrasted with Anna as more natural, fresh, spontaneous, juvenal. Whereas Anna has "the unnatural whiteness of flowers forced in the dark,"[51] Sophy is described in Dianic terms: she looked as if she had been "plunged into some sparkling element which had curled up all her drooping tendrils and wrapped her in a shimmer of fresh leaves" (36). When a lock falls over her ear, "it danced . . . like the flit of a brown wing over flowers" (31). In caressing her, "Darrow felt as if he had clasped a tree and a nymph had bloomed from it . . ." (262, Wharton's ellipsis).

The latter allusion signals to us that Wharton is presenting in *The Reef* a patriarchal inversion of the ancient Daphne myth. As noted in chapter 1, that story concerns the unsuccessful pursuit by Apollo of Daphne, a "follower of Artemis," who is turned into a tree by her mother, Earth, to save her from Apollo. As recorded by Ovid in the *Metamorphoses,* the separatist matriarchal roots of the story are clear: one male suitor of Daphne, who disguised himself as a woman to be near her (since she hated men), is killed by Daphne's virgin companions when his identity is discovered (Rose, 141). I have noted a local-colorist version of the myth in Freeman's "Old Woman Magoun," where mother Earth kills the Daphne-daughter to prevent rape-abduction by the Apollonian father. In Wharton's version of the myth the powers are held by the patriarch; it is he who transforms a tree into a "nymph" in order that he may seduce her, and as in *Ethan Frome,* "there is no mother earth."[52] The powerful green-world mothers of the local colorists are dead. With Demeter out of the way, Persephone is fair game for Hades, and George moves in on Sophy without a struggle. In their early days together they see the play *Oedipe* (50)—probably Corneille's 1659 version of *Oedipus Rex*—which underscores the oedipal theme of Wharton's novel.

Sophy is presented as an unmediated preoedipal, preliterate figure: "She was one of the elemental creatures whose emotion is all in their pulses, and who become inexpressive or sentimental when they try to turn sensation into speech" (262). George watches her trying to write a letter: "she was really powerless to put her thoughts in writing, and the inability seemed characteristic of her quick impressionable mind, and of the incessant come-and-go of her sensations" (44). In other words, Sophy harks back to the marginal world of the nineteenth-century women's literary culture, always in danger (according to Wharton) of succumbing to silence or sentimentalism, the "rose-coloured" vision.

By contrast, Anna has learned patriarchal discourse; her letters are notable for "the clear structure of the phrases" (45), yet they, like Anna herself, seem cut off from genuine expression of authentic feelings. "[A] veil . . . had always hung between herself and life" (86); "she learned to regard the substance of life as a mere canvas" (87). The latter comment suggests a conception of art that is considerably removed from the powerful sources of emotion that animate Sophy's writing, however inchoate and inarticulate it may appear to the patriarchal observer. Anna's "art" is, unfortunately, closer to Wharton's than is Sophy's. The extent to which Wharton suspected this identification or intended it is not clear. Both Sophy and Anna are, however, compelled by the governing ideology to seek their salvation in a male, George Darrow, who manages to deceive each of them in turn.

In the year following *The Reef,* Wharton published her harshest view of capitalist-patriarchal America. *The Custom of the Country* (1913) depicts a fallen, rapaciously materialistic world similar to that seen in *The House of Mirth.* Both novels are set in New York City, the capital of commercial imperialism, a patriarchal society based, as we have seen, upon the exchange of women.

Undine Spragg, the "negative hero" of this work, is, however, unlike Lily Bart, able to survive and triumph in this social-Darwinist jungle. She is, in one respect, a product of assimilationist feminism; she has adopted the behavior and values of men without challenging the system in which they operate, and without retaining ties to the maternal, private world where humane personalist values remain marginalized. As Ammons points out, she is "her father's daughter" (108). She is a capitalist who has learned to play the only market available to women— the marriage market. She sells herself as a commodity and she rises, ruthlessly, on the ladder to commercial success through a succession of marriages to wealthy men. As Wolff notes, "Undine is the spirit of competition imbued with a voracious appetite" (253), and, we might add, unchecked by any feminine-maternal moral scruples. These have been left behind in the private sphere. Indeed, Wharton ascribes to the old-world aristocracy, which is giving way to nouveaux-riches "Invaders" such as the Spraggs, a moral integrity not seen in the latter. Under the old ethic we learn there was "an archaic probity that had not yet learned to distinguish between private and 'business' honour."[53]

As in such stories as "Afterward" and "The Descent of Man," Wharton decries the public-private split, the separation of life into distinct spheres for men and women, with its attendant divergence in ethics, the one an amoral social-Darwinist struggle for survival cast in economic terms, and the other the women's caring ethic of concern, relegated to an ineffectual marginal existence. This was a central concern of the nineteenth- and early twentieth-century cultural feminists. The "custom of the country" that Wharton abhors is, in fact, the confinement of women to the private sphere, to the dependent status of the wife in marriage. It is this "custom" that creates figures like Undine; she is a "monstrously perfect result of the system" (208). Wolff points out that the phrase "custom of the country" derives from a Fletcher and Massinger play (of the same title) that concerns a realm where "women's virtue is no more than a piece of property." It is "a world whose moral center has been lost—a world where everything is for sale" (Wolff, 247).

Like Clemence Verney in *Sanctuary* (where a maternal ethic reclaims the central character from the "descent of man"), Undine's god is material success. She recalls the stock figure, the gold-digger, of scores of eighteenth-century novels of manners but seems a particularly American version, a capitalist "reptile" of the sort condemned by Cather in *My Ántonia*. Cut off from nature, her responses are aesthetic and amoral. Unlike a childhood friend who "played Atalante to all the boyhood of the quarter . . . Undine's chief delight was to 'dress up' . . . and 'play lady' before the wardrobe mirror" (22). It is an early rehearsal of the role she will play in life, like Lily, an object in the patriarchal exchange of women; but unlike Lily she is willing to sell herself as a commodity and therefore to manipulate the market to her own gain. It is a particularly chilling vision, exceeded in its pessimism only by *Summer*, Wharton's next novel.

Shortly before *Summer*, Wharton published a strange story entitled "Kerfol" (1916), which, like most of her other ghost tales, concerns demonic female revenge, in this case against a patriarch who violates the precultural bond between women and animals. Set in seventeenth-century Brittany, the story bears some resemblance to Susan Glaspell's celebrated "A Jury of Her Peers," published the following year.

Anne de Berrigan is a child bride to an aging patriarch who keeps her "like a prisoner."[54] Her only companions in her isolation are her dogs. When her husband discovers that she has given the collar of a pet to a young (male) friend who is leaving on a trip, he strangles the dog in a fit of jealousy and leaves it on her pillow. He continues this unpleasant ritual with a succession of dogs. One day, however, he is found murdered; the wounds look like bite marks. At her trial Anne claimed he was killed by a pack of dogs—the ghosts of her strangled pets. She spends the remainder of her days in seclusion, perceived by the community as "a harmless madwoman" (300).

Summer is a classic text in women's literature because it is so archetypally expressive of the psychic transition treated in this study; it is a repetition of the rape of Artemis-Persephone and the death of Demeter. Set in a sterile New England village similar to Starkfield (Wharton called it her hot *Ethan Frome*), the story concerns a young girl, Charity Royall, a Dianic figure who thirsts for wider knowledge and longs to escape from North Dormer, where she works in a library, her "prison-house."[55] The novel has overtones of incest, because Charity's abductor/seducer is her foster father. Paternal incest had indeed become one of Wharton's preoccupations; the celebrated Beatrice Palmato fragment, recently discovered, is thought to have been written in 1918 or 1919, shortly after *Summer*.[56]

In the beginning of the novel Charity retains connections with the green-world bower: "she loved the roughness of the dry mountain grass . . . the smell of the thyme . . . the fingering of the wind in her hair and through her cotton blouse" (21). "She often climbed up the hill and lay there alone for the mere pleasure of feeling the wind and of rubbing her cheeks in the grass. Generally at such times she did not think of anything, but lay immersed in an inarticulate well-being" (21). She is reminiscent of Sylvia in Jewett's "A White Heron" (1886), who is similarly in tune with nature, which she understands in a preverbal, preoedipal way (Wharton's descriptions are somewhat more sensuous than Jewett's, however). Like Sylvia's, Charity's "awakening" is precipitated by a young urban visitor, a green-world lover, Lucius Harney. Unlike Sylvia, who rejects the visitor to her rural realm, Charity engages in an affair with him. In Jewett's story, too, there is no overlooming patriarchal figure such as Charity's foster father, lawyer Royall. There indeed are no patriarchs at all in "A White Heron"; its world remains a matriarchal sanctuary. There Artemis-Persephone remains inviolate in preliterate communion with animals and vegetation.

Charity is, by contrast, under patriarchal domination from the beginning. A central, poignant image in the novel makes this clear: one
day while communing in nature, Charity felt "merged in a moist
earth-smell that was like the breath of some huge sun-warmed animal" (54). Suddenly, however, "there came between her eyes and [a]
dancing butterfly, the sight of a man's foot in a large worn boot" (54).
This image symbolizes the forces that operate in the novel: the patriarchal boot obliterating women's connection with rural, matriarchal
roots. Charity recalls the image when her foster father Royall proposes to her for the second time: "As she listened, there flitted
through her mind the vision of Liff Hyatt's muddy boot coming down
on the white bramble-flowers" (118).

In this novel the mothers are reduced to nearly nonhuman status:
Charity encounters her own mother only after she is dead (where her
corpse is compared to a dead animal). The only other mother figure
in the work is Verena Marsh (whose name recalls the green-world
bower), a servant woman in the Royall household. She is "a deaf
pauper" (38) who lives in the attic. Her presence engenders silence
and ignorance. "Verena's deafness prevented her being a source of
news, and no one came to the house who could bring enlightenment"
(109). In short, she is the ultimate Wharton image of the atrophied,
marginalized mother.

When Charity learns that she is pregnant (by Harney) and that he is
going to abandon her for another, she tries to seek out her natural
mother. Like Lily Bart, when the patriarchal powers become oppressive, she seeks (also unsuccessfully) the maternal bower. She had occasionally in the past wondered who her mother was; she knew she had
been adopted by Royall when her father, an alcoholic convict, had
asked the lawyer to retrieve the child from her mother, one of the
mountain people who lived as half-civilized "swamp-people" in the
wilderness near North Dormer (86). In her troubled state Charity
determines to return to the mountain to save her child (238) and to
find her mother (240). Her impulse is therefore to reestablish the
mother-daughter connection, to return to the marginal matriarchal
wilderness, to reunite with Demeter. After a long, arduous journey,
Charity finally reaches her mountain home, but she is too late. Her
mother, Mary Hyatt, has just died. Charity observes, "there was no
sign of anything human [in her face]: she lay there like a dead dog in a
ditch" (250).

A brief moment of female connection occurs after her mother's funeral when a kindly elderly woman takes Charity in: "in silence she and Charity walked away together through the night" (259). However, Charity experiences estrangement from her own mother: she "herself felt as remote from the poor creature she had seen lowered into her hastily dug grave as if the height of heavens had divided them" (259).

At this moment, with Demeter dead and her world demolished, Hades moves in. Lawyer Royall comes up the mountain to retrieve Charity, who by then had begun to feel alien among the mountain people; for the third time he proposes, and this time, worn down and with no alternatives, abandoned and totally estranged from the matriarchal community, Charity accepts. "[S]he followed Mr. Royall as passively as a tired child" (274). Earlier in an "Old Home Week" celebration in North Dormer for which, ironically, Charity had prepared hemlock garlands (symbols of death), she had fallen in a faint "face downward at Mr. Royall's feet" (199). In the marriage ceremony Charity finds the liturgy reminds her of the burial rhetoric used at her mother's entombment. "[R]eading out of the same book [the] words . . . had the same dread sound of finality" (278). Patriarchal words, which Wharton herself had seen as analogous to the pomegranate seed, are here seen as casting and ratifying Persephone-Charity's final captivity. "For an instant the old impulse of flight swept through her; but it was only the lift of a broken wing" (280).

Summer records the demise of the nineteenth-century women's community of Demeter and the abduction of Persephone, whose doom, as Wharton recognized in the playlet "Pomegranate Seed," published shortly before, is henceforth forever cast in the world of the dead.

The thematic patterns laid out in earlier works—the myth of the fall, the mother-daughter connection, and the theme of Diana—are continued in *The Age of Innocence* (1920), which many consider Wharton's greatest work. Like most Wharton novels, this one is told from the point of view of the central male personage, Newland Archer, a device that reflects Wharton's continuing male identification. The novel, nevertheless, centrally addresses the women's issues considered in this study. The ironic title refers to a prelapsarian age; the novel is set in New York in the 1870s, but the "innocence" of the title is seen by Wharton to be fraudulent, a further expression of her emphatic rejection of the world of the mothers.

As in several earlier Wharton works—*The Bunner Sisters, The Fruit of*

the Tree, Ethan Frome, The Reef, and "The Letters"—this novel centers
upon a primary mother-daughter competition. In this respect *The Age
of Innocence* seems closest to *The Fruit of the Tree.* Once again two
women are contrasted and set in implicit competition: the one, a representative of the "older" traditional woman, May Welland, is drawn
against Ellen Olenska, something of a new woman who has moved out
of the maternal bower into new realms of knowledge and experience,
and therefore, like her author, a daughter figure. May Welland resembles in some ways Bessy Westmore; she is a sheltered, childlike type of
woman but is more compassionate, less materialistic, less selfish than
Bessy, and therefore more sympathetic. Ellen Olenska, separated
from her husband, a "brute . . . who kept her practically a prisoner,"[57]
is able, like Justine Brent, to bear the brunt of social opprobrium
without collapsing. She moves beyond Justine, however, in being able
finally to make it independently; by the end of the novel she is living
in a room of her own.

As in *The Reef* and other works, there is an inherently "oedipal"
competition in *The Age of Innocence* between the old woman and the
new, the mother and the daughter, for the favors of a man. The title,
therefore, takes on the added irony that in a truly nonoedipal,
prepatriarchal, prelapsarian world, as seen in the literature of the
local colorists, there is no such competition. The mother-daughter
bond remains primary.

In a few earlier works—notably *The Fruit of the Tree,* "The Hermit
and the Wild Woman," and *Summer*—Wharton had presented authentic Dianic daughter figures who, if doomed, were nevertheless in occasional connection with the maternal green-world bower. In this novel,
the Dianic world is seen as fraudulent, associated with the marginal,
ineffective, static women's sphere Wharton feared and rejected.

The opening scene of the novel initiates the theme. Newland Archer is at a performance of the opera, Gounod's *Faust.* It is the garden
scene where (Wharton does not specify) Faust, the patriarch, is seduc-
ing Margaret, an innocent preliterate Artemis-Persephone, which
leads to her ruin/fall. In this context Newland observes May Welland
across the hall; she is "a young girl in white" (3), carrying, as she
always does, white flowers (4). The association is clear; like Margaret,
she too is an Artemis-Persephone. Later in the novel Wharton returns
to the garden scene, this time accentuating the seduction aspect: "the
same large blonde victim was succumbing to the same small brown
seducer" (323). The Margaret figure is, however, presented as having

"*affected* a guileless incomprehension of [Faust's] designs" (4, my emphasis), which suggests Wharton's central perception that the innocent naiveté presumed in the Dianic woman is fraudulent. This is consonant with Wharton's insistence elsewhere that Persephone was at least a half-willing victim, and with her emphatic rejection of any "rose-coloured" visions that impute a basic goodness to human character as sentimentalist and false.

As Newland cynically remarks, in reflecting upon May's apparent innocence, "all this frankness and innocence were only an artificial product. Untrained human nature was not frank and innocent; it was full of the twists and defences of an instinctive guile" (43). He is particularly "oppressed by this creation of factitious purity, so cunningly manufactured by a conspiracy of mothers and aunts and grandmothers . . . because it was supposed to be what he wanted . . . in order that he might exercise his lordly pleasure in smashing it like an image made of snow" (43). Now we have the point of view of Hades, complaining that the matriarchs have seduced him into raping-seducing Persephone! In other words, the Persephone-Hades myth is here cast as just another game in the exchange of women, a ritual in which women are seen as being as complicit as men. Wharton softens the point somewhat by having Archer suggest that women's wiles are necessitated by the patriarchal system they are "enslaved" in: "A woman's standard of truthfulness was tacitly held to be lower: she was the subject creature, and versed in the arts of the enslaved" (308).

It is in this context that May is set up, negatively, in the Diana role. At a dinner before their marriage she is presented "in her dress of white and silver, with a wreath of silver blossoms in her hair[; she] looked like a Diana just alight from the chase" (62; also 309). Even after her marriage, "in her white dress, with a pale green ribbon about the waist and a wreath of ivy on her hat, she had the same Diana-like aloofness as when she [appeared] on the night of their engagement" (211). After she wins an archery competition, May is given as a prize a "diamond-tipped arrow" (214), a further ironic allusion to Artemis-Diana.

The denouement of the novel is less harsh than in *The Fruit of the Tree*. While May dies, she is not murdered, and beforehand there had been glimmers of compassion and sisterhood between May and Ellen. Indeed, Ellen's decision to break off with Newland and return to Europe is precipitated by a conversation she has with May. It is clear that Ellen cannot bear the betrayal of May that her relationship with

Newland has entailed, especially after she learns that May is pregnant (328–29, 346). Thus, while the traditional world of the mothers is rejected in this novel in favor of the new woman who has ventured into new realms of experience, the theme is handled more gently and with a remote hint of, if not mother-daughter reunion, at least something short of mother murder.

In an interesting analysis of this novel, Elizabeth Ammons suggests that the fundamental split in the work is between "the realm of Diana, chaste and rule-bound" and "the world of art, dangerously sexual and full of mystery and adult knowledge," to which women are denied entrance.[58] Ellen Olenska in this view represents the daughter-artist struggling to enter the mainstream oedipal world of artistic production. As in "Life and I," the opposition is cast between the preliterate, preoedipal world of traditional mothers and the patriarchal oedipal world of the Symbolic. According to Wharton, for the woman artist to survive she must eat the pomegranate seed.

Interestingly, while she was working on *The Age of Innocence*, Wharton published one of her few stories that concern a woman writer, "Writing a War Story" (1919). This piece, somewhat reminiscent of "A Poetess," shows Wharton's ambivalence about *women* writers. It concerns Miss Ivy Spang, who writes sentimentalist (and therefore, according to Wharton, poor) verse. During World War I, while serving as a nurse in Paris, she is asked to write a war story. This proves a very difficult task, but with the help of a French woman who had written down some of the patients' stories, she manages to produce one. As with Betsey Dole, the patriarchal authorities (here a male novelist on the ward, as well as other male patients) put down her work. They do, however, like the photo of her that accompanies it. This enrages Ivy. In commenting on her anger the novelist observes, "Do you wonder that we novelists have such an inexhaustible field in Woman?"[59]

Thus, while Wharton unleashes heavy and contemptuous satire against Ivy throughout the story, in the end her sympathies are with the woman because of the men's attempt to reduce her to an object (the photo), reinscribing her in the system that treats women as objects for exchange. While one could hardly call this story feminist, it, like *Age of Innocence*, suggests a softening of Wharton's attitude toward femaleness and the female identity, which she previously rejected.

Adeline R. Tintner has pointed out in a perceptive article that a "persistent" theme in Wharton's novels of the twenties is "the strained relationship between mothers and daughters," within which is an implicit "struggle for the father."[60] As we have seen, that struggle is an inherent issue in nearly all Wharton's work, not just her late novels. Tintner focuses on three works—*The Old Maid* (1922), *The Mother's Recompense* (1925), and *Twilight Sleep* (1927)—where the struggle is literally between mothers and daughters.

The Old Maid is a particularly poignant work that repeats the script of the young woman rejecting the old. In this case because of a fear of scandal, Charlotte Lovell gives her illegitimate daughter over to a cousin, Delia Ralston, to raise, remaining in the household as the child's "aunt." Charlotte longs to intensify her relationship with her daughter, but the girl gradually grows away from "Aunt Chatty," seeing her as a repressed old maid. In reaction, Charlotte, "abrupt, passionate and inarticulate, knew of no other security than to wall herself up in perpetual silence."[61]

When Chatty suggests taking Tina, the daughter, away from New York and living in the country (the dream of the mother-daughter reunion in Demeter's garden), Delia fears "the change might only precipitate a tragedy . . . vague visions of revolt and flight—of a 'fall' deeper and more irretrieveable than Charlotte's—flashed through her agonized imagination" (123).

What is this "fall" that Delia so fears? Is it of the mother-daughter reunion, or is it of a violent daughter rebellion? Apparently, the latter. In any event, it is clear that powerful mythic female forces continue to inform Wharton's work: Delia senses that "the blind forces of life [are] groping and crying underfoot" (129).

The title of *The Mother's Recompense* (1925), Wharton's next novel, is, as Tintner points out, an ironic allusion to Grace Aguilar's 1847 novel of the same title, which conceived the maternal purpose as that of getting daughters safely married—a topos in the novel of manners. In Wharton's handling, the mother and daughter are overtly engaged in the oedipal triangle we have seen as covert in early Wharton works. This time mother and daughter have the same male lover (not at the same time). The picture of Beatrice Cenci, the legendary victim of father-daughter incest, that appears in this novel points once again to patriarchal incest as the central theme, this time seen from the mother's horrified point of view.

Twilight Sleep (1927) is another overdone satire of the busybody society lady, but underneath there remains the question of the mother-daughter relation. Here the sympathy is with the daughter, Nora Manford, who is described as a "bewildered little Iphigenia," one of those children who had to serve as "vicarious sacrifices" to their parents. Iphigenia is, of course, in classical myth, an Artemis figure who is sacrificed literally by her father, Agamemnon, in order that he may proceed to war. None of these novels is particularly profound, but they do indicate that the problematics of the repressed mother-daughter relationship remain a central Wharton concern. Two stories published about this time (1925) similarly concern repressed female powers. They are "Miss Mary Pask" and "Bewitched," both ghost stories about female revenge.

But in Wharton's final novels the Furies are transformed into positive, redemptive female powers.[62] While her final stories, "Pomegranate Seed" (1931) and "Roman Fever" (1934), discussed below, suggest that Wharton remained ambivalent toward the world of the mothers, *Hudson River Bracketed* (1929) and especially *The Gods Arrive* (1932) present a kind of recantation of previous rejections of the matriarchal and an embracement of "the Mothers" as the ultimate redemptive source.

The two novels concern the long dark night of artist Vance Weston's soul. Weston is Wharton's male persona, and his thoughts on writing throw further light on the complex problem of the woman writer in a patriarchal culture: the voice is that of the daughter-artist who has consumed the pomegranate seed but finds herself in darkness.

Hudson River Bracketed opens with Weston recalling his powerful grandmother Scrimser (his mother's mother). With this key sounded, Weston proceeds, the waters of inspiration drying up, until one day in reading the second part of *Faust* he discovers "the mysterious Mothers, moving in subterranean depths among the primal forms of life."[63] He begins to sense that authentic art comes up from "invisible roots [which] struck down, in the depths ruled by the Mothers" (391).

This theme continues as central in the next novel, *The Gods Arrive,* which really concerns Persephone-daughter Wharton's reunion with the Demeter sources of female creativity. I suggested in Chapter 1 that the muse is female, a manifestation of maternal-lesbian passion. In her last published work Wharton seems to be presenting this intimation.

Weston flounders around, unhappy with his latest work, but still aware that real art comes from the maternal "depths" (71, 183). At one point he questions who his audience is. "What's the use," he wonders, "of doing anything really big? If I ever do, nobody'll read it. . . . Well, and if they don't? Who am I writing for, anyhow? Only the Mothers!" (72).

As in her early novella *The Touchstone* (1900), Wharton here seems to be posing the central question of the female artist: how to render female experience authentically without casting it in words, in symbols, acceptable only to a patriarchal audience; how to remain faithful to the feminine without consuming the pomegranate seed, without betraying it through the use of patriarchal systems of discourse. In this novel Wharton suggests that the answer to this complex question is to write from and for the mothers.

In the process of his soul-searching, Weston reenters the green-world bower and reconnects with its Dianic power (here presented positively, unlike in *The Age of Innocence*). The incident occurs in the forest at Fontainebleau: "The forest seemed endless; it enclosed him on every side. He could not imagine anything beyond it. In its all embracing calm his nervous perturbations ceased . . . he felt the same deep union with earth that once or twice in his life he had known by the seashore" (111).

There he encounters a girl asleep. He thinks of "Dryads" (114)—whom we last encountered as a negative comment on Lily Bart; the girl is a "Diana . . . vanishing in a silver mist" (114). That night he wakes up suddenly: "the moon [a symbol of Diana] streamed across his bed. . . . 'Diana after all!' he thought, his brain starting into throbbing activity" (116). Thus, Wharton exclaims, in a profound statement of reunion with the matriarchal bower she had so emphatically rejected through most of her artistic life: "Diana after all!"

The next day Weston finds himself reinspired. "That girl in the forest. He knew now why she had been put there. To make his first chapter out of . . ." (118). He feels tremendous inspiration and writes freely. "You have to go plumb down to the Mothers to fish up the real thing," he reflects (118). He makes "the descent to the Mothers, the crux, the centre of the book" (380).

His final redemption is precipitated by a reunion with his dying grandmother, Mrs. Scrimser. "He buried his face in those tender searching hands, feeling the warm current of old memories pass from her body to his, as if it were she who, in some mystical blood-transfusion, was calling him back to life" (402).

Thus, in her final works Wharton picked up the intuition of a powerful prelapsarian matriarchal order that had run in one form or another through most of her previous work. But this vision is not conclusive. For two of her most powerful stories published in the thirties return to a vision of a fallen state of patriarchal captivity.

"Pomegranate Seed" (1931) engages in the gender reversal seen in other works: here the Persephone figure is a male and the Hades figure a female (it is this kind of compromise/betrayal done to disguise female realities and appease patriarchal authorities that Wharton herself repudiated in *The Touchstone* and *The Gods Arrive*).

The plot is that Kenneth Ashby, now happily married to his second wife, begins receiving ghostly letters from his first wife, who is dead. He finally disappears; the day before, his wife had felt his handclasp as "the clutch of a man who felt himself slipping over a precipice."[64] When Kenneth does not return, his wife, Charlotte, turns in desperation to his mother, a Demeter figure. "Old Mrs. Ashby sat by her bright fire, her knitting needles flashing steadily . . . her mere bodily presence gave reassurance to Charlotte" (782). When Mrs. Ashby realizes what has happened, "her glossy bloom was effaced by a quick pallor; her firm cheeks seemed to shrink and wither" (784).

In this story Wharton turns the mythical Persephone-Hades abduction into a parable about the seizure by the terrible mother. It is a rehearsal of the *Ethan Frome* script, cast in terms of the Persephone myth. Hades is now the terrible mother; the victim is once again the estranged daughter (cast here, as often, as a man).

"Roman Fever" (1934), curiously one of Wharton's most anthologized works, is another bleak story about the fallen condition of women in patriarchal culture: that their allegiance must always be to men and never to one another, that their struggle for survival (as seen in *The Custom of the Country*) means marketing themselves to a man.

The story takes place in Rome, where two elderly women sit reminiscing. Unlike Jewett's matriarchal "Miss Tempy's Watchers" (1888), which at first this story resembles, the women do not form a bond with one another; rather, they end in a head-on competition, fully estranged.

In their reminiscing they recall that when they had visited Rome years before they had been in competition for the same man, Delphin Slade. The future Mrs. Slade, Alida, then engaged to him, had sent a forged letter to Grace, purporting to be from Delphin asking her to meet him after dark at the Colosseum. The idea behind this trick was that a great aunt of Grace's had sent a female competitor of hers out after dark to the Roman Forum. The woman had caught the malarial "Roman fever" and died. Alida hoped the same thing would happen to Grace. The plot was somewhat foiled since Grace responded to the letter and Delphin did meet her at the Colosseum, though he later married Alida. In telling this miserable story to Grace, years later, Alida cried, "I hated you, hated you. I knew you were in love with Delphin—and I was afraid. . . . I wanted you out of the way, that's all. Just for a few weeks; just till I was sure of him."[65]

The "Roman fever" to which these women succumbed was really the ideological atmospheric premises unquestioned in a patriarchal society, that women are natural enemies, cast so by the governing exchange system. Unfortunately, as seen in this study, Wharton herself, like many of her characters, was a victim of Roman fever. Only in her last novel did she appear to emerge into matriarchal "health," and even then the connection with the "mothers" is mediated through a male persona. Probably, as Sharon O'Brien suggests of Willa Cather, Wharton "employed a male consciousness in part as a defense against fusion with a maternal presence."[66] The fear of engulfment, entrapment by the mother, remained powerful in Wharton's final works. But it was not just personal fear of her own mother's control that motivated her; as I have suggested throughout, the fear was that she would be sucked back into the traditional, circumscribed female role, which she despised. Her political rejection of what she saw as an insipid, childlike state may certainly be appropriated to liberal feminism. However, the rejection of the mothers and their values, entailed in assimilationist feminism, means emotional alienation from the maternal bower and from maternal sources of inspiration—the muse. This Weston seems to realize in *The Gods Arrive*.

Personally, however, I sense a certain artificiality in Weston's rediscovery of the mothers.[67] The idea is, after all, derived from Goethe's *Faust*—not from Jewett's *Country of the Pointed Firs*. It does not reflect a genuine reconnection with feminine literary traditions, nor does it seem to reflect a genuine emotional transformation in Wharton.

It nevertheless seems probable that Wharton had come to the intellectual decision that the world could no longer afford the exclusion of the mothers' humane ethic. Living in Europe in the thirties, Wharton was surely aware of the rise of fascism, an egregiously male-supremacist ideology, and perhaps like Virginia Woolf in *Three Guineas* (1938) felt that it could in part be explained as the final result of the revalorization of the masculine that characterized early twentieth-century ideologies (as discussed in chapter 1). This, at any rate, is how I would explain Wharton's turn toward the "mothers" in her late novels.[68]

4

Willa Cather:
The Daughter in Exile

*Ears were only a tradition there, fabulous fruits like the golden
apples of the Hesperides. . . . Sometimes, the . . . corn leaves whis-
pered to each other that once, long ago, real yellow ears grew in
the . . . valley.*

—*Willa Cather, "El Dorado: A Kansas Recessional" (1901)*

As in the works of Edith Wharton and Ellen Glasgow, her sister realists in the early twentieth century, there is a pervasive sense of a fall in
the fiction of Willa Cather. Despite her reputation for romantic descriptions of nature—especially of the Great Plains—more often than
not the picture Cather gives of the prairie is of a place of exile, barren,
bleak, soul-destroying. Her pioneer characters often pine for the cultural communities they left back home; in the mythography of
Cather's early works, East is Eden. And the plains is a place of patriarchal exile, where the daughter is estranged from matriarchal roots.

The fall that is mythically recorded in the fiction of Willa Cather is
the destruction of the nineteenth-century women's community, which
was animated by the intense passion of "romantic friendship" and
sealed by the mother-daughter bond. The nostalgia characters feel for
a lost Eden is infused with the loss of that "female world of love and
ritual" that "new women"—Demeter's daughters—were experiencing

in the declining years of the nineteenth century as they left their mothers' bowers. Cather belongs to this historic moment in women's cultural history.

Cather's fiction is centrally focused upon the daughter in exile, whether lured into the traffic of heterosexist commerce and thus, like Persephone, doomed, or embarked upon assimilationist career courses such as becoming a successful writer or artist—and thus pursuing an ambivalent, independent, ofttimes male-identified tack. In nearly every work a contrast is drawn between a pre- or nonoedipal communitarian female/maternal world, which retains an edenic integrity and purity and is the source of true artistic inspiration, and a fallen patriarchal, capitalist world, where people are motivated by greed, ambition, and selfish egotism.

Like Wharton, Cather had to confront the problematic of being a female artist in a patriarchal culture. Like Wharton, Cather seems to have felt the need to adopt a masculine self-identity in order to take herself seriously as a writer and to be so taken by others. In this sense she too swallowed the pomegranate seed; at least in the early years she absorbed a cultural ideology that esteemed the male and denigrated the female. It is well known that as a youth Cather adopted masculine styles in dress and coiffure, preferred to be called "William," and endorsed liberal, masculinist notions of scientific progress.

Her 1890 high-school graduation speech is characteristic in this regard; it defends the use of scientific experimentation on animals, in particular vivisection, a practice she evidently had engaged in herself. "Scientific investigation," she claims, "is the hope of our age." "The boy who . . . tries with bungling attempt to pierce the mystery of animal life . . . is [considered] cruel . . . [but] if we bar our novices from advancement, whence shall come our experts?" She concludes by raising the ethical question of whether anyone "has . . . a right to destroy life for scientific purposes?" Her answer is in the affirmative.[1]

This statement could be dismissed simply as the hackneyed paean to science characteristic of the commencement-address genre. However, that these words were spoken in 1890 by a woman registers a significant break with women's cultural traditions, indeed, a rebellion against them. These are the words of the "new woman," embracing an assimilationist course, endorsing a masculine cultural endeavor, and rejecting the feminine. In particular, it marks an attack on women's cultural tradition of identification with animals and resistance to scientific and other abuse of them; in the late nineteenth century this tendency materialized in the antivivisection movement, a cause that was dominated by women, as Coral Lansbury has recently shown, and which represents another aspect of women's resistance to the mathematization of the world addressed in chapter 1.[2]

In women's literature the tradition is manifest in, for example, the eagle-trees episode in Harriet Beecher Stowe's *Pearl of Orr's Island* (1862), where a girl protests against a boy's destruction of an eagle's nest, and in Sarah Orne Jewett's celebrated "White Heron" (1886)—a direct descendent of Stowe's piece—where a young girl protects a bird from the designs of an ornithologist. (Stowe also wrote an "animal rights" manifesto: "Rights of Dumb Animals" [1869].) Cather herself in her fiction continued this tradition, for example, with the use of the woodpecker in *A Lost Lady* (1923) and in numerous similar treatments of animals. So, it is significant that in her early years Cather rejected this feminine sympathy/identification with animals (probably seeing it as too sentimental) and endorsed the detached, unemotional masculine project of scientific experimentation. It is a sign of the masculine identification that characterized her early years, a pose that continued well into the first decade of the twentieth century.

Like Wharton, too, Cather engaged in the use of male personae in her fiction, although she has fewer insufferable "old-boy" narrators in the Jamesian style. Also like Wharton, Cather rejected the sentimentalist tradition in women's literature. Her (unfair) dismissal of Kate Chopin's novel, *The Awakening* in an 1899 review is characteristic.[3]

Unlike Wharton, however, Cather did not reject the local-color tradition in women's literature as "rose-coloured" or sentimentalist. On the contrary, Cather had read Jewett's *Country of the Pointed Firs* with enthusiasm shortly after it was published (in 1896), and she found Jewett's *Country Doctor* admirably "austere and unsentimental."[4] Later she wrote Jewett that she always carried a copy of "A White Heron" (1886) and "The Dulham Ladies" (1886) with her when she traveled and that she had brought them, along with Jewett's "Flight of Betsey Lane" (1893), with her on a trip to Italy.[5] Significantly, Cather called Jewett's "Martha's Lady" (1897) "the saddest and loveliest" of stories, one that inspired her "to begin all over and try to be good."[6] Cather later included these stories in the Jewett anthology she prepared in 1925.

These remarks were transmitted to Jewett in a series of letters written in late 1908 after Cather had met her idol in Boston. There is no question—as numerous critics and biographers have stressed[7]—that the brief encounter Cather had with Jewett was probably the most important literary event of her life. In particular, advice Jewett gave Cather in her celebrated letter of 13 December 1908—a letter E. K. Brown has characterized as "the most important letter, beyond a question, that Willa Cather ever received"[8]—has been seen as decisive. In it Jewett warned Cather that her gifts were not maturing "as they should" and advised her that she should retire from her newspaper work (Cather was then on the staff of *McClure's Magazine* in New York) and devote full time and concentration to her fiction. She also suggested that Cather use her "Nebraska life," her "child's Virginia," as well as her Bohemian New York world as fictional milieus.[9]

In an earlier and perhaps even more significant letter, dated 27 November 1908, Jewett had responded to Cather's story "On the Gulls' Road," published the next month in *McClure's*. "It made me feel very near to the writer's young and loving heart," Jewett wrote. However, she criticized Cather's use of a male persona.

> The lover is as well done as he could be when a woman writes in the man's character—it must always, I believe, be something of a masquerade. I think it is safer to write about him as you did about the others, and not try to be he! And you could almost have done it as yourself—a woman could love her in that same protecting way—a woman could even care enough to wish to take her away from such a life, by some means or other. But oh, how close—how tender—how true the feeling is![10]

The word *masquerade* had at the time the connotation of cross-dressing and female/male impersonation—a topic Jewett had treated comically in earlier stories, "An Autumn Holiday" (1880) and "Hollowell's Pretty Sister" (1880), as noted in chapter 2. The currency of the term is indicated in a 19 January 1901 article in the *New York Times* about a woman, Murray Hall, who had "for Years . . . Masqueraded in Male Attire," according to the headline.[11] A similar case of a Boston woman came to light in October 1901, also reported by the *New York Times* as a "Woman Who Masqueraded as a Man."[12]

This connotation suggests once again that Jewett was writing from a viewpoint that accepted intense female relationships as a norm, but that she was quite aware of the pressures to disguise such relationships, cautioning nevertheless against capitulation. The story itself,

"On the Gulls' Road," does involve intense passion. At one point the male narrator says, "she must have known that I loved her."[13] "I kissed her hair, her cheeks, her lips, until her head fell forward on my shoulder" (91). Jewett therefore is saying that this is perfectly normal behavior between women; why disguise the narrator (Willa's persona) as a man? Indeed, in this story, as in numerous later Cather works that use male personae, the denouement is implausible. The two lovers supposedly cannot run off together because she is too old and sick (she is only twenty-six) and he is too young (he's roughly the same age). The real reason they cannot run off is that Cather was writing a disguised lesbian story, and she could not project two women running off together as passionate lovers, one abandoning her husband. But Jewett could.

Nothing could illustrate more dramatically the cultural transition between Jewett's era and Cather's than Jewett's critique of this story. As I have noted in chapters 1 and 2, and as Sharon O'Brien notes in her review of the problematic relation of Cather's lesbianism to her fiction, "feminine friendship" was clearly considered "unnatural" in Cather's formative years.[14] "Unlike Jewett, [Cather] could not write unconflicted, unselfconsciously affectionate or passionate letters to a woman she loved"—in this case Louise Pound, with whom Cather was infatuated in the early 1890s.[15] Nor could she deal with passion between women in her fiction. With the exception of two early stories, "Tommy, the Unsentimental" (1896) and "The Joy of Nelly Deane" (1911)—the latter probably written under the influence of Jewett's advice—it always remained disguised, "something of a masquerade."

Nevertheless, Jewett's influence was profound. It moved Cather beyond the Jamesian hold manifest in Cather's fiction in the early years of the twentieth century, and led directly to the creation of Cather's first great novel, *O Pioneers!* (1913). Cather later remarked that she dedicated that novel to Jewett because "I had talked over some of the characters in it with her one day . . . and in this book I tried to tell the story of the people as truthfully and simply as if I were telling it to her by word of mouth."[16]

Thus, by 1913, when this interview was recorded, Cather was locating herself within a feminine literary tradition. Art is perceived as one woman talking to another—in this case to a direct literary foremother. Cather had found her literary mother in a sister lesbian writer, who became the primary source of her inspiration, a maternal muse.

Cather notes further in this interview that, until she met Jewett and had become aware of her writings, she had despaired of treating her Nebraska material authentically.

> Then I had the good fortune to meet Sarah Orne Jewett, who had read all of my early stories and had very clear and definite opinions about them and about where my work fell short. She said, "Write it as it is, don't try to make it like this or that. You can't do it in anybody else's way—you will have to make a way of your own. . . . Don't try to write the kind of short story that this or that magazine wants—write the truth and let them take it or leave it."[17]

In other words, do not capitulate.

Therefore, like Wharton, Cather wrestled with the problems of masculine self-identification in the early twentieth century. But unlike Wharton, she established a primary connection with a literary mother, and also, unlike Wharton, both she and that "mother" were lesbians, at least emotionally.[18] This may account for the fact that Cather's rejection of male identification and her move toward a reappreciation of the feminine-maternal occurred much earlier than Wharton's. From *O Pioneers!* on it is a central issue, and after 1922—the year Cather claimed "the world broke in two"—reconnection with the maternal became the primary concern. As Ellen Moers noted, "All the fiction from Willa Cather's greatest period centers on the death of a mother-figure" and "the daughter's ambivalent anguish."[19] More precisely, one could say that nearly all Cather's mature fiction deals with the question of the daughter's exile from the feminine/maternal world of "love and ritual," from Demeter's bower, and the quest of the new woman, the daughter, to retrieve its inspirational sources, without being swallowed up in its passion.

For also central in Cather, as numerous critics have pointed out, is the quest for individual autonomy and integrity, the quest of the new woman.[20] How to reconcile and integrate these two realms of feminine experience—that of the nineteenth-century mother with that of the twentieth-century new woman–daughter—is the central issue in Cather's fiction. It is dealt with but still not resolved in her final story, "The Best Years" (1945).

Several of the stories Cather wrote and published in the 1890s and early 1900s establish the issues that preoccupy Cather throughout her career. "The Clemency of the Court," one of Cather's earliest stories and an extraordinary one, was published in the *Hesperian*, the college literary journal at the University of Nebraska, in 1893, when Cather was an undergraduate. Located within the women's thematic tradition of animal identification, it anticipated Susan Glaspell's "Jury of Her Peers" (1917), as well as Wharton's "Kerfol" (1916). Unlike Glaspell and Wharton, however, Cather uses a male protagonist, Serge Povolitchky, a rude, illiterate peasant of Russian descent who works as an indentured servant on a farm on the plains. His only love is a dog, Matushka, "which was the name by which he always thought of his [dead] mother."[21]

His boss kills the dog one day in front of him; Serge grabs the hatchet and splits the man's head, for which he is sentenced to life in prison. As a child his stepmother had told him life was much better in the United States than under the tsar because in America "the State" took care of people. Serge envisioned "the State" "as a woman with kind eyes, dressed in white with a yellow light around her head, and a little child in her arms, like the picture of the virgin in the church" (518). In prison Serge is eventually strapped up by his arms in solitary confinement. Thus he dies, thinking of the plains and his dog; and thus "the State, took this wilful, restless child of hers and put him to sleep in her bosom" (522).

The fierce irony in this story, revolving around mother deprivation, tells us something about Cather and the "new woman's" state of mind during this period. The dog, identified with the mother, is killed, and Serge's dream of the state as a comforting matriarch proves bitterly fraudulent. As with Lily Bart, only in death does the child return to the maternal sanctuary. Here, as elsewhere in Cather's fiction, the plains proves to be a place of exile, of alienation, ruled by hostile, loveless authorities.

"The Burglar's Christmas" (1896), published pseudonymously, also concerns a quest for the maternal bower; once again the protagonist is male. In her analysis of the story, O'Brien proposes that Cather's use of male personae was a device to keep the mother at bay, so to speak, to keep from being engulfed by maternal/erotic passion—an interesting theory that further suggests the power of the maternal attraction.[22]

This peculiar story can be read allegorically as the exiled new woman–daughter's quest for the mother. It concerns a young panhandler in Chicago who, desperately hungry, decides to commit a burglary. He inadvertently chooses his parents' apartment (they had moved since he was last in touch with them). His mother discovers him but forgives all; what transpires is an archetypal return to the mother by the prodigal child. In her arms "that whole miserable, futile, swindled world of Bohemia seemed immeasurably distant and far away, like a dream that is over and done."[23] Thus, the careerist world into which the youth had ventured is seen as fallen and fraudulent; the return to the mother's world, redemptive.

Another peculiar story, allegedly for children, published the same year repeats, if interpreted allegorically, the division of experience between the maternal bower and the world beyond. This time, however, the appeal of freedom and autonomy is sounded, and the security of the maternal sanctuary rejected. Nevertheless, freedom is seen as dangerous, and those who choose it are doomed. The details concern reindeer who run freely over the plains: "[T]he reindeer love their freedom more than any other animal, and swift motion, and the free winds."[24] When stabled they are "homesick for their freedom and their wide white snow plains" (444). Unfortunately, however, while running they fall through thin ice and drown—a prefiguration literally and symbolically of the demise of another free spirit, Lucy Gayheart. The remaining reindeer hesitate to offer Santa assistance (the story revolves around getting the gifts delivered on Christmas) because "they all loved their freedom . . . and were loath to give it up even for the snug, warm stables of Santa Claus" (447).

A story published the same year that is similarly revealing of its author's psyche is "Tommy, the Unsentimental" (1896). This piece concerns a tomboyish young woman who works in a bank and is more competent than her male coworkers. Significantly, her mother is dead and the old businessmen in town "had rather taken her mother's place."[25] She is indeed not just in a motherless world but in a womanless one as well. "She knew almost no women, because in those days there were few women in Southdown who were in any sense interesting, or interested in anything but babies and salads" (474)—a repudiation of the trivial business of the traditional woman. She was one of the boys: "she played whist and billiards with them, and made cocktails for them, not scorning to take one herself occasionally" (474).

One year she goes back East to school, but the old boys do not approve: "it was a sign of weakening, they said" (475). Thus, the East is associated with a weaker, "feminine" culture, and the West with macho masculinity—a continuing theme in Cather's work. When Tommy returns, she brings with her "a girl she had grown fond of at school, a dainty, white, languid bit of a thing, who used violet perfumes and carried a sunshade" (476). This woman, "Miss Jessica," is a type figure satirized throughout women's literature, the female quixote; an early American version appears in Caroline Kirkland's frontier fiction (1839).[26]

It is odd, however, that "unsentimental" Tommy, a Cather persona, would be attracted to this type. "The Old Boys said it was a bad sign when a rebellious girl like Tommy took to being sweet and gentle to one of her own sex, the worst sign in the world" (476). Presumably here the "Old Boys" are condemning the relationship as lesbian. But the deeper question is why a practical competent like Tommy would be attracted to an ultrafeminine incompetent like Jessica. It suggests the power the traditional feminine world—particularly its romanticism and promises of emotional fulfillment—had over Cather.

For the denouement involves Tommy saving a weak male coworker and then matching him up with Jessica, whom she describes apologetically to him as "essentially romantic"—and therefore his type (479). Tommy sees herself as different. Thus, the story divides the world into ineffectual romantics and practical achievers; the latter, though admirable because they have the (masculine) skills to survive in the harsh environment of the West, nevertheless are strongly attracted to the former for aesthetic and emotional reasons. This division of experience—masculine autonomy and achievement versus feminine culture and beauty—becomes a central perspective in Cather's work, especially evident in her masterpiece *My Ántonia* (1918).

The first story that shows what appears to be a Jewett influence is "A Resurrection," published in 1897, the year after Jewett's *Country of the Pointed Firs*. It opens in a fashion characteristic of the local-color format that Jewett often used: two women gossiping (in this case as they arrange flowers in church). One of them is Margie, a thirty-year-old spinster whom life seems to have passed by. Her plight occasions a disquisition on the world's waste of women: "She was one of those women . . . fashioned for the fullness of life . . . but condemned by circumstances to poverty, obscurity and all manner of pettiness." These women "were made to rule, but . . . are doomed to serve. There are plenty of living masterpieces that are as completely lost to the world as the lost nine books of Sappho. . . . The world is full of waste of this sort."[27]

Cather's lament for the loss of Sappho's poetry was registered earlier in a review of "three women poets" published in the *Nebraska State
Journal* (13 January 1895). She wrote: "If of all the lost riches we could
have one master restored to us . . . the choice of the world would be
for the lost nine books of Sappho. . . . Twenty centuries have not
cooled the passion in them."[28]

More important is the verbal echo in this passage of a similar observation in *Pointed Firs,* where the narrator notes: "It was not the first
time that I was full of wonder at the waste of human ability in this
world, as a botanist wonders at the wastefulness of nature, the thou-
sand seeds that die, the unused provision of every sort."[29] The elegiac
tone in Cather's story is markedly like that in Jewett's great work.

The story contrasts the fallen present with a nobler, purer world.
Today the town is dominated by "river rats" (430), mercenary Ma-
chiavels. In contrast is the river itself, an early Cather adumbration of
a natural green world that represents the Dianic realm—source of
feminine creativity.

> To all who follow it faithfully, and not for gain but from inclina-
> tion, the river gives a certain simpleness of life and freshness of
> feeling and receptiveness of mind not to be found among the
> money changers of the market place. . . . It gives [its dis-
> ciples] . . . something of that intimate sympathy with inanimate
> nature that is the base of all poetry. (433)

Thus, Cather is here articulating an idea similar to that espoused by
Wharton in *The Gods Arrive:* that the sources of creativity come from a
reconnection with the marginal green-world font, by being faithful to
the realm of Diana/Demeter.

A story published the following year, "The Way of the World"
(1898), also focuses upon gender roles but ends on a misogynist twist.
Several boys set up a toy town and exclude Mary Eliza from their play.
She finally convinces them to allow her to join them (the assimilationist goal): "For all boys will admit that there are some girls who
would make the best boys in the world—if they were not girls."[30] But,
as the boys fear, Mary Eliza eventually brings "disaster and ruin upon
the town of Speckleville" (401). First, she overpowers them; then she
abandons them for a dandy from Chicago (the feminine East). Here
Cather devolves into the Eve stereotype, the seductive but fickle female, which she had also used in "A Resurrection," where a frivolous

woman who neglects her maternal responsibilities is similarly casti-
gated. The point of view in this story is that of the aggrieved males, a
probable sign of Cather's continuing male identification.

The next story that reveals a Jewett influence is "Eric Hermannson's
Soul." Published in 1900, shortly after Jewett's "Martha's Lady," it offers a similar scenario but disguises a female-female liaison as heterosexual, another "masquerade." Eric, the protagonist, corresponds to Martha in Jewett's story, and Margaret Elliot, an eastern sophisticate, recalls
Helena Vernon, the vibrant Boston visitor who enlivens Martha's mun-
dane rural world. In Cather's more negative handling, Margaret becomes a new-woman type, reminiscent of Ibsen's Hedda Gabler. She
"was one of those women of whom there are so many in this day, when
old order, passing, giveth place to new; beautiful, talented, critical,
unsatisfied, tired of the world at twenty-four."[31]

She nevertheless brings hope and life to Eric, who, as a Norwegian
on the Divide, is in a place of exile.

> But the sad history of those Norwegian exiles, transplanted in
> an arid soil and under a scorching sun, had repeated itself in
> his case. Toil and isolation had sobered him, and he grew more
> and more like the clods among which he labored. . . . It is a
> painful thing to watch the light die out of the eyes of those
> Norsemen, leaving an expression of impenetrable sadness,
> quite passive, quite hopeless, a shadow that is never lifted. (369)

Eric had converted to a strict, puritanical gospelism and had vowed
never to indulge in music again (he had destroyed his violin and given
up dancing). Margaret brings him back to life and gets him dancing
again. The dance scene includes a grim description of the exiled lives
of the plains women: "Torrid summers and freezing winters, labor
and drudgery and ignorance, were the portion of their girlhood; a
short wooing, a hasty, loveless marriage, unlimited maternity, thank-
less sons, premature age and ugliness, were the dower of their womanhood" (374–75). Theirs the fate of Persephones condemned to
heterosexist commerce.

While Eric and Margaret share a romantic passion, a "romantic
friendship," they are unable to consummate it or to run off together.
It is not clear why, except that their alien cultures, eastern and western, and class might preclude it. The subtextual reason, however,
once again, is that this is a disguised lesbian story, and once again

Cather is unable to realize the relationship (undisguised) in print. Jewett once said, "Nobody must say that Martha was dull, it is only I." Willa Cather might similarly have remarked of Eric, "it is only I," the exiled daughter in search of redemptive feminine passion.

"El Dorado: A Kansas Recessional" (1901) further clarifies Cather's mythographic landscape. The western plains are described as arid, lifeless, dried up; while eastern valleys are thought of as home, as green-world maternal bowers. The corn (Demeter's symbol) on this land is "only a tradition"; there are only memories of a time when "real yellow ears grew."[32] It is a land made barren by Demeter's curse.

El Dorado, an obviously ironic name, was once "the Queen City of the Plains," but it is now a fallen shell. The protagonist, a victim of a fraudulent investment scheme, is nostalgic for his Virginia home. "To every exile from the Valley of Virginia that sound [of the Potomac and Shenandoah rivers] is as the voice of his mother . . . forever calling him to come home" (306).

Cather's first story set in Pittsburgh is also pervaded by a sense of failure and of a fall. "The Professor's Commencement" (1902), published, like "El Dorado," in the *New England Magazine,* concerns a teacher who despairs of the materialism of his students. "I suppose we shall win in the end," he muses, "but the reign of Mammon has been long and oppressive."[33] The professor does not win, however; he is a failure, he thinks, because of the "woman's heart" in him (291). The professor's failure is paralleled by the corruption and degeneration that has corroded the town, fallen from a wilderness paradise. "The beautiful valley, where long ago too limpid rivers met at the foot of wooded heights, had become a scorched and blackened waste" (286). Once "shining," the river no longer had "one throb of its woodland passion" left when it arrived in the city (287). Again a natural and pure green world is contrasted to a wasteland, fallen prey to commercial interests. The further implication is that those with "women's hearts" are doomed, but that those who adopt masculine/capitalist skills are corrupt.

One of Cather's most significant early stories and one of the first to be set autobiographically in her childhood Nebraska home is "The Treasure of Far Island" (1902). It is also the first to use a device Cather was to use in later work (notably *My Ántonia*) and which she may have borrowed from Jewett—that of the return of the native, now an educated sophisticate, who serves as narrator. Jewett used this effectively in *Pointed Firs* and other works: in her case the figure is nearly always a woman; in Cather's it is nearly always a man.

This story opens with Douglass Burnham, a successful playwright and an obvious Cather persona, returning to his Nebraska home to revisit a childhood bower, Far Island, a sandbar in the Nebraska River. He also rediscovers a childhood friend, Margie Van Dyke, a Dianic figure, who accompanies him on his return to the childhood haven.

Margie is another of those "mannish" girls who are generated, Cather seems to feel, by the conditions of pioneer life. As a girl, the narrator notes, Margie had "never exactly stood in need of masculine protection. What a wild Indian she was! . . . I never found such a mind in a girl. But *is* she a girl? I somehow always fancied she would grow up a man."[34] Another Nan Prince.

> There was a wholesomeness of the sun and soil in [Margie] that was utterly lacking in the women among whom he had lived for so long. She had preserved that strength of arm and freedom of limb . . . which modern modes of life have well-nigh robbed the world of altogether. Surely, he thought, it was like that that Diana's women sped . . . down the slopes of Ida. (278)

Thus, the narrator contrasts the realm of this Diana with the fallen present, where "modern modes" dominate. Margie is further associated with the preoedipal green-world bower where the two played as children. It is a place "where the grass is greener" and "trees . . . and certain spots . . . are in a manner sacred, like the sacrificial groves of the Druids" (275).

On their return the two realize that this was an edenic spot and that their lives since have been spent in exile. They reflect that they have "shut the gates of Eden behind us." "And now we are only kings in exile" (281). Nevertheless, in a blaze of ecstasy they kiss and become engaged (282): "these two looked about over God's world and saw that it was good" (282).

This story may be interpreted on a number of levels. On the one hand it may be seen as another masqueraded lesbian fantasy; on another it may be seen as the fantasy of the careerist new woman reconnecting with the lost Dianic realm. Finally, it may be a manifestation of the author's subconscious desire to reconnect with that aspect of herself, the Dianic green-world self, threatened with extinction by the "modern modes" Cather was by this time fully engaged in (she was working in Pittsburgh as a journalist and a high school teacher during this period).

If we interpret Douglass and Margie as two aspects of Cather's self, a central interpretive problem in the story is explained. That problem is why such an energetic, competent woman as Margie had languished on the plains, waiting for his return, while Douglass went East to pursue a career. In other words it answers the question of why Margie, otherwise so similar to Nan Prince, remained inactive, the woman left behind in the waiting mode.[35] She indeed compares herself in the third person to Penelope: "the years she has waited have been longer than the waiting of Penelope. . . . I could not play anything alone. You took my world with you when you went and left me only a village of mud huts and my loneliness" (282).

But if Douglass and Margie represent two aspects of Cather's self—the career-oriented assimilationist side (the masculine) and the side that remains in touch with the nurturing feminine bower—the story represents the desired reconnection of these two sides of the psyche. It further suggests that each side is stunted without the other. The masculine remains disconnected from the preoedipal sources of inspiration; the feminine risks losing itself in cycles of repetition and waiting, the traditional female plight.

Several of Cather's following stories, written between 1902 and 1904, were collected in *The Troll Garden* (1905). The epigraph to that volume is taken from Christina Rossetti's *Goblin Market* (1859), a poem usually interpreted in lesbian terms. It concerns two sisters who are tempted by the "goblin men" to buy their fruits. One sister succumbs and nearly dies. The other resists and in the end rescues her sister. Symbolically, this scenario seems to reflect the threat to "romantic friendship" posed by the patriarchs, "goblin men," and the choices women have of remaining faithful to one another, to their own female world, or of capitulating to patriarchal hegemony.

Cather's epigraph—"We must not look at Goblin men, / We must not buy their fruits; / Who knows upon what soil they fed / Their hungry thirsty roots?"—seems to advocate a course of female identification. The other epigraph, from Charles Kingsley, refers to a magical troll garden—another apparent allusion to a special green world apart from the fallen present.

The first published of the *Troll Garden* stories seems to amplify the Rossetti theme; indeed, it is Cather's first overt elaboration of a

Persephone figure, Katharine Gaylord. The story opens with Everett Hilgarde in a train returning West. In the railroad he hears a tune written by his brother Adriance, a famous composer. It is the "Spring Song from *Proserpine*."[36] As he descends from the train in Cheyenne, he encounters a woman in white, who is lurking in the shadows—a clear allusion to the Persephone myth. It is Katharine, who had been seduced and abandoned by his brother and is now dying of consumption.

She speaks nostalgically about New York, which is (ironically but characteristically, given Cather's edenic view of the East) seen as a green-world font: "Are the trees still green," she asks, "in Madison Square . . . ? Does the chaste Diana on the Garden Theatre still keep her vestal vows?" (206). The image of Diana contrasts markedly to her own plight. For she had been a singer in Adriance's entourage and became "one of the broken things his . . . imperious speed had cast aside and forgotten" (210). Yet, Katharine acknowledges that she had consumed the pomegranate seed willingly: "I fought my way to him, and I drank my doom greedily enough" (215).

Two other stories in the collection—"A Wagner Matinee" (1904) and "The Sculptor's Funeral" (1905)—similarly depict the West as barren ground and the East as the source of cultural life. The latter story, which Jewett praised as standing "a head higher than the rest" of the *Troll Garden* stories,[37] repeats a number of early Cather themes. The contrast is drawn between the commercially corrupt West and the artistically creative East; and the world of the traditional woman is drawn negatively, its conditions seen as creating harsh, loveless mothers, sounding once again the motif of the absent, nonresponsive mother.

The story opens in a fashion similar to Jewett's "Miss Tempy's Watchers" (1888): mourners gather (in Cather's story) to await the arrival of a coffin at a railroad station in Kansas. It contains young Harvey Merrick, a successful sculptor who had escaped to Boston from the "dung heap" of his childhood.[38]

This "dung heap" fosters Machiavellian commercialism in the men and stony heartlessness in the women. Harvey's mother, the presiding matriarch, is one of Cather's harshest depictions of a woman character (similar in some regards to Sapphira Dodderidge). "There was a kind of power about her face—a kind of brutal handsomeness, even, but it was scarred and furrowed by violence, and . . . coloured and coarsened by fiercer passions. . . . She filled the room; the men were obliterated, seemed tossed about like twigs in an angry water" (176).

This avenging matriarch resembles in some respects Wharton's Zeena Frome. An embittered Demeter, she casts a pall upon the landscape; when the coffin arrives, she engages in "an orgy of grief" (177). But, an observer also comments, "the old woman is a fury. . . . She made Harvey's life hell for him when he lived at home" (178). As a child Harvey had once sculpted a boy who was trying unsuccessfully to get his mother to glance up from her sewing to look at a butterfly (178).

The mother-child dynamic here is troubled: the mother is obsessively attached to the boy but in her bitterness has become a hellhound, a Hecate, such that his only course is to escape. Here the suggestion, new in women's literature, is that the mother's oppressive soul-numbing control forced the child to leave, to seek artistic autonomy, rather than, as in *Ethan Frome*, the daughter's quest for autonomy having occasioned the mother's revenge. That the young sculptor found his creative sources in Boston, where Cather herself located her own literary foremother, indicates that he/she found a substitute mother in the East that enabled him (as her) to create. That Jewett, Cather's literary mother, singled this story out suggests a shock of recognition, though it seems more likely that her appreciation of the story was more for its craft, in particular for Cather's realistic use of detail and effective use of tone. (It must be said, however, that the story is flawed thematically and that the above interpretation is based upon fragments that do not entirely cohere).

In the years 1905 to 1908 Cather published several Jamesian stories, which are probably the ones that prompted Jewett to warn her that she was getting off track. E. K. Brown speculates that "The Namesake" (1907) and "Eleanor's House" (1907) must have particularly displeased Jewett, in addition, of course, to "On the Gulls' Road."

Happily, however, in 1909 Cather completed an excellent story, in her own vein, that undoubtedly was a response to Jewett's counsel: "The Enchanted Bluff." She sent the story to Jewett in January 1909, and one only hopes that Jewett had a chance to read it, for in the spring of that year Jewett suffered a stroke from which she never recovered. She died in June.

"The Enchanted Bluff" is similar to "The Treasure of Far Island" in that it evokes the same sandbar as a paradisiacal refuge. Also nostalgic in tone, it recalls a final moment childhood friends spent on the island in which they shared their dreams for the future. One dream in particular sticks out because it is Cather's first use of the pre-

Columbian southwestern cliff-dwellings as an image of a destroyed idyllic, female civilization.

In this story the "enchanted bluff" is described as a place where peaceful Indians had once lived. They had ascended the bluff as a refuge from a war taking place below. One day while the males were out hunting, a storm destroyed the steps up to the mesa, leaving only the women, children, and the aged on top. Eventually, they starved to death. No one has been there since. It is another image of a doomed, feminized utopia on the margins of a violent patriarchal culture.

At this point Cather must only have read about the cliff-dwellings, for she did not visit them herself until 1912. The image remained a powerful one for her, however; she used it to great symbolic effect in a number of works, most notably *The Song of the Lark* (1915), *The Professor's House* (1925), and *Death Comes for the Archbishop* (1927). As Ellen Moers notes, in the former novel it presents "the most thoroughly elaborated female landscape in literature."[39]

Shortly after Jewett's death Cather published "The Joy of Nelly Deane" (1911), which seems, like "The Enchanted Bluff," to have been written in direct response to the criticism voiced in Jewett's December 1908 letter. This time the I-narrator (another educated, traveled "native") is a woman, and this time she reflects directly about her childhood love for another girl—the only time (with "Tommy, the Unsentimental") love between women, or "romantic friendship," is dealt with in Cather's fiction. It is also a story of the fall—the destruction of that female world and the victimization of the woman (Nelly) who chose the Persephone route, dominance by a man in marriage.

In recalling their relationship the narrator remembers a night they had spent together as adolescents—the night when Nelly announced her engagement. The description of Nelly is done in unusually sensual terms. As she spoke, she was "flushing all down over her soft shoulders."[40] "She seemed so changed to me by the warm light in her eyes and the delicate suffusion of color. I felt as I did when I got up early on picnic mornings in summer, and saw the dawn come up in the breathless sky above the river meadows and make all the corn fields golden" (61).

The image of the golden corn and sunlit summer suggests Demeter before the fall, and indeed this recollection is of a prelapsarian connection between two women: one of the few glimpses of the nineteenth-century world of "love and ritual" in Cather's works. But it is doomed: "in that snug, warm little bed I had a sense of imminent change and danger. I was somehow afraid for Nelly when I heard her breathing so quickly beside me, and I put my arm about her protectingly as we drifted toward sleep" (61).

While the narrator goes off to college, Nelly stays behind, is abandoned by one man, and marries another who is "taciturn and domineering" (58), "grim and saturnine" (62)—a Hades figure. Because of his intransigence and unconcern she dies in childbirth. Eight years earlier, she had borne a daughter, whom she had named after the narrator. The only respite in her harsh life had been her relationship with a mother figure, her mother-in-law. A neighbor woman later tells the narrator, "I never saw anything like the love there was between those two . . . she looked to Mrs. Spinny [her mother-in-law] for everything" (65). On a visit home just before Nelly's marriage, the narrator "remembered sharply how much I had loved her" (63).

This story remains strangely schizophrenic: on the one hand is the doomed Persephone figure; on the other is the careerist new woman who avoids the former's fate but who remains alienated from the traditional female bower, from Demeter's world. Cather, like Wharton, fears the cultivation of traditionally feminine attributes as weakening and sees the traditional female course as destructive; survival depends upon the development of masculine autonomy. Yet this route too is destructive, alienating and corrupting (recall "The Professor's Commencement," where the protagonist's failure is due to his "woman's heart," or Tommy, who survives because of her masculine skills). In her great novels, however, *O Pioneers!* and *My Ántonia*, Cather is able to synthesize the two sides of modern women's experience.

Cather said she was inspired to write her first novel, *Alexander's Bridge* (1912), while sitting at Jewett's desk on a visit to Jewett's home in South Berwick, Maine, in the summer of 1911. Jewett's "spirit, which filled the place," she said, "warned her that time was flying"; it "goaded" her to proceed with the novel, which she began to write in South Berwick. (She also spent a week with Annie Fields—Jewett's long-term companion—in Boston at this time.)[41]

The novel is indeed principally set in the Beacon Hill area of Boston, where Annie Fields lived, and there is no question that the world described in the novel is the drawing-room milieu of "148 Charles Street" (which Cather later described—in *Not Under Forty* [1936]—in an essay of that title; see also her essay "Miss Jewett" in that collection).[42]

Alexander's Bridge was originally entitled *Alexander's Masquerade* (as published in the spring 1912 issues of *McClure's*).[43] This direct echo of the phrase Jewett used to criticize "On the Gulls' Road" must have been intentional; it gives us open license to interpret the central character as a woman, indeed as a Cather persona. It even suggests a kind of inside joke between Cather and Fields (or perhaps with Mary Rice Jewett, Sarah's surviving sister, who may also have known of the Jewett-Cather disagreement about "masquerading").

The story concerns Bartley Alexander, a Faustian engineer, who is torn between two women and the worlds they represent. One is the proper Bostonian world of his wife, Winifred; the other is that of the Irish actress Hilda Burgoyne, who lives in London. The former woman is urbane, dry, somewhat cold; the latter is emotional, energetic, and rural (Hilda's roots are rural Irish, and in the play Bartley sees early in the novel she portrays a peasant girl). In short, as Bernice Slote has suggested, Hilda is a Diana figure, and Winifred represents the "civilized" world of Jewett and Fields's Boston.[44]

The Jewett presence in this novel is a complex one. On the one hand, the work involves a repudiation of her Boston milieu as too stiff, too repressed, too "Apollonian" (to use the Nietzschean distinction between the Apollonian and the Dionysian, a concept Cather, like many in her generation, seems to have absorbed). In this perspective Hilda represents an acivilized rural energy. On these premises one would have to read the novel as a rebellion against Jewett and Boston (a switch from Cather's earlier identification of Boston as a cultural Eden).

On the other hand, Jewett herself counseled authenticity and advised Cather to return to her rural roots to find authentic sources for her art. Moreover, Jewett herself was ambivalent about Boston. While she enjoyed its sophistication and culture, her own art is set in rural Maine, and indeed *The Country of the Pointed Firs* concerns an artist whose sources of inspiration have dried up in the city and who returns to the country, where she is reinspired, principally by Demeter-matriarch Almira Todd. In this sense, *Alexander's Bridge* is a ratification of the Jewett influence. For Bartley leaves the Boston world because it lacks "energy"; it cannot inspire.[45] Speaking of Hilda's influence, Bartley says:

> Sometimes I get used to being dead inside, but lately it has been as if a window beside me had suddenly opened, and as if all the smells of spring blew in to me. There is a garden out there . . . where I used to walk. . . . I can remember how I used to feel

there, how beautiful everything about me was, and what life
and power and freedom I felt in myself. . . . But that garden is
closed to me. (99–100)

Hilda represents the Dianic green world, source of artistic inspiration. Recall that Cather had stated that before she met Jewett she had
felt blocked in her writing, in particular in her attempts to treat Nebraska. In this sense Hilda may represent the world opened to Cather
by the Jewett influence. Winifred and Boston, however, represent
civilization, which is of course patriarchal and Apollonian, the realm
of the logos, the Symbolic.

That Bartley is torn between the two worlds suggests the psychic
split that existed in Cather herself, between the Dionysian energy of
the Dianic green world and the power and established authority inherent in the publishing world of Boston, which Annie Fields/Winifred
represented. That Bartley fails to integrate these two worlds must also
be interpreted symbolically. The bridge of the title refers to a literal
bridge that he had engineered which collapses, occasioning Bartley's
death. But the bridge also has the metaphorical meaning of the connection between the two options open to women in the early twentieth
century. The central problem was how to integrate the world of patriarchy, to which the new woman–daughter had assimilated, but which
was inherently alienating, and the green world of rural energy and
emotional fulfillment, Demeter's world. Hilda appears to have accomplished that integration herself; however, since the novel focuses primarily on the male protagonist, her life is not fully detailed in the
novel. She merely represents one side of Bartley/Cather's psyche.

The reason, I suggest, that Bartley dies, that the integration of the
two sides fails in this novel, is that Cather had not yet figured out how
to manage that integration in her fiction. But in her succeeding novels, written under Jewett's immediate influence, which include two of
her masterpieces—*O Pioneers!* (1912) and *My Ántonia* (1918)—as well
as a lesser work, *The Song of the Lark* (1915), that integration is more
successfully accomplished.

Like *My Ántonia, O Pioneers!* is based upon the feminine resurrection
myth, the cycle of Demeter and Persephone, itself based, as all rituals of
rebirth, upon the vegetative transitions of the year. The novel opens in
winter. The Nebraska land where the novel is set is harsh, hostile, and
bleak: it is a "stern frozen country," a place of "sombre wastes."[46] It is a
world reminiscent of Starkfield in *Ethan Frome.*

The protagonist's given name, Alexandra, is a variant of Bartley's surname in *Alexander's Bridge*, which suggests a certain kinship between the two characters. Indeed, she is also a figure who negotiates between two worlds—the matriarchal, a realm of herbal rebirth, and the patriarchal, a world of winter, of doom.

Her first appearance marks her as one of Cather's competent "mannish" girls, a survivor. "She wore a man's long ulster (not as if it were an affliction, but as if it . . . belonged to her; carried it like a young soldier)" (6). She rejected a street flirtation "with a glance of Amazonian fierceness" (7). And the ending of the first episode finds her driving her wagon home in the cold evening "alone," "going deeper and deeper into the dark country" (16). The land was alien: "mischance hung over it." To humans, "its Genius was unfriendly" (18).

In this dark, wintry moment—the nadir of the agricultural cycle, the period of death—Alexandra's father dies; it is a repetition of the ancient dying year-god ritual. As he dies, he hands his authority to Alexandra, betokening a change of regime. Henceforth, the cycle rises into summer, the period of rebirth—the reign of Demeter. Alexandra knew that "down under the frozen crusts, at the roots of the trees, the secret of life was still safe, warm as the blood in one's heart; and the spring would come again! Oh, it would come again!" (172).

The characters in *O Pioneers!* fall into two sets, representing opposing forces. On the one hand are Alexandra's brothers Lou and Oscar and a neighbor, Frank Shabata. These figures tend to be divorced from nature, heartless, brutal, and opportunistic. They represent the masculine. On the other hand are characters such as Crazy Ivar, Marie Tovesky, and, to an extent, Emil, Alexandra's younger brother, whom she treats as her child. These figures are marginal, acivilized, in connection with nature, but in some senses weak and vulnerable. They are to the feminine side of the spectrum. Emil, for example, is described as "tender-hearted" (47). Alexandra's strength lies in an ability to negotiate between the two sides and in the end to integrate or synthesize them, something in the manner of Nan Prince.

An early episode reveals how this subtextual dynamic operates in the novel. It concerns a visit—one might say a pilgrimage—Alexandra makes with her brothers to the sod hut of Crazy Ivar, an eccentric Norwegian hermit who lives out on the plains in a half-animal existence. Significantly, it is July, several months after her father's death.

Ivar is something of a descendent of Jewett's hermit Joanna in *The Country of the Pointed Firs,* as well as of numerous other marginal witch-

women in the fiction of the women local colorists (I think particularly
of Mary E. Wilkins Freeman's "Christmas Jenny" [1891]). Like them,
Ivar lives in the company of animals, "in the clay bank, without defil-
ing the face of Nature any more than the coyote" (32). He is the
unofficial veterinarian of the region and is opposed to hunting; his
religion is a sort of "immediate" animism (33). In short, he is an
exemplar of the feminine tradition of interspecies holism. Alexandra
respects him and follows his advice (to give her hogs more space),
while her brothers ridicule him. Eventually, Alexandra provides a
sanctuary for Ivar in her home, saving him from being sent to an
asylum. She identifies with him and recognizes that there are forces at
work bent on destroying what he represents; those forces are the
imperialist spread of patriarchal capitalist-industrial hegemony resisted so fiercely in nineteenth-century women's local-color literature,
and epitomized in the institutional discipline of the asylum, as Foucault has pointed out.

Carl Linstrum, Alexandra's male counterpart, has gone East to urban metropolitan centers, where he encountered their alienation, returning to the rural world with renewed appreciation (perhaps a sign
of Cather's own shifting attitude). In the city, he laments, "we are all
alike; we have no ties; we know nobody. . . . When one of us dies, they
scarcely know where to bury him" (105). Alexandra is somewhat ambivalent, however, about the land. On the one hand, she has moments
when "it seemed beautiful to her, rich and strong and glorious" (56).
On the other, she sees that it can breed the hardness and ignorance
characteristic of her brothers and Frank Shabata. She wants Emil to
escape, to go to college, to become "cultured."

Marie Tovesky, like Ivar, is associated with natural life, in particular
with plants, fruit, and trees. In the tradition of Stowe's eagle-trees
episode and Jewett's "White Heron," she is distressed when Emil shoots
some ducks. Like Ivar, she seems attracted to a kind of animistic religion and speaks sympathetically of the pre-Christian Bohemian tradition of tree-worshiping. Marie is also feminine in the sense that "Miss
Jessica" is in "Tommy, the Unsentimental" or that Nelly Deane is. She is
romantic, delicate, vulnerable, and ultimately doomed. For on a mythic
level Marie represents the Persephone portion of the resurrection cycle
in *O Pioneers!*—the cycle of death.

In "The White Mulberry Tree" segment of the novel, she and her
lover, Emil, reenact the classical Pyramis and Thisbe legend—young
illicit lovers who die under a white mulberry tree, their blood turning

the tree's berries thenceforth to red. In Ovid's version the lovers commit suicide; in Cather's they are killed by Marie's vengeful husband, Frank, as they lie together under the tree. This episode has a striking similarity to the sledding accident in *Ethan Frome*. Both incidents are associated with a matriarchal tree of life (the mulberry was sacred to the Great Goddess) that has consummated the characters' doom. And in each episode the woman has been reduced by violence to a whimpering animal-like status.

The difference between the two works is, however, significant. *Ethan Frome* remains fixed in winter, fixed in death, whereas the redemptive cycle continues in *O Pioneers!* Alexandra survives and in herself seems to integrate the Artemisian daughter with Demeter the mother, resulting in a triumphant feminine resurrection.

Alexandra's attitude toward Marie is revealing. One the one hand, she is crushed by her and Emil's deaths. And she "hated to think" that "warm-hearted . . . impulsive" creatures like Marie were automatically doomed (252). At the same time, she partially blames Marie for Frank's behavior. She is angry that Marie deceived her about her relationship with Emil (257), and she also views her as something of a temptress who lured Emil to his fate (259). She visits the prison where Frank is held and forgives him, saying Marie and Emil to some extent deserved his wrath.

Alexandra's character is such that she must reject Marie's Persephone path; she cannot taste the pomegranate seed (here representing heterosexual passion or indeed passion of any kind, if one chooses to interpret the Emil-Marie episode as another masquerade, reflecting perhaps Cather's sense that in patriarchal culture lesbian passion too is doomed). Alexandra retains an intellectual autonomy, characteristically seen as masculine, as well as other masculine survival skills; she becomes a shrewd businesswoman. Unlike natural creatures like Ivar and Marie, therefore, Alexandra learns to function in a capitalist male world. At the same time, she retains a connection with the natural realm; she does not become a hardened, disconnected opportunist like her brothers.

Two images in the work particularly illuminate Alexandra's character. One is that of a self-sufficient wild duck whom Alexandra had watched one summer day with Emil. Such days Alexandra recollected "as peculiarly happy; days when she was close to the flat, fallow world about her, and felt, as it were, in her own body the joyous germination in the soil" (173), a clear image of the fecund earth mother, Demeter.

On one such day she saw "a single wild duck . . . swimming and diving and preening her feathers, disporting herself very happily in the flickering light and shade. . . . No living thing had ever seemed to Alexandra as beautiful as that wild duck" (174). "Years afterward she thought of the duck as still there, swimming and diving all by herself in the sunlight, a kind of enchanted bird that did not know age or change" (175). This image symbolizes the autonomous, self-sufficient, and essentially happy person Alexandra had become.

Another figure that helps explain the mythic dynamics of this novel is the "green-world lover" Alexandra occasionally fantasizes about.[47] Alexandra imagines this maternal creature cradling her and carrying her "swiftly off across the fields" (176). The figure is "yellow like the sunlight, . . . [with] the smell of ripe cornfields." It carried her "as if she were a sheaf of wheat" (175). Strangely, Alexandra believes "it was a man, certainly, who carried her, but he was like no man she knew" (175). That is understandable, because on a mythic level the figure is really not a man; rather, it is the embracing corn mother. It is Demeter carrying her daughter home. Alexandra's fantasy is that of the autonomous daughter being returned to the arms of all-embracing Demeter.

While the novel ends with the return of Carl Linstrum and the prospect of her marriage to him, Carl is such a disembodied figure that his final appearance in the novel remains improbable, tacked on—a deus-ex-machina ending, a masquerade whereby Cather capitulated once again to heterosexist ideology. Had Jewett still been around to critique this novel, I suspect she would have said: Why make the fantasied lover a man? A woman could love her in that same protecting way. And why bring in the man at the end? Why not leave her alone, "mateless and appealing"—the powerful words by which Jewett described her monumental matriarch at the conclusion of *The Country of the Pointed Firs*.

Cather's great novel *My Ántonia* (1918) is an even more direct literary descendent of Jewett's *Pointed Firs*. Both works concern the return of sophisticated natives, who serve as narrators, to a rural homeland, where they reconnect with matriarchal sources—Demeters—who reinspire them in their work and life. In Jewett's case the narrator/persona is a woman author; in Cather's, it is a male lawyer, Jim Burden, whose autobiography closely parallels Cather's own. Once again Cather chooses to "masquerade" behind a male persona. Why she continued to do so is a complex issue and has been much discussed. It seems likely, however, that it reflects a continuing discomfort with traditional female identity (a theme quite pronounced in the narrative itself) and therefore is a sign of her continuing male identification, or at least identification with masculine autonomy (see Sharon O'Brien's discussion of the issue in *Willa Cather,* pp. 217, 369). It may have enabled her to keep a necessary distance (once again the daughter's imperative) from the all-powerful mother that Ántonia becomes by the novel's end, where Jim is a kind of profane initiate to the mysteries of Ántonia.

Over a decade ago Evelyn Helmick identified the underlying ritual pattern in *My Ántonia* as that of the Eleusinian mysteries—the ancient religious rite based upon the Persephone-Demeter myth.

> The earth goddess motif builds in *My Ántonia* to those rituals in the final chapter through parallels between Ántonia's story and Persephone's, beginning with the ritual of the "marriage of death." Ántonia's abortive alliance with Larry Donovan, her union with her mother, the birth of her child, her later fecundity all connect her story with the ancient myth.[48]

As in *O Pioneers!* the cyclical pattern of death and rebirth is evident. In this novel too "the first sacrifice must be . . . that of the European father, in order to allow the female rule so prominent in agricultural society" (174). The European father in this novel is Mr. Shimerda, Ántonia's father, who, unable to bear the harshness and brutality of the plains or the loss of the civilized, feminine values of the Dionysian music of his old-world home in Bohemia, commits suicide.

Mr. Shimerda is another of those open, vulnerable feminine figures in Cather's fiction who are doomed because they cannot cultivate the masculine, capitalist skills necessary for survival on the frontier. As in *O Pioneers!* the characters tend to fall into two camps: on the one hand those like Mr. Shimerda; on the other, the opportunistic, heartless survivors, which include Ántonia's mother and her brother Ambrosch; the moneylender Wick Cutter, who tries to rape Ántonia; and Krajiak, who fleeces the Shimerdas of their money. The latter is appropriated to the rattlesnakes that populate the plains, who take advantage of the vulnerable prairie dogs.[49]

Snakes, of course, have a mythic association with the Judeo-Christian Garden of Eden, and the episode in Jim's childhood when he killed a rattlesnake, as well as his grandmother's continual elimination of them, suggests symbolically an attempt to keep the land in its edenic state.

Thus, there is a dialectic between rattlesnakes and prairie dogs, and one of Ántonia's accomplishments is that, like Alexandra, she is able in the end to transcend the vulnerability of the feminine prairie dog without adopting the characteristics of the snake. Jim's grandmother, too, seems to exhibit realism, or what she calls "horse-sense" (she fears the Shimerdas lack it); at the same time she remains emotionally open and retains her ties to nature. She speaks of a badger who watches her garden: "In a new country a body feels friendly to the animals. I like to have him come out and watch me when I'm at work" (17).

After her father's death Ántonia, like Alexandra, has to learn masculine survival skills. In the summer following his death Jim finds her plowing in the fields. "She wore the boots her father had so thoughtfully taken off before he shot himself. . . . She kept her sleeves rolled up all day, and her arms and throat were burned as brown as a sailor's" (122). "I can work like mans now," she asserts (123). Like Alexandra, she becomes a capitalist of sorts: she "could talk of nothing but the prices of things, or how much she could lift and endure" (126). Jim sees her transformation somewhat negatively. "Ántonia ate so noisily now, like a man" (125), and his grandmother worries lest she lose the feminine graces (125).

At the same time, she retains qualities that link her with the feminine; indeed, in some aspects she recalls Marie Tovesky. She is strongly identified with nature. One episode that particularly draws attention to this quality is when one summer day, barefooted, "while we were lying there against the warm bank," she notices "a little insect of the palest, frailest green." It appears vulnerable and sits there "antennae quivering, as if . . . waiting for something to come and finish him" (39). Ántonia, however, in maternal fashion saves the cricket, making "a warm nest for him in her hands" and talking to it in Bohemian, which symbolically seems to signify a preoedipal "language." Soon it begins to chirp, and she gives it a home in her hair. She says that the cricket reminds her of an herb woman, "Old Hata," who lived in her village in Europe.

The incident with the cricket puts Ántonia on the side of the compassionate maternal/feminine figures who identify with vulnerability, and with nature, another link in the women's tradition of ecological holism.

Significantly, after this episode the narrator engages in a paean to the afternoon sun and golden cornfields: "The blond cornfields were red gold, the haystacks turned rosy and threw long shadows. The whole prairie was like the bush that burned with fire and was not consumed. . . . It was a sudden transfiguration, a lifting-up of day" (40). Ántonia here clearly becomes associated with the transfiguring agricultural ritual of rebirth—a prefiguration of her final role as Demeter.

But in her early phases Ántonia also retains a resemblance to Marie in her attraction to a kind of Dionysian romanticism; and, as with Marie, this quality leads to her doom. It engages her in the Persephone phase of her life cycle. Like Marie, Ántonia is highly emotional: "Everything she said seemed to come right out of her heart" (176). And she loves to dance. In this, like the other "hired girls," she hovers on the edge of respectability in the Apollonian eyes of the town. It is at a dance that she meets Larry Donovan, "a kind of professional ladies' man" (223), who Helmick suggests is identified "with the underworld and hence with the drama of Persephone" (180).

Ántonia is seduced and abandoned by Donovan, and her experience with him is like a trip to the underworld. Her return, as Helmick notes, is in May, and she is "wearing the veils which often distinguish statues of the earth goddess in classical sculpture" (180). "The strongest echo of the Demeter-Persephone" myth occurs, suggests Helmick, in the Widow Stevens's recollection of the event: " 'Jimmy, I sat right down on that bank beside her and made lament.' Here she is mother Demeter mourning the abduction of her daughter, just as later Ántonia mourns the loss of her own daughter, even to a happy marriage: 'I cried like I was putting her in her coffin' " (180).

The final section of the novel, "Cuzak's Boys," follows the traditional stages of the Eleusinian rituals, explained by Helmick in great detail. One of the final images of Ántonia is in an apple orchard—an edenic image—where she "kept stopping to tell me about one tree and another. 'I love them as if they were people,' she said, rubbing her hand over the bark" (340). The comment suggests the religion of animism that attracted Marie and Crazy Ivar in *O Pioneers!* and, of course, recalls the golden apples in *A Country Doctor*, similarly emblematic of the matriarchal community. Ántonia, reborn, explains to Jim that she has grown particularly sensitive to natural life; she now rejects hunting. "Ever since I've had children, I don't like to kill anything" (242). And Jim's concluding observation is: "She had only to stand in the orchard, to put her hand on a little crab tree and look up at the apples, to make you feel the goodness of planting and tending and harvesting at last. All the strong things of her heart came out in her body, that had been so

tireless in serving generous emotions" (353). Ántonia now fully represents the feminine/matriarchal principle.

Perhaps the ultimate explanation for Cather's choice of a masculine
persona is that it represents the logos. Jungian theorist Erich Neu-
mann proposes in *Amor and Psyche: The Psychic Development of the Feminine* that "the masculine mystery is bound up with the active heroic
struggle of the ego. . . . But the primordial feminine mysteries have a
different structure. They are mysteries of birth and rebirth."[50]

Jim represents the autonomous daughter who has developed the
powers of the logos in her assimilation into patriarchal culture; her
return to the realm of Ántonia signifies a reunion with the matriarchal mysteries—the repetitive cycle of birth and rebirth that characterizes the nonoedipal feminine condition. In this sense, the structure of
My Ántonia repeats the pattern seen in Jewett works and in Wharton's
ambivalences, where the daughter must engage in patriarchal production, develop the logos, learn patriarchal language in order to transcribe the matriarchal mysteries in order to inscribe them in history.
For without the traveling daughter those mysteries remain silent, marginal, not named (as noted in chapter 1).

The final passages of this novel include an apparent reference to
Jewett as mentor. Jim speaks of studying Virgil in college under the
aegis of a teacher named Cleric. He learned in his studies of Virgil's
desire "to bring the Muse into [his] own country" (264). Jim wonders
whether Cleric had tried to bring the muse to "that particular rocky
strip of New England coast" that was his home—a clear allusion to the
Maine seacoast of Sarah Orne Jewett (265). In further reflections
upon the muse Jim realizes that it is the power of the feminine that
provides the inspiration for poetry like Virgil's (270). And he resolves
to carry the face of Ántonia "at the very bottom of my memory" (322).

His final comment, after his rediscovery of Ántonia many years
later—"I had the sense of coming home to myself"—expresses the
primordial reunion of the daughter-artist with the matriarchal sources
of creation. This rediscovery of and reconnection with the feminine
side of the psyche, which Jim's return to Ántonia symbolizes, is the
dynamic that informs this great novel with feminine power. In the end
the work itself is a celebration of the mysteries of triumphant Demeter.

Between *O Pioneers!* and *My Ántonia* Cather published a novel that is
not of their stature, but which concerns many of their themes and
reflects Jewett's continuing influence. *The Song of the Lark* (1915) tells
that part of the tale that Jewett never told: what happens to the

daughter-artist once she goes to the big city. In this respect it resembles Mary Austin's *A Woman of Genius* (1912), published shortly before, and Ellen Glasgow's *The Descendant* (1897) and *The Wheel of Life* (1906), all of which concern the struggles of young women artists (somewhat peripherally in Glasgow's case, however).

The strain of romantic elitism, always a leitmotif in Cather's works, is particularly strong here: Thea Kronberg is seen as endowed with special talents that set her apart from the mediocrity of the sluggish masses. Otherwise, like Nan Prince, she is "not the marrying kind" (her father says)[51] but is oriented toward a (musical) vocation at an early age. A suitor, Ray Kennedy, is conveniently killed, leaving her six hundred dollars, enough for her to pursue her career in Chicago.

During a period when her enthusiasm seems to ebb, and seeking reinspiration, Thea visits the southwestern site of the ancient cliff-dwellers, Panther Canyon. This section is another repetition of a feminine ritual, a mother-daughter reunion in which the daughter is reinspired by her reconnection with the powers of Demeter. It is a process by which the ego, the logos side of the personality, is dissolved. As she approaches the region, "the personality of which she was so tired seemed to let go of her" (296).

Deep within this feminine landscape, described as a "V-shaped inner gorge," "a hollow (. . . like a great fold in the rock)" (297), Thea establishes herself in a "rock-room," a cave—always a feminine symbol—surrounded by flowers that are "sickeningly sweet after a shower" (299). Here she meditates in solitude, loses herself in the sounds of nature, reconnects with the ancient Indian women, and takes ritual baths.

> On the first day that Thea climbed the water-trail she began to have intuitions about the women who had worn the path, and who had spent so great a part of their lives going up and down it. She found herself trying to walk as they must have walked, with a feeling in her feet and knees and loins which she had never known before. . . . She could feel the weight of an Indian baby hanging to her back as she climbed. (302)

Thus, Thea absorbs the maternal powers of the traditional women whose lives she imagined were bound by cycles of repetition. Thea herself regularly bathes in a stream that expresses "a continuity of life that reached back into the old time." "Thea's bath came to have a

ceremonial gravity. The atmosphere of the canyon was ritualistic"
(304).

In an epiphanic moment she reflects upon the Indian women's
pottery, "their most direct appeal to water, the envelope and sheath of
the precious element itself" (303). "[W]hat was any art but an effort to
make a sheath, a mould in which to imprison for a moment the shining, elusive element which is life itself. . . . The Indian women had
held it in their jars" (304). Thea applies this realization to her own art;
thus occurs the desired reinspiration. As O'Brien suggests, this moment provides Thea "with a connection to feminine creativity outside
the patriarchal artistic tradition." Cather felt that "in the Cliff-
dwellers' civilization, unlike her own, 'woman' and 'artist' were not
conflicting identities."[52]

Thea's feminine rebirth, accomplished through reconnection with
the ancient mothers, enables her to return to her career, which she
pursues thenceforth successfully. Near the end of the novel, however,
a new issue is raised—one that will become increasingly significant in
Cather's later works—whether devotion to art should take precedence
over a commitment to life. When her mother is dying, Thea cannot
come to her side because she has "an unhoped-for opportunity to go
on in a big part" (403). An old suitor finally recognizes that her primary commitment has been not to other people but to her art (466).
Her "selfishness" had been signaled earlier when she had refused to
sing at a family friend's funeral because she was saving her voice
(221).

The rebellion against the traditional feminine relational ethic, of
putting the collective before the self, is another aspect of the daughter-
artist's quest for autonomy (seen as early as such nineteenth-century
künstlerromans as Elizabeth Stuart Phelps's *Story of Avis* [1877]). Emphasis upon the self's autonomy, however, inevitably occasions the experience of guilt, which is the voice, so to speak, of the collective echoing
within. It arises whenever bonds with others are ruptured.

David Stouck suggests that Cather's late works reflect a sense of
guilt toward her own mother; they were written, he suggests, in a
"spirit of self-exorcism."[53] Moreover, they question the choice made
by Thea (and presumably by Cather herself), that of a commitment to
art over life. Instead, Stouck contends, "The priority of life over art
and achievement is implicit throughout Willa Cather's last four
books."[54]

I propose, however, that the real opposition was not so much between "art" and "life" as between art mediated by the masculine logos, autonomous art done by the individual in isolation—that is, Western "masterpiece" art—and art done in the context of the collective, anonymous art, in other words, women's traditional folk art.

In 1927 Cather commented, "The German housewife who sits before her family on Thanksgiving Day a perfectly roasted goose, is an artist."[55] Such an intuition is already evident in Thea's appreciation of the Indian women's pottery in *Song of the Lark*. Ordinary women's art is integrated in a way that the art practiced by the daughter-artists under the sway of patriarchal stylistics is not. The work produced by the German housewife, the Indian women, as well as that of Ántonia and Alexandra, seems integrated with its natural sources in a way that the art of the sophisticated daughters does not; in the latter there is always a disconnection, an alienation, the intervention of the logos, the "male narrator." Cather's dissatisfaction with this intervention becomes apparent in her final works, to be treated at the end of this chapter.

Meanwhile, in the 1920s Cather produced three important novels: *One of Ours* (1922), *A Lost Lady* (1923), and *The Professor's House* (1925). Cather's celebrated comment that "the world broke in two in 1922 or thereabouts"[56] may be (and has been) interpreted variously. It can be seen as a general comment about the dramatic transitions that were occurring in the world in the wake of World War I; it may refer to Cather's realization of the fall upon which this study is predicated, that by 1922 the world of the mother's garden had been fully destroyed and that the daughter was henceforth fully dissociated from it; or it may be a more personal remark, relating to the break-up of her relationship with Isabelle McClung, itself a friendship that harked back to the passionate bonds formed by nineteenth-century women.[57] Little precisely is known about their relationship because most letters have been destroyed; however, it is well known that Isabelle's marriage in 1917 was devastating to Cather. What is rarely noted, however, is that Willa had moved out of the McClung household in 1906 to follow her own career in New York. Perhaps it was this that undermined the relationship, and perhaps this is the reason for the underlying sense in Cather's work that pursuit of a career means destruction of the personal bonds of "home" (and vice versa). In any event, the observation about 1922 clearly expresses a sense of fracture, that something whole has been destroyed, henceforth leaving alienation, dissociation, the phenomenology of the fall.

While it earned Cather the Pulitzer Prize, *One of Ours*, the novel published the year the world "broke in two," has not been judged by critics as one of her major works and has sometimes been dismissed as an unsuccessful attempt at a war novel. However, when set in the thematic contexts being explored in this study, the work is of considerable significance. It continues, indeed intensifies, the mother-daughter dialectic seen in earlier works. As with *Alexander's Bridge*, the protagonist is a man, Claude Wheeler, who is torn between two feminine options— the one represented by his mother and her world; the other by his wife, Enid Royce. And as in the former novel, the character is unable to negotiate the two worlds and this occasions his death. If once again we may interpret Claude as a Cather persona, we see that the work exhibits the psychic split seen in much of Cather's work.[58] The novel is dedicated to Cather's mother, and indeed a central figure in the novel is Claude's mother. She represents the traditional female world of the home, domestic life, peace, and order. She and Mahailey, an old servant woman, constitute the feminine/maternal cosmos of the novel.

Mahailey is reminiscent of the servant woman Verena Marsh in Wharton's *Summer*. Both are partially deaf, both are associated with attic sanctuaries, both represent maternal-domestic traditions. But Wharton's figure is far more negative, suggesting an absence, something failed. Cather's Mahailey, although also marginal, is a positive power, a Hestia, who keeps the feminine-maternal spirits alive. She helps the mother raise Claude (the father, like most Cather patriarchs, is rarely at home and is emotionally remote); she consoles the mother; she cooks; and in one symbolic episode she refuses to bequeath her mother's quilts to Claude's brother Ralph, another ruthless masculine entrepreneur, a type figure in Cather's repertoire of characters. Mahailey's gesture of preserving her mother's art, refusing to turn it over to a patriarchal authority, is another expression of the archetypal feminine artistic problem faced by women writers during this period— seen so dramatically in Wharton's early novellas, *The Touchstone* and *Sanctuary*. In *One of Ours* capitulation is resisted; the feminine-maternal artistic tradition (symbolized by the quilts) is preserved. Significantly, Claude sees Mahailey and his mother as "children of the moon," always a symbol of the feminine and closely associated with the Demeter-Persephone-Artemis myth.[59] Here Claude uses the term to suggest that the women are repressed, denied, marginal figures, too sensitive for the rough-and-ready patriarchal world into which they have been cast.

Claude and his mother's relationship is intense. In one episode after a heart-to-heart talk: "For a moment they clung together in the pale, clear square of the west window, as the two natures in one person sometimes meet and cling in a fated hour" (87). Their selves merge—a striking image of the mother-daughter reunion, or perhaps of the two aspects of the author's psyche, logos and the collective, reconnecting. During a later period Claude, who has reluctantly had to abandon his university studies, lives idyllically on the farm with his mother and Mahailey. She says, "It's almost like being a bride, keeping house for just you, Claude" (78)—another image of merging.

But Claude has something of the daughter's spirit in him too. He is restless and ambitious (52), and at the university he learns that scholarship is an exercise of the logos; one must purge it of personal feelings. In working on a paper on Joan of Arc, Claude prides himself "that he had kept all personal feelings out" (61). (*Song of the Lark* also evokes the Joan of Arc legend, that of a Dianic witch-woman eventually destroyed by patriarchal powers.)

Claude finds, however, "that after all his conscientious study he really knew very little more about the Maid of Orleans than when he first heard of her from his mother, one day when he was a boy" (62). He had found "a picture of her in armour, in an old book," and had taken it "down to the kitchen where his mother was making apple pies. . . . [A]nd while she went on rolling out the dough and fitting it to the pans, she told him the story" (62). Thus, it is not patriarchal knowledge derived from the objective modes of university learning that Claude finds most powerful; rather, it is the tradition of oral feminine knowledge that has remained persuasive in his memory. That tradition had been evoked earlier by Cather when she said she wrote *O Pioneers!* as if she were telling it to Jewett.

Enid Royce, the woman Claude marries, is a peculiar character. At first, she is presented sympathetically; before their marriage, when Claude is injured in a farming accident, she visits him faithfully, in accord with the traditional feminine relational ethic, which arouses his interest in her. But later, especially after the marriage, she becomes increasingly negative, almost a stereotype of the heartless, rigidly ambitious career woman. Claude continually compares her with his mother; on their wedding night, when Enid refuses to sleep with him, he is overcome by a wave of homesickness: "he could see the light in his mother's window . . . [and] the glow of Mahailey's lamp" (196).

Enid is a negative portrait of the new woman. She is involved in various causes, especially prohibition. She spends most of her time going to meetings in her electric car, neglecting her husband. "It seemed" to her father "as if his daughters had no heart" (250). She finally abandons Claude by going to China to tend her missionary sister—also a new woman far from the hearth. One senses that there is a personal model for the figure of Enid—perhaps Isabelle McClung— and that Claude's feelings of bitterness and desolation reflect Cather's sentiments at Isabelle's perceived desertion: "He wondered how he was to go through the years ahead of him, unless he could get rid of this sick feeling in his soul" (223). His solution provides what appears to be a deus-ex-machina ending; he enlists in the army and is killed in World War I.

But when he leaves his home he notices a black barn cat—always a symbol of the Hecate witch (associated, as noted, with Zeena Frome)— and takes it with him. Claude laughs at the idea that it is a supposed symbol of bad luck (224). The cat is, however, an ironic prefiguration of the end, for, once again, it is a symbol of the disconnection of the mother and the daughter and of the daughter-death inherent in that ritual cycle, represented in this novel by Claude's death and Enid's disappearance. The final scene indeed suggests maternal transcendence: it is of the mothers at home. Mahailey has the last line: she observes that God is "directly overhead, not so very far above the kitchen stove" (459). Rather, it is the feminine-maternal goddess who has arisen and is in her place, triumphant.

A Lost Lady (1923) is conversely about the destruction of the feminine and the triumph of the patriarchal, a repetition of the myth of the fall. Marian Forrester, the bittersweet protagonist of this novel, is a Persephone figure reminiscent of Marie Tovesky, except that Marian appears to be more of a willing victim. But the point of view has changed. Where Marie's fate is told more or less neutrally in the third person, Marian's is presented from the point of view of a judgmental youth, Niel Herbert, a Cather persona, who condemns her fall as a capitulation. "In the end, Niel went away without bidding her good-bye. He went away with weary contempt for her in his heart."[60]

Evelyn Helmick, in another perceptive article, argues that the "fall" registered in the novel is from a matriarchal to a patriarchal society, and from a value system that respects nature to one that would dominate and ultimately destroy it.

The opening scene is emblematic: it depicts an atrocious incident in which Ivy Peters, one of a group of young boys that includes Niel Herbert, maims and tortures a female woodpecker by slitting its eyes.

Ivy does this with tools from his taxidermy kit, which connects him with the vivisectionist Cather lauded in her male-identified graduation speech, as well as with the ornithologist in Jewett's "White Heron." Here, however, there is not even the pretense of scientific purpose; it is an example of gratuitous cruelty. Significantly, the episode takes place on the Forrester marshland, a green-world female sanctuary. The woodpecker symbolizes the feminine. Niel cries, "It's a female," while Ivy sarcastically calls it "Miss Female" (23).

As an adult, Ivy becomes a lawyer-entrepreneur who cheats Indians and takes advantage of the Forresters' financial difficulties by buying their marshland, draining it, and using it for hunting (which they had forbidden him as a boy). Helmick analyzes Peters's draining of the marsh as follows: "The swamp stage of civilization . . . represents the early matriarchate, its drying up is a symbol not only of the human dominance of nature but also of the male drive for knowledge that succeeds the female acquiescence to nature."[61] It also recalls the allusion to Faust's drainage enterprise echoed ironically in Wharton's *Fruit of the Tree*.

Niel's final disillusionment with Marian occurs near the end of the novel when she adopts Peters as her lawyer, and indeed appears to be having an affair with him, symbolizing her final capitulation to patriarchal control. Meanwhile, the script has followed the stages of her fall.

Like Marie Tovesky, Marian is a magical personality who animates everything, a romantic who loves to dance. But like other Dionysian figures, her warmth is blotted out by the bleakness of the plains, especially in winter. It is a place of exile. The pivotal experience in Marian's fall is an adulterous affair with Frank Ellinger, who seduces and abandons her. Reminiscent of Larry Donovan, he is a Hades figure. In the wake of this disaster Marian begins to degenerate; she drinks excessively. "She had ceased to care about anything" (139).

Where Ántonia rose from her underworld, Marian remains fixed. Where *My Ántonia* affirms the transcendence of Demeter, *A Lost Lady* laments the betrayal of Persephone. And, as Helmick suggests, Marian's capitulation has wider implications: it reflects the destruction of the nineteenth-century agricultural matriarchy and its replacement by patriarchal hegemony, the unholy alliance of science and capitalism represented by Ivy Peters; the tyranny of the masculine logos imposing its destructive forms on nature, no longer restrained by a feminine value system.

Thus, Niel's condemnation of Marian is more than just a puritanical rejection of her adultery, and more than a Hamlet-like oedipal discomfort with/attraction to maternal sexuality; the subtextual meaning is that he is condemning the failure of Marian to stand up for her feminine heritage—symbolized by the marshland—allowing it instead to be destroyed by patriarchal imperialism. In this novel Cather returns to the ethic proposed in the works of the local colorists, where such capitulation (recall Jewett's "White Heron" or Freeman's "Christmas Jenny") is condemned.

Cather's next novel, *The Professor's House* (1925), deals, allegorically, with the attempt by the daughter to connect her art with maternal sources, and with the tenuous nature of that connection. The protagonist is a professor, Godfrey St. Peter, another Cather persona. His financial success has allowed him to build a new house, but when the time comes to move he finds he cannot leave his old study, which is located in an attic.

Also in the attic are dressmaker forms used by Augusta, his wife's seamstress. The attic, the female forms, and Augusta constitute the maternal/preoedipal/matriarchal realm to which the professor is attached, some critics say infantilely.[62] The subtextual reason for the professor's apparently "infantile" regression, however, is that the attic is the site of the maternal muse, which the professor (the artist) fears losing if he moves (disconnects) from it. If, as Hélène Cixous has suggested, women's ink is white because it comes from the mother's milk,[63] the concern of the professor, who represents Cather, is understandable. Significantly, when he and Augusta start to pack up for the move, he notices that their papers are all mixed together. He says, "I see we shall have some difficulty in separating our life work, Augusta. We've kept our papers together a long while now."[64] This integration suggests the desired synthesis Cather is coming to wish between the art of the daughters and that of the mothers, as seen in the German housewife's goose, the Indian women's pottery, and Mahailey's quilt.

Later, in another significant episode, the professor is elated when he finds that Augusta believes the Blessed Virgin had "composed the Magnificat" "just as soon as the angel had announced to her that she would be the mother of our Lord" (100). He repeats the information to himself and feels that it has "brightened" his study: "(Surely she had said that the Blessed Virgin sat down and composed the Magnificat!)" (100). The reason the professor (Cather) is elated is that the image is one of a mother creating art, indeed that her maternity is the source of her inspiration. This idea is reinforced as the professor recollects how in the past, while he worked in the attic study, the sounds from the domestic world below had filtered up, helping him to feel in touch with it.

> Just as, when Queen Mathilde was doing the long tapestry now shown at Bayeux,—working her chronicles of the deeds of knights and heroes,—alongside the big pattern of dramatic action she and her women carried the little playful pattern of birds and beasts that are a story in themselves: so, to him, the most important chapters of his story were interwoven with personal memories. (101)

This wonderful epic simile is a paradigmatic description of the dynamic in women's art between the marginal green world of the mothers, on the one hand—"the little playful pattern of birds and beasts that are a story in themselves"—and on the other the central masculine scripts—"the deeds of knights and heroes"—that have traditionally been considered the stuff of great (patriarchal) art. The image of Queen Mathilde surreptitiously slipping in marginal feminine matter is poignant. Like Claude Wheeler's study of Joan of Arc, the professor finds that in his own work "his most important chapters" are those informed with the personal, which derives from feminine-maternal tradition.

Tom Outland, a precocious student of St. Peter's, who represents the next generation, is similarly moved by a quest to integrate the maternal into his life and work. Tom represents the post–World War I daughter figure, but like others in that generation (Claude Wheeler and Lesley Ferguesson in "The Best Years") he is doomed (like Claude, he is killed in the war).

The professor, himself but tentatively connected with the maternal, is especially worried about the new generation and about the transition of (women's) art to future generations. In speaking of his elaborate garden, to which he is as attached as he is to his attic, he comments, "What am I to do with that garden in the end . . .? Destroy it? Or leave it to the mercy of the next tenants?" (77). His anxiety recalls Evelina's concern in the Freeman story discussed in chapter 1.

Book 2 of the novel (the novel has a tripartite structure) is a first-person narration told by Tom to St. Peter (recall Cather's desire to narrate her novel directly to Jewett). His story is a repetition of the cliff-dweller narrative seen in other works. Like Thea Kronberg's,

Tom's discovery of this ancient feminine utopia is epiphanal. He learns they were a people who lived "an orderly and secure life . . . [and who] developed considerably the arts of peace" (219).

In his exploration of the ruins of their deserted cave city, Tom discovers a female mummy—another symbol of the feminine-maternal on the order of the dressmaker forms. But like them she is only a partial representation, in a state of disintegration, the apparent victim of violence. "We thought she might have been murdered; there was a great wound in her side. . . . Her mouth was open as if she were screaming, and her face, through all those years, had kept a look of terrible agony" (214). The suggestion is of a primal fall; indeed, the cliff-dwellers had been destroyed by a horde "without culture or domestic virtues" (221)—another image of patriarchal capitalism. Tom and his companion nickname the mummy "Mother Eve" (214).

Tom keeps a journal (his art) of his days in the Southwest, and when he leaves the area he secretes it in a niche near Mother Eve, another gesture that suggests an attempt to integrate daughter-art with the maternal source. Later he and St. Peter retrieve it. Before he returns East for good, Tom spends a summer alone on the mesa. His experience is similar to Thea's; it provides a kind of spiritual rebirth: one moonlit night, "It all came together in my understanding, as a series of experiments do when you begin to see where they are leading. Something had happened in me that made it possible for me to coordinate and simplify, and that process . . . brought with it great happiness. . . . It was my high tide. . . . I had found everything" (250–51). The experience of integration suggests a dissolution of the masculine logos and a discovery of intellectual holism—the feminine way.

In Book 3 the professor works on editing Tom's journals (Tom is now dead). In that process and in the process of his own dying, St. Peter too moves toward an experience of integration; it involves a shedding of his surface, civilized, oedipal self and a return to his "primitive" core. "He was a primitive. He was only interested in earth and woods and water. Wherever sun sunned and rain rained and snow snowed, wherever life sprouted and decayed, places were alike to him. . . . He was earth, and would return to earth" (265). It is an image of Demeter triumphant.

Significantly, in his final reflections St. Peter feels that in his process of growing up he had adopted a false self: "adolescence grafted a new creature into the original one" (267). He decides that "the complexion of [one's] life was largely determined by how well or ill [one's] original self and [one's] nature as modified by sex rubbed on together" (267). Here Cather seems to be saying that entrance into patriarchal culture—the infernal city of heterosexist commerce—forces individuals to assume culturally prescribed roles (women as exchange objects) that are inauthentic, an idea proposed by numerous feminist theorists, especially those like Gayle Rubin and Juliet Mitchell who combine a psychological (Freud) and an anthropological (Lévi-Strauss) perspective.[65] Cather's suggestion here is that by shedding those selves, by somehow returning to the preoedipal or the nonoedipal, to the matriarchal, one rediscovers "Desire under all desires, Truth under all truths" (265).

The novel thus follows the mythic ritual of death and resurrection, Persephone and Demeter, seen in so many Cather works. Its tripartite structure suggests a thesis-antithesis-synthesis pattern. Book 1 concerns the retention of the maternal; Book 2, the death of the daughter; Book 3, the integration of the insights of the daughter with those of the mother, the reabsorption of the daughter into the maternal, into transcending Demeter.

Cather's handling of these issues became increasingly pessimistic in three works completed in the latter phases of her career: two stories, "Old Mrs. Harris" (1932) and "The Best Years" (1945), and a novel, *Lucy Gayheart* (1935). *Sapphira and the Slave Girl* (1940), Cather's last novel, also deals with mother-daughter conflict and mother-daughter reconciliation, but because it has been treated sufficiently elsewhere, I will not discuss it here.[66]

"Old Mrs. Harris" was written at about the time of Cather's own mother's death, which occurred in 1931 and had a "profound effect" on her, according to Edith Lewis.[67] The story is a valorization of a mother figure, Grandma Harris, who is not appreciated by her daughter and granddaughter, the latter of whom is bound for college and selfishly absorbed in that process.

The story is set in Colorado and includes several of Cather's earlier motifs: nostalgia for an eastern edenic green world, this time Tennessee (the grandmother had worked there as a backwoods nurse); the sense of the passing of an old order based on a personalist relational ethic to a secular, demythologized commercial realm; and the association of the matriarchal figure with animals (Grandma Harris's primary attachment is to her cat). The piece ends with the grandmother's death and with the prediction that the daughter and granddaughter "will come closer and closer to Grandma Harris . . . they will regret that they heeded her so little."[68]

Lucy Gayheart (1935) and "The Best Years" (1945) deal with doomed daughters in exile. Lucy Gayheart, as her name implies, is another of Cather's lyrical Dionysian figures who struggle to experience passion in a world that is dried up, bleak, lifeless, fallen. Her moving life story somewhat resembles that of the similarly named Katharine Gaylord in "A Death in the Desert," characterized explicitly by Cather as a Persephone. Lucy is also a Persephone figure, doomed apparently by her pursuit of heterosexual passion and careerist ambition.

Lucy's fall is not, however, condemned as Marian Forrester's was; rather, it is described with sympathy. Nor is she the victim of a seduce-and-abandon rake; rather, she chooses to involve herself with Clement Sebastian, a famous singer, who is kindly and otherwise inoffensive (if somewhat paternalistic).

The novel is set in the early years of the twentieth century, partly in Nebraska, partly in Chicago, where, like Thea, Lucy goes to pursue her (musical) career. Like many of Cather's young women and like Nan Prince, Lucy, whose mother is dead, has a boyish character. An old suitor recalls that he had first seen her, "a slip of a girl in boy's overalls," barefoot, "watering the garden."[69] Clement finds her "rather boyish" (80). And when she is first in the city she exults in the experience of masculine autonomy. "[F]or the first time in her life she could come and go like a boy; no one fussing about, no one hovering over her" (26). Indeed, speaking as a decided "new woman," Lucy rejects the domestic world as oppressive. In a striking reversal of traditional feminine imagery, she exclaims: "Family life in a little town is pretty deadly. It's being planted in the earth, like one of your carrots there. I'd rather be pulled up and thrown away" (134).

But such deracination cannot be sustained, Cather seems to imply. Both Lucy and Clement, in separate incidents, die in accidental drownings. While their fates suggest, many critics have proposed, Cather's condemnation of all-engulfing passion, I suggest that unconsciously her condemnation is of the heterosexist route to passion, a surrogate route that supplants the feminine-maternal, the lesbian, and wrongly channels women's desires for collective engagement.

For even in her early days in Chicago, at the height of her careerist ambitions, Lucy longs to merge her self in something larger, to, as Cather put it elsewhere, "be dissolved into something complete and great" (*My Ántonia,* 18). "If only one could lose one's life," Lucy reflects, "and one's body and be nothing but one's desire; if the rest could melt away, and that could float with the gulls, out yonder where the blue and green were changing!" (102). Her meditation recalls St. Peter's desire to shed his surface selves.

After Clement's death, Lucy returns defeated to her hometown on the prairie. That section of the novel opens, significantly, with the point of view of a neighbor woman, Mrs. Alec Ramsay, a matriarchal figure, solidly rooted in her rural environment. The name Ramsay must recall Virginia Woolf's great figure, Mrs. Ramsay, in *To the Lighthouse* (1927), and surely Cather's choice of name is not accidental. Indeed, mutual influences appear to have passed between Cather and Woolf—a topic that has not yet been investigated (Leon Edel suggests that the structure of *To the Lighthouse* reflects the influence of *The Professor's House*).[70]

Back home Lucy feels alienated; the only areas where she feels happy are the attic and the orchard—two realms that symbolically connect in Cather's mythography to the maternal, to Demeter's green world. The apple orchard becomes a sacred sanctuary to Lucy, recalling Ántonia; there, as Nan Prince with her apple trees, Lucy receives redemptive knowledge. "Out here in the orchard she could even talk to herself; it was a great comfort" (157). "She would come out here under the apple trees, cold and frightened and unsteady, and slowly the fright would wear away and the hard place in her breast would grow soft" (158).

The pivotal event during Lucy's homecoming is her sister Pauline's decision to have the orchard cut down for financial reasons. Lucy and Pauline had always been alienated; Pauline, who resented what she saw as Lucy's favoritist treatment in the family, is something of an entrepreneur; at least, her judgments are often materially based. The confrontation over the orchard, reminiscent of Chekhov's *Cherry Orchard* and, more importantly, of the conflict over the marshland in *A Lost Lady*, is symbolically over the destruction of the matriarchal green-world bower. Lucy begs her sister to preserve the area, which Pauline agrees to do, for at least a year.

Meanwhile, Mrs. Ramsay, the voice of the mother, has advised Lucy to choose life over "accomplishments." "Nothing really matters," she says, "but living, and I know. Accomplishments are the ornaments of life, they come second." She encourages Lucy to revive from her despondency. "There's a long summer before you, and everything rights itself in time" (165). It is the wisdom of Demeter.

Finally, Lucy accepts Mrs. Ramsay's advice. Intuitively, she experiences a great desire to go on living, but she wonders, "How could she go on, alone" (184). The answer also comes to her: "What if—what if Life itself were the sweetheart?" (184). It is an affirmation that suggests a holistic transcendence, the joy of Demeter. However, not long after this, Lucy drowns in a skating accident. The contrast between this ending and that of Jewett's *Country Doctor,* where Nan Prince, who had come to a similar wisdom as Lucy, thanks God for her future, is marked. Lucy, Cather observes, "was like a bird being shot down when it rises in its morning flight toward the sun" (207). The image culminates the identification of women and vulnerable natural creatures noted as characteristic in women's literature. But, again, where in Jewett's imaginative construction the white heron is saved, in Cather's final vision, a similar representation is doomed. The reason for this depressingly pessimistic view, I suggest, is that Cather and her characters existed in a fallen world where contact with redemptive feminine passion was no longer possible. The daughter's exile was complete.

"The Best Years" (written in 1945), apparently Cather's last story, published posthumously, is a similarly bleak evocation. Set in 1899 in Nebraska, it concerns a new woman, Lesley Ferguesson, who teaches in a rural school. The story opens when Evangeline Knightly, the local school superintendent, comes to inspect Lesley's school. Afterward she gives a homesick Lesley a ride back to town. Once home, Lesley "gave herself up to the feeling of being at home, like getting into a warm bath when one is tired. She was safe from everything, was where she wanted to be, where she ought to be. A plant that has been washed out by a rain storm feels like that, when a kind gardener puts it gently back into its own earth with its own group."[71] This highly significant passage recalls St. Peter's desires and reverses the image of deracination seen in *Lucy Gayheart.* Cather's final vision is one of being rerooted in the mother's garden.

Lesley's own mother is the typical rural matriarch. And, as elsewhere in Cather's work, the attic signifies a place of maternal retreat. In later years, after the family had moved, the mother recollects: "And I can almost think I am down there, with my children up in the loft. We were very happy" (137). After Lesley becomes a teacher, however, "her mother had said she must have a room of her own" (110)—another verbal echo from Virginia Woolf, this of her essay on the woman writer's need for independence, *A Room of One's Own* (1929). But Lesley is not happy about being cut off from the collective space, a further hint that Cather is questioning the notion of autonomous art and its compatibility with feminine traditions and psychic needs.

At home Lesley experiences the epiphanal mystical merging of the self that recurs in Cather's work. "[S]itting in the warm sun . . . she almost ceased to exist. The feeling of being at home was complete, absolute: it made her sleepy" (112).

The story then switches abruptly. From Demeter's warm sun we are transposed into a winter blizzard. Evangeline Knightly is at a convention in Lincoln, where she is snowbound. On her way back on the train she learns that Lesley had been isolated in the school during the storm, had contracted pneumonia, and had died three days later.

Twenty years later Evangeline (now married) returns to visit Mrs. Ferguesson, who is still lamenting the death of her daughter: "there's nothing in all my life so precious to me to remember and think about as my Lesley" (134). Her final meditation is on the death of a matriarchal symbol: "You know," she says, "cows will cross the road right in front of a car. Maybe their grandchildren calves will be more modern-minded" (138). Thus, in her final work Cather continues her concern about the destruction of the matriarchal, the mother's garden, by the forces of modernity, and about the exile and death of the daughter Persephone. While Mrs. Ferguesson survives, she is not a joyously transcendent Demeter; rather, it is Demeter in mourning. This is Cather's final vision.

Why, then, when Wharton returned in the thirties to at least a tentative embrace of redemptive maternal sources (although, as indicated, she also continued in her late stories to transmit uncritically a patriarchal or male-identified vision—seen in "Roman Fever"), did Cather end on this resigned, pessimistic note? One can only speculate that perhaps it was the influence of world events; after all, "The Best Years" was written during World War II, in 1945, the year of Hiroshima and Nagasaki. Surely, the healing vision of Demeter had never been more in eclipse; perhaps this knowledge became inscribed in Cather's final work.

5

Ellen Glasgow:
Beyond Barren Ground

> *[I]n her heart of hearts she had never really liked men. . . . [S]he*
> *had never enjoyed [her husband] as naturally as she enjoyed Lou-*
> *isa. For more than fifty years Louisa had understood her more*
> *absolutely than any man can understand the woman he loves. Beau-*
> *tiful as this long association had been, it was fortunate, Victoria*
> *reflected now, that it had come to flower before the serpent of Freud-*
> *ian psychology had poisoned the sinless Eden of friendship.*
>
> —*Ellen Glasgow*, They Stooped to Folly (*1929*)

The works of Ellen Glasgow transcribe a fall from the world of the
mother's gardens, which is presented for the most part negatively as a
cloistered hothouse where ignorance and "evasive idealism" hold
sway, to a Darwinistic social jungle that is governed by the laws of
heterosexist commerce based upon the exchange of women.[1] Like
Wharton and Cather, therefore, Glasgow dealt centrally in her fiction
with the dilemma of the new woman–daughter, who in rebelling
against her mother's ethos finds herself a Persephone in patriarchal
captivity. Only those who learn to negotiate the streets of capitalist
patriarchy (and once again, as in *The House of Mirth*, the underground
captivity is often located by Glasgow in New York City) survive; but
their survival depends upon having retained a connection with "some

buried self . . . some ancient instinct which was as deep as the oldest forests of earth . . . a buried forest within [one's] soul."[2]

This buried forest symbolizes the preoedipal green-world realm of matriarchal energy—the world of Demeter. Those characters who retain or develop a connection to this world, associated in Glasgow's work, as in Cather and the local colorists, with rural life and the land, manage to prevail. As with Cather's characters Alexandra Bergson and Ántonia Shimerda, Glasgow's triumphant women are those who can operate among the strong without losing the sensibilities of the weak. They emerge out of the Persephone cycle strengthened and empowered; attached to the feminine myth of resurrection, they arise as Demeter.

However, much of Glasgow's attention is devoted to the rejected world of the mothers, who are seen as ineffectual at best, otherwise neurasthenic and morbidly self-sacrificial, and at times demonic, given to revenge. Sometimes their target is appropriately a patriarchal oppressor; other times they simply attempt to control and destroy whoever is about.

As with Cather—and to a lesser extent Wharton—empathy with animals is an important visible sign that a character has retained a connection to the "buried forest" of matriarchal integrity. Occasionally men manifest this sensibility—those who are opposed to hunting, for example. These men are usually mouthpieces for the author's own inclination, which was toward the interspecies integration characteristic of the green-world vision. Glasgow herself, like many authors in the women's local-color tradition, was an animal lover (Harriet Beecher Stowe and Elizabeth Stuart Phelps wrote what today would be called animal-rights tracts; Jewett was involved with her state Society for the Prevention of Cruelty to Animals [SPCA]). Glasgow was president of the local SPCA, to which she left a bequest in her will; her dogs are buried with her.

Glasgow was more politically active than Cather or Wharton. She participated in the suffrage campaign, and women's rights are explicitly presented as positive ideas in some of her early novels (for example, *Romance of a Plain Man* [1909], *The Miller of the Old Church* [1911], *Virginia* [1913], and *Life and Gabriella* [1916]). Like Wharton, she saw herself in rebellion against the New England local-color school, because of its "genteel tradition," its "refined realism," and its alleged sentimentality.[3] The title of an early novel that she burned was *Sharp Realities*, an indication of her determination to shatter "rose-coloured" visions. Nevertheless, she singles out Jewett and Freeman for praise in an article entitled " 'Evasive Idealism' in Literature" (1917), in which she damns what she sees as an American cultural tendency to ignore evil and suffering by means of rationalizations.[4]

However, the dominant intellectual influence upon Ellen Glasgow was, as she acknowledged, Charles Darwin. She visited his grave on a trip to England in 1896. The realism she espoused in rebellion against sentimentalist foremothers was Darwinian.

At times Glasgow expresses a Darwinism that is close to the "phallic worship" Charlotte Perkins Gilman decried in Freudianism, where a powerful, "virile" male is advanced as the plot's most compelling fig-ure because of his biological status. Other times Glasgow seems to have absorbed Gilman's own version of social Darwinism. In *Virginia* (1913), for example, Glasgow argues that social life is organized around the principle of the "sacrifice of the fittest" women. In gen-eral, the more "male-identified" Darwinism is evident in her earlier works.

Indeed, feminist critic Linda Wagner has argued that the male identification evident in Glasgow's early work continues until the novel *Virginia,* in which she dropped her "condescending attitude toward women"; there "the imitative, pseudomasculine voice gives way to a feminine perspective."[5] But in the 1890s and early 1900s Glasgow, like Cather and Wharton, felt the compulsion to adopt as an author a masculine self-identity. As Wagner notes, Glasgow "may have been a woman writer, but during the 1890's she was a woman writer trying desperately to pretend that she was . . . a liberal well-educated man" (22). "She began her career . . . when being mistaken for a male writer was the highest praise." In her early novels, "all attention, all interest, lay in the male protagonist" (ix).

While Wagner's statement is largely true, there are a number of interesting women in the margins of Glasgow's early plots, and pat-terns that link even Glasgow's early work to the dynamics of women's literary history being charted in this study. Despite her desire to be treated as a male (i.e., serious) writer, Glasgow's thematic concerns link her primarily to her sister women realists of the day, Wharton and Cather.

Glasgow's first novel, *The Descendant,* published in 1897 and set in the early 1890s, is in many respects a remarkable work; like many of her early novels, it is set in New York City and concerns one of Dar-win's "fittest," Michael Akershem, a Nietzschean superman who rises to success despite poor environmental conditions. His early years as a poor orphan outcast are described in a section entitled "Variations from Type"—an obvious reference to the *Origin of Species*. By the age of twenty-six he has become a famous journalist and radical social critic in New York.

The novel also concerns, however, the fortunes of a new-woman artist, Rachel Gavin. Like Nan Prince, Rachel is set upon a career; indeed her fervent prayer ("Give me my ambition . . . and nothing else—nothing else, O God!")[6] recalls Nan's heartfelt gratitude at the conclusion of *A Country Doctor* that her ambition has been realized. At first Rachel seems as positively self-sufficient as Nan Prince; but her declaration to Michael that she has no need for love because "I adore myself" (102) suggests that Glasgow finds her ambitions tainted with hubris, and indeed Rachel's road to success is much rockier than Nan's.

The influence of Elizabeth Stuart Phelps is clear in this and other early Glasgow novels: the central female script is the career-versus-love plot seen as early as Phelps's *Story of Avis* (1877). Like Avis, Rachel cannot complete a painting of (ironically) the Magdalen once she engages in her affair with Michael. The script is complicated by the fact that, since Michael, as a radical who has taken a public position against marriage, cannot marry or he will lose his following, Rachel is reduced to being his mistress and therefore is, as a Magdalen herself, blackballed by society.

Other women figures in the novel, however, show that the plight of the "true woman" is probably worse. A woman in Rachel's building whose artistic ambitions have been destroyed by marriage is a victim of wife abuse.

During the period of Rachel's disgrace, she wanders the streets of New York, anticipating Lily Bart, similarly fallen and reduced to the status of commodity in heterosexist exchange. While in the end Rachel is triumphant, and Michael dies, the novelist's sympathy in this book is clearly with the male protagonist. Indeed, an aside early in the novel suggests that even by 1897 the "female world of love and ritual" had disintegrated for the women of Glasgow's generation. Michael is described as having an affection for a friend whom he loved "as a man loves a man . . . which passeth the love of woman for woman" (65)—an interesting verbal echo of David's comment to Jonathan (2 Samuel 1:26) and an inversion of the idea of the superiority of romantic female friendship seen in earlier centuries, which Lillian Faderman adapted as the title of her study *Surpassing the Love of Men*. This authorial comment suggests that Glasgow, like her character Rachel, had long since left the nineteenth-century women's bower and had absorbed the male-supremacist ideologies of her day.

Glasgow's second novel, *Phases of an Inferior Planet* (1898), reinforces this impression. Once again the central figure is a Nietzschean male, an iconoclast scholar, Anthony Algarcife, who is working on an aspect of Darwin's theory of heredity but is reduced by circumstances to teaching a bowdlerized version of it at a women's college, which is seen as beneath him. Once again the author's sympathies are with the male protagonist, who, one suspects, is something of a Glasgow persona. His philosophy is one of respect for nature: "toads," he says, "have an equal right with ourselves to the possession of this planet."[7] He claims to "have two passions . . . —a passion for books and a passion for animals" (73). Unlike "fox-hunting heroes" who exemplify the masculine ethos, Anthony seems a new kind of sensitive male, whose attitudes would be branded "effeminacy" by the Teddy Roosevelt majority (74).

Contrasted with Anthony is one of Glasgow's most negative women characters, Mariana Musin. Something of a Hedda Gabler figure, she is a caricature of Kierkegaard's "aesthete": she disdains public transportation, which requires sitting next to Irish women (8); she is self-absorbed, aspires to be an opera singer but apparently has little talent; her main impulse is "to flee from poverty and ugliness to beauty and bright colors" (175).

Unlike Anthony, who waters her geranium back to life (34, 42), she is cut off from the natural world. Where he deplores caged birds, her canary dies; "everything that belongs to me always dies, sooner or later," she admits (74). While in later novels Glasgow suggests that social causes contribute to the development of such egregiously unattractive female types, here the blame is largely on Mariana.

Her relationship with Anthony is cast, nevertheless, in Darwinian terms, which may suggest that Glasgow sees her character as to some extent a result of her female biological fate. She has, for example, a "natural" susceptibility to her environment (which is cast as one of commercial mediocrity), as opposed to Anthony, who is oblivious to it, driven from within (43). In conversation "she adapted herself instinctively to whatever he might mean" (47). Moreover, "the power of his will . . . enthralled her, and she felt strangely submissive" (47).

In the end, they marry and have a child, a girl whom Mariana rejects and who eventually dies (symptomatic of the destruction of female matrilineal bonding). Bored with her leisure-class existence, Mariana leaves Anthony, aspiring to greater opulence. He becomes a minister engaged in slum work, assuming the traditional women's caring role, where she remains a materialist social climber on the order of Undine Spragg, though not quite so unredeemed.

The three Virginia novels Glasgow published in the early years of the twentieth century—*The Voice of the People* (1900), *The Battle-Ground* (1902), and *The Deliverance* (1904)—are more in the genre of conventional romance than her earlier works and may have been an attempt to attract a popular readership.[8] All concern cross-class liaisons between powerful male protagonists and more or less traditional women. In the latter two novels the woman's love redeems the hero, which places them within the confines of the traditional sentimentalist format. While these novels are not without merit, because their pertinent themes are more fully developed in later works, I will not discuss them here.[9]

Like *The Descendant*, *The Wheel of Life* (1906) is a somewhat daring novel for its time; it treats of cocaine addiction, adultery, and sex. Also like *The Descendant* it is set in New York and has a strong Darwinian imprint to the point again of "phallic worship." Much space is devoted, for example, to the virility of a central male character, Arnold Kemper: there is a "compelling animal magnetism . . . behind the masculine bluntness of manner."[10] Laura Wilde, his fiancée, "found suddenly that almost in spite of herself she was rejoicing in the masculine quality of his presence—in his muscular strength . . . in the ardent vitality with which he moved" (183). Another male figure, when angered, is described as feeling "quick animal passion—the passion of the enraged male" (246).

The novel, however, indicates a shift in Glasgow's attitude toward her women characters, a hint of the more "woman-identified" vision found in her later works, beginning primarily, as Wagner notes, with *Virginia*. Once again, the central dilemma for the woman is love versus artistic career. The woman in this case is Laura Wilde, who is an established and successful poet. Counterposed against her is a minor character, Christina Coles, who aspires to be a writer but who apparently lacks the talent and therefore lives on the edge of starvation in a New York City flat. And there is Laura's aunt Angela, almost a stereotype of the washed-out spinster, who, seduced and abandoned in her youth, has become a recluse, "cold, white, and spectral" (23)—a reminder to Laura of what happens to women who renounce men.

The other major woman character is Laura's friend Gerty, whose husband is a handsome philanderer and whose marriage is burned out. She does, however, have a passion of sorts for Laura: "Laura was not only the woman whom she loved, she had become to her at last almost a vicarious worship" (349).

Laura is herself somewhat unorthodox: she "read Plotinus at her dressmaker's. She says he helps her to stand the trying on" (225). Although she agrees to marry Kemper, as the event approaches she begins to feel trepidation, recognizing implicitly that the "exchange of women" turns them into commodities and throws them into competition with one another. "She understood . . . the relentless tyranny which clothes [which commodify women] might acquire—the jealousy, the extravagance, the feverish emulation, and the dislike which one woman might feel for another who wore a better gown" (403). "A shiver of disgust went through her . . . she longed for her old freedom of spirit, and instead she struggled helplessly in the net" (404). She especially fears that a competitiveness could be set up between her and Gerty.

After much agonizing Laura breaks her engagement, and after a suicidal period in which she is missing for several days, she reunites with Gerty, who grasps Laura in her arms, crying "Dearest!" "[T]he two women kissed in that intimate knowledge which is uttered without speech" (462). After a renewal in the "green natural world" (468), Laura decides to devote herself to helping the poor, similar to Anthony in *Phases of an Inferior Planet*, rejecting heterosexual romantic love as narcissistic and deceptive (474). Thus, in a novel published the same year as *The House of Mirth*, Laura achieves perceptions that might have saved Lily Bart. The relationship between the two women in *The Wheel of Life* is, however, somewhat anomalous in Glasgow's fiction, though the disillusionment with heterosexual romance becomes a dominant theme.

The central female figure in Glasgow's next novel, *The Ancient Law* (1908), is more typical in this respect. Emily Brooke is indeed the prototype of the powerful independent women of Glasgow's later works, such as Dorinda Oakley of *Barren Ground*. These women are autonomous, rooted in the soil, but unaffiliated with other women. As with most of Glasgow's characters, Emily belongs to a family that had seen better times and had fallen in social and economic status. The sense of a fall from a previous condition of plenitude that pervades Glasgow's works may, of course, be appropriated to the white southern cultural sense of a historical fall associated with the Civil War and Reconstruction; however, the fall is also connected with the cultural transition in women's history treated in this study.

While the protagonist of *The Ancient Law* is another of Glasgow's exceptional outcast men, Daniel Ordway, a reformed ex-convict, the women characters are of central interest. For the first time Glasgow draws a strong contrast between two types of women: one represents the mother's generation, and the other the daughter's. Emily is of the latter breed: strong and competent, she does much of the physical labor on the Brooke estate, which is marked by "age and decay." It is she who (by teaching) supports the other members of her family, who include Emily's incompetent wastrel brother, Beverly, and his neurasthenic wife, Miss Amelia.

Glasgow's satirical treatment of the latter is so heavy-handed as at times to be comical. Amelia is another attic-bound woman who has carried the negative traits of the "mothers" to the point of self-destruction. She spends most of her time upstairs "prostrate . . . with her head swathed in camphor bandages."[11] During her chronic headache spells, she "conjured up dozens of small self-denials which served to increase her discomfort while they conferred no possible benefit upon either her husband or her children. Her temperament had fitted her for immolation. . . . The rack would have been to her morally a bed of roses" (105). Glasgow targets this tendency toward obsessive self-sacrifice on the part of the mothers in much of her remaining work. In *Barren Ground,* for example, Dorinda "sometimes felt that the greatest cross in her life was her mother's morbid unselfishness."[12] Similarly Emily feels "that Beverly's selfishness was less harmful in its results than Amelia's self-sacrifice" (105). But Amelia is a figure from the past: "she appeared . . . as the disembodied spirit of one of the historic belles . . . [giving a] ghostly impression" (175).

Daniel's wife, from whom he had been separated for many years, is of Amelia's ilk. Her "health . . . wrecked" (293), she spends her days dressed in black veils languidly reading romantic novels (318). Although she has a "vein of iron," by which Glasgow means a genetic disposition to survive and triumph in the struggle for existence, it has hardened into compulsive hate—mainly against her husband—and thus condemns her to a life of meaningless stasis.

In the end Daniel is trapped by his ties to this environment, the decadent aristocracy of the mothers, and is unable to break away to join Emily, the new woman in her democracy of labor. The tension between the two worlds reflects psychic realities the author understood: the entrapment/seduction posed by the mother's sphere versus the freedom/autonomy of the daughter's. Here as in much of the literature by women of Glasgow's generation—as opposed to those of Jewett's—the mother's world is depicted negatively.

Glasgow's next two novels are romances between sensitive animal-loving green-world men and women. *The Romance of a Plain Man* (1909) centers upon the Horatio Alger rise of another self-made man, Benjamin Starr, who has the inner genetic disposition to rise and triumph in the capitalist jungle. The woman he eventually marries, Sally Miekleborough, is associated in her youth with an "enchanted garden"—symbolizing once again the world of the traditional mothers.[13] Benjamin and Sally's bond is forged over their concern about animals. She early gives him strays to care for; in exchange for the right to spend time in her garden, he promises never to kill a cat; he refuses to work for a butcher (68); she finally decides she loves him after seeing him chastise a porter for overworking his horse (185, 195–96).

The contrast between the garden and the jungle is sharply drawn in this novel. Also clear in this work is that Glasgow is beginning to espouse a kind of assimilationist liberal feminism: that the solution to women's problem is for them to be let out of the garden and into the jungle. That it is a Darwinian world in which men express their primordial desires to win life's competition is seen in Benjamin's passionate energies. He felt "a fierce, almost a frenzied, desire for achievement. Here, in the little world of tradition and sentiment [the women's garden], I might show still at a disadvantage, but outside . . . I could respond freely to the lust for power, to the passion for supremacy, which stirred my blood" (421).

But Sally, despite her sheltered upbringing and generally traditional orientation, comes to realize, "All of us have an ambition, you know, women as well as men" (414). Rejecting a great-grandmother who was so submissive that when asked if she had a toothache she had to ask her husband (171), Sally exclaims, "women must have larger lives—they mustn't be expected to feed always upon their hearts. . . . How can they . . . when love isn't there—when it's off in the stock market or the railroad . . . ?" (399). The latter comment refers to the basic bone of contention between her and Benjamin, that he spends too much time at work, neglecting her, a failing he vows to correct at the novel's end.

Sally's movement may in part be due to the absorption of some of her aunt Matoaca's feminist ideas. An ardent suffragist, she maintains "taxation without representation is tyranny" (94)—repeating a standard motto of the suffrage campaign. In her youth Matoaca had rejected Benjamin's mentor, General Bolingbroke, a prototypical capitalist entrepreneur, who cites Machiavelli's observation that "Fortune's a woman" who must be battered into compliance in order for a man to succeed (140). Bolingbroke roundly condemns the women's rights movement: "When a woman once gets that maggot in her brain, she stops believing in gentleness and self-sacrifice . . . and ceases to be a woman" (180), an echo of the "mannish" charge that Nan Prince managed to withstand.

The Miller of the Old Church (1911) is a kind of romance in which a Dianic antimale woman, Molly Merryweather, finally marries Abel Revercomb, a rural miller who is the type of green-world lover found elsewhere in women's literature.[14] He, for example, at one point maternally nurses an orphaned robin: "Like all young and helpless things, it aroused in him a tenderness which, in some strange way, was akin to pain."[15] One suspects that Molly is primarily attracted to his womanly qualities, which leads one to wonder if this is not another of those "masquerades" decried by Jewett.

Various characters comment on Molly's strong bonding with other women. Abel says, "You were a friend to every woman" (364). Another character makes a powerful observation about women's silenced relationships with one another, and how they are rooted in the earth, recalling the Demeter bond.

> The relation of woman to man was dwarfed suddenly by an understanding of the relation of woman to woman. Deeper than the dependence of sex, simpler, more natural, closer to the earth, as though it still drew its strength from the soil, he realized that the need of woman for woman was not written in the songs nor in the histories of men, but in the neglected and frustrated lives which the songs and the histories of men had ignored. (410)

Since this observation is completely out of character for the speaker, a superficial roué and womanizer, one must assume that it is an awkward authorial interjection. Its lack of integration with the plot suggests something of the struggle Glasgow must have been undergoing to rise beyond the male-identified perspective that dominated the cultural ideology of her time. The growing identification with women seen in her next novel, *Virginia*, is also evident in her portrait in this novel of a minor character, Aunt Keziah.

Where earlier negative images of women were presented *in isolatione*, with no explanatory cultural context, Keziah, another washed-up spinster, is presented from a (liberal) feminist point of view. A would-be artist, she was prevented as a youth by custom and by her rootedness from studying in Paris. "A man would have struck for freedom, and have made a career for himself in the open world, but her nature was rooted deep in the rich and heavy soil from which she had tried to detach it" (79). "[S]he had pulled in vain at the obstinate tendrils that held her to the spot in which she had grown" (79).

This image is strikingly reminiscent of that in Freeman's "Evelina's Garden" in which the younger Evelina had to destroy the roots in the mother's garden in order to escape. Here those roots are seen negatively as bonds that prevent Keziah from adopting an assimilationist course: leaving her home and embarking, autonomously, upon a career.

A similar set of contrasting options is presented in *Virginia* (1913), but the prevailing perspective is somewhat different. This work effectively integrates many of the themes that are tentative in earlier works: the condemnation of the traditional woman's mode of self-sacrifice, but also ambivalence about the new woman's mode of assertive autonomy. The novel presents three generations of women, from Virginia's mother to her daughters, the latter of whom are exemplars of the new woman. Virginia herself is caught in between. The novel plots the pattern of a fall from the (false) innocence of the sheltered garden of Virginia's youth, presented in a section entitled "The Dream," to the disillusioned "Reality" (the title of the next section) Virginia becomes aware of as she matures.

The novel opens in 1884 in a backwater town in Virginia. "[A] quarter of a century had passed since 'The Origin of Species' had changed the course of the world's thought, yet [people there] had managed to evolve without being aware of it"[16]—a sign, according to Glasgow, of the regressive ignorance of the place. Virginia is educated by Miss Priscilla Batte, Mary E. Wilkins Freeman's New England nun gone south, who dotes on a caged canary and whose theory of education was "that the less a girl knew about life, the better" (20). "Knowledge of any sort . . . was kept from her as rigourously as if it contained the germs of a contagious disease" (20). Again, patriarchal education—knowledge of such things as Darwin's theories—is seen as emancipatory, an unquestioned assumption of liberal feminism that Glasgow clearly espouses. Virginia spends her time reading romances like the *Heir of Redclyffe,* a novel that Jewett had put down in her youth as sentimentalist trash. Virginia's "bookcase . . . was filled with sugared falsehoods about life" (132).

By contrast, a central young male character, iconoclast Oliver Treadwell, who endorses progressive ideas and whom Virginia later marries, rejects the popular sentimentalist novels of Mrs. E.D.E.N. Southworth. Once again, we see the rejection by Glasgow's generation of their sentimentalist literary foremothers (Cather had a regressive character in *A Lost Lady* reading Augusta Jane Evans's *St. Elmo* [1866], one of the most notorious and most popular of the sentimentalist extravagances—a nevertheless intriguing novel). Oliver even raises the issue of women's rights, of which Virginia is ignorant. He says, "I've always had a tremendous sympathy for women because they have to market and housekeep. I wonder if they won't revolt some time?" She responds, "But don't they like it?" (65).

Virginia does have a romantic friendship with a schoolmate named Susan. At one point Susan asks Virginia to "promise . . . that [you'll] never let anybody take my place." Virginia promises, "and they kissed ecstatically. 'Nobody will ever love you as I do. [Susan responds] And I you, darling!' " (27).

But the main thrust of Glasgow's description of this early life is to condemn the "evasive idealism" of the mothers, which effects their capitulation not only to their own oppression but to other evils that exist around them, such as animal abuse and slavery. "Directly in their line of vision, an overladen mule with a sore shoulder was straining painfully under the lash, but none of them saw it, because each of them was morally incapable of looking an unpleasant fact in the face" (60). For, Glasgow acridly asserts, "to be feminine . . . was to be morally passive" (135).

On a trip to the market where butchered animals are on sale, Virginia is repulsed by the "slaughtered animals," the "pathos of the small bleeding forms" (62), though she does nothing about it. But her mother rationalizes their fate. "If Mrs. Pendleton had ever reflected on the tragic fate of pullets, she would probably have concluded that it was 'best' for them to be fried and eaten. . . . So, in the old days, she had known where the slave market stood, without realizing in the least that men and women were sold there. 'Poor things, it does seem dreadful, but I suppose it is better for them to have a change some-times' she would have reasoned" (61). Glasgow thus joins Wharton in an uncompromising condemnation of the mothers' willful ignorance of and therefore collaboration with evil.

Not surprisingly, Mrs. Pendleton's primary counsel to Virginia when she marries is to capitulate to her husband. "His will must be yours now, and wherever your ideas cross, it is your duty to give up. . . . It is the woman's part to sacrifice herself" (181). The author observes, "It was characteristic . . . of most women of her generation, that she would have endured martyrdom in support of the conse-crated doctrine of her inferiority to man" (182).

Virginia's letters home after her marriage are full of homesickness for her mother; the mother-daughter bond remains primary, and Vir-ginia repeats the pattern of her mother's life. Mother and daughter "were so alike . . . they might have represented different periods of the same life. . . . Both were trained to feel rather than think" (285)—again the authorial voice of liberal feminism. In one letter to her mother, Virginia dutifully criticizes a college-educated woman she meets who is always "trying to appear as clever as a man" (198); whereas, she, Vir-ginia, is so housebound "she would never cross [the] threshold if Oliver didn't make me" (199). Significantly, Virginia's first child is a daughter, named after her mother. During labor, she later writes her mother, "The whole time I was unconscious I thought you were here. . . . I was calling 'Mother! Mother!' all that night. Nothing ever made me feel as close to you as having a baby of my own" (206). She becomes fully immersed in motherhood to the exclusion of her husband. Oliver mean-while seems to have forgotten his earlier feminist inclinations, having absorbed the social-Darwinist creed (now, however, presented ironi-cally by Glasgow): for Oliver "true womanliness was inseparably associ-ated . . . with those qualities that had awakened for generations the impulse of selection in the men of his race. . . . [E]volution . . . had left his imagination still cherishing the conventions of the jungle in the matter of sex. He saw women as dependent upon man" (278).

The central tension in the novel, therefore, develops between Vir-ginia's mother—representing matriarchal lineage and values—and Virginia's husband, who represents the public world of patriarchal attitudes. In a pivotal scene Virginia determines to win back the attention of her husband, who had felt left out of the mother-daughter-granddaughter "world of love and ritual" that emerged with the child's birth. In order to show Oliver that she is one of his (patriarchal) kind, Virginia agrees to go on a fox hunt, always in Glasgow an emblem of the worst of the masculine ethos.

Virginia's own evasive idealism enables her to participate in the event. On hearing of the fox's death, "the casual cruelty of the words awoke no protest in her mind, because it was a cruelty to which she was accustomed." If she had heard of it happening in a remote place, "she would probably have condemned it as needlessly brutal" (296). Glasgow observes that Virginia "regarded 'the rights of the fox' " with something of the attitude of scornful amusement "with which her . . . grandmother had once regarded 'the rights of the slave' " (297). Thus, like her mother, Virginia, primarily through ignorance and faulty education, acquiesces in evil.

The hunt itself, a central patriarchal ritual, functions as Laura's engagement—another patriarchal rite—had in *The Wheel of Life.* It sets her in competition with another woman for Oliver's attention. To win the fox hunt and receive the trophy—the fox's tail—becomes for Virginia a means of winning back male approval. This competition drives her to win the race: "[T]here stirred faintly the seeds of that ancient lust of cruelty from which have sprung the brutal pleasures of men" (298). A spirit "had driven her . . . in a chase that she despised, toward a triumph that was worthless" (299).

Here for the first time we begin to sense in Glasgow a rejection of the assimilationist mode, for the fox hunt is a masculine game. Glasgow senses here that foxes and women have common cause against patriarchal oppressors and that Virginia's joining the fox hunt signifies a fundamental betrayal of that bond. Indeed, in later works, especially *Vein of Iron,* the hunter-hunted theme becomes explicit, and Glasgow herself opens her autobiography with a powerful scene of empathy with a dog being chased by townspeople: "I have seen what it means to be hunted. I run on with the black dog. . . . I am beaten with clubs and caught in a net."[17] She later concluded, she says, that life is divided between "the stronger and the weaker. . . . Either by fate or by choice, I had found myself on the side of the weaker."[18]

The division in Virginia occasioned by this event is exploited by her husband, who is delighted with the competitiveness she shows at the hunt and encourages her toward further assertions of independence. In particular, he urges her to leave the children for a short trip with him to Atlantic City. She is torn and at the last minute decides to stay with the children, while Oliver goes by himself. As it turns out, one of the children develops diphtheria and nearly dies. During this three-day period Virginia experiences a kind of dark night of the soul in which she emerges fully committed to the realm of the mothers, implicitly rejecting the way of independence and autonomy—the companionate marriage her husband wants. During her ordeal she longs "to throw herself into her mother's arms" (325)—and the episode has the effect of psychologically doing just that. When later her mother dies, Virginia recalls that she had once thought there was one thing she could not bear "and that is losing my mother" (362). Now that she is gone Virginia realizes that "whatever the years brought . . . they could never bring her a love like her mother's" (362). So the intensity of female bonding—especially the mother-daughter bond—remains primary in this novel, but the tensions tending to destroy it are vividly dramatized. Like *The House of Mirth*, "it is a pivotal text in the historical transition . . . from the homosocial women's culture and literature of the nineteenth century to the heterosexual fiction of modernism."[19]

Virginia's daughters, particularly Jenny, are almost a stereotype of the new woman; Jenny goes to Bryn Mawr and majors in biology. She rejects her mother's traditionalism with science and rationalism (392). Her "attitude toward life was masculine rather than feminine" (412). In her letters home, which contrast to Virginia's letters to her mother, there is no "sentiment," no "plaintive homesickness" (412). She preferred "the active rather than the passive side of experience" (412).

Glasgow seems to suggest that such is the tide of the future and that the processes of evolution are weeding out "weak" figures like Virginia. Of another "free woman," who has seduced Oliver in New York, we learn "her freedom . . . had been built upon the strewn bodies of the weaker. . . . The justice . . . of nature, was on her side, for she was one with evolution" (442). Whereas, Virginia has refused to engage in the Darwinian, masculinist struggle, and therefore in the end she is defeated: "What she longed for was not to fight, not to struggle, but to fall, like a wounded bird, to the earth" (473).

Thus, *Virginia* presents the first clear articulation of what becomes Glasgow's central thesis: that to survive women must engage in the real world, which is conceived as a Darwinian jungle governed by a patriarchal ethic. They can no longer remain in the sheltered garden, for to do so is in effect a form of suicide. And, in any event, its innocence is compromised by collaboration with and capitulation to patriarchal evil. At the same time, Glasgow's sympathy for Virginia is clear; the emotional intensity of which she is capable, the ethical sensibility that is at least there—even if veiled and compromised—are clearly preferable to the daughter's disembodied rationalism. (The fact that Jenny majored in biology is, of course, significant; it means she has adopted the masculinist mode of the scientific epistemology and presumably engages in vivisection, which was, as noted earlier, anathema to large numbers of turn-of-the-century women,[20] presumably including Glasgow.)

In her next novel, *Life and Gabriella* (1916), also a powerful exploration of the tensions between new and true womanhood, Glasgow furthers the thesis that women must learn to deal with the public world of capitalist patriarchy if they are to survive. Once again the novel is structured on the pattern of a fall. The first section is entitled "The Age of Faith"; the second, "The Age of Knowledge."

Glasgow's satire of the helpless, incompetent traditional woman is merciless in this novel. One representative has a "pretty vacant face . . . [which] resembled a pastel portrait in which the artist had forgotten to paint an expression."[21] Another "loved inanimate things with [a] passion" (14). When she has to sell her knickknacks it is "as if the very roots of her being were torn up" (14). "[A]ny change in her surroundings produced a sensation of shock" (15). "It was distressing to her to be obliged to move a picture" (16).

Gabriella is, however, the opposite. "From the moment of her birth . . . she had begun her battle against the enveloping twin forces of decay and inertia" (16). She is thus temperamentally or genetically (she has a "vein of iron" [30, 112, 242, 440]) disposed to compete in the struggle for survival. Gabriella assertively rejects her mother's mode and her mother's world. But the means by which she does so is to marry an alien patriarch—thus following the Persephone pattern of a descent into patriarchal captivity. Once again the setting is New York City; her husband, appropriately, is a stockbroker. That he subscribes to an oppressive patriarchal ethos is early apparent when he announces, "A mannish woman is worse than poison, and the less you know about stocks the more attractive you will be" (102). Gabriella's growing disillusionment occurs in moments of perception such as one where her husband, George, is (symbolically) standing on a bearskin rug smoking a cigar and discussing big-game hunting with an old crony. "For a flashing instant of illumination" Gabriella thought "he looked stupid" (150). George turns out to be a philanderer, a drunkard, and a wastrel, and eventually they divorce, but Gabriella vows not to become a victim (201). Instead, she gets a job, is able to support her children, and feels a certain pride in her success; her philosophy is characteristically individualistic: "Nobody, except myself, is ever going to make me happy" (334). In a moment of sexual harassment, she asks a business colleague to treat her as a "gentleman" (364). But the episode depresses her enormously: she had a "sodden sense of loss, of emptiness, of defeat" (365)—largely because of the gender ambivalence her new life-style has effected.

Her salvation is to embrace fully the Darwinist philosophy of life as a struggle; she agrees to marry a prototype of Darwin's fittest, a robust, virile entrepreneur who has risen through the commercial jungle and whose struggle excites Gabriella, making her further reject the feminine world of her youth: "So that is a man's world [she thought] . . .: What a mean little life I have been living" (420). Her final philosophy is: "What do any of us get out [of life] . . . except the joy of triumphing? It's overcoming that really matters. . . . I am happy because in my little way I stood the test of struggle" (474).

Glasgow published several stories at this time; her short pieces are atypical of her work as a whole because they operate more on a psychic symbolic level than on the level of mimetic realism. Three stories in particular evoke "The Yellow Wallpaper" in their sense of women's psychic oppression and concomitant desire for vengeance against their oppressors. In "The Shadowy Third" (1916) a woman believes her husband, a famous surgeon, has murdered her daughter. The woman is committed to an asylum, where she dies, but he falls to his death after tripping on a child's jump rope—the revenge of the daughter. Thus, the mother-daughter bond prevails in this story against the intrusion of the male professional.

In "Dare's Gift" (1917), a powerful and effective story, the revenge theme is even more pronounced. In this case, the husband is a corporate lawyer who hunts. The wife, Mildred, is given to nervous breakdowns. To help her recuperate he leaves her on a rural Virginia farm, which had been the site of an earlier betrayal by a woman of her lover during the Civil War. In that case, the woman was a Confederate fanatic and her lover a Union soldier, who sought asylum in her house; however, she turned him over to the Confederates to be shot. A parallel situation occurs between Mildred and her husband. When she learns that he has unethically decided to defend clients who have engaged in illegal practices, she betrays him by revealing his complicity to a newspaper. Naturally, when he finds out, he decides she is mad; locals wonder whether she might not have been influenced by the ghost of the Confederate woman. In any event, the story is one of feminine revenge.

"Whispering Leaves" (1923) is another story that can be interpreted symbolically as expressing psychic feminine powers. Also a "ghost story," it deals centrally with a fall from a past paradisiacal garden world to a corrupt, menacing present. The plot is that Clarissa, Pelham Blanton's first wife, has died; she was a gardener who planted a lush garden that is no longer cared for. When she died she entrusted the care of her son to Mammy Rhody, a black servant woman, who also is tied to the matriarchal green world: she is intimately connected with animals, birds, flowers. "[T]he woods . . . are still full of the ghosts of Mammy Rhody's pets."[22] After her death Mammy Rhody continues as a ghost to care for the boy. When his stepmother orders his pet puppy killed, Mammy Rhody saves it. When there is a fire in the house, she saves the child. Thus, the story affirms the existence of green-world feminine powers who care for the young, for animals and vegetation, recalling the Great Goddess of ancient myth, the consoling Demeter.

The two novels Glasgow published after *Life and Gabriella*—*The Builders* (1919) and *One Man in His Time* (1922)—were written in collaboration with her lover of the time, Henry Anderson. Therefore, one hesitates to attach too much weight to them. They deal centrally with noble Nietzschean supermen, who are seen as "the builders" of society in the novel of that title. It is believed that Anderson, himself a successful politician, was the model for these figures. *The Builders* presents one of Glasgow's most negative images of women in Angelica Blackburn, who is a sort of cross between Zeena Frome and Bessy Westmore in Wharton's *Fruit of the Tree,* an exemplar of the demonic reaches to which the housebound mother can go in her suppressed exertion of power, but by this time something of a commonplace.

One Man in His Time is a more interesting work in that it advances Glasgow's vision of the autonomous woman who connects with the green-world mythos, thus anticipating the protagonists of her great novels *Barren Ground* and *Vein of Iron.* This figure is Corinna Culpepper, a beautiful forty-eight-year-old artist who is also a successful but compassionate businesswoman (she subsidizes restored row houses, which she rents to the poor). Like other successes in Glasgow's world, Corinna has "fighting blood in [her] veins" (103), and "from the inherited instinct for selection" that she received from her forebears, she struggles "against the tyranny of mediocrity" (104).

Corinna has a sense of living in a fallen world: "Futility—weariness—disenchantment" (119). "All was tawdry, all was tarnished, all was unreal" (120). Her nephew Stephen, upon whom much of the novel centers, similarly feels that "every apple has turned into Dead Sea fruit" (84).

Corinna, however, who is compared with Diana (52) and Artemis (314), retains a connection to "a buried forest within her soul," but it remains hidden; "she had never discovered" it (282). Perhaps this is why she feels an affection for Polly Vetch, one of Stephen's loves. Polly too is associated with the forest world, with the acivilized: "she had the look of a small wild creature of the forest" (128). When she is first observed she is in the process of trying to save a wounded pigeon. And in front of the Vetch house is "a fountain of [a] white heron" (234)—surely an allusion to Jewett's story.

Corinna takes Polly on as a kind of daughter protégé, which thrills the young girl, who is something of an outcast (the identity of her parents is uncertain). Corinna's gesture of adoption makes the world for Polly "as if by miracle, less impersonal and unfriendly. . . . It was like first love. . . . It was like a religious awakening. . . . Nothing, she felt, could ever be so beautiful again!" (160). Thus, the novel deals at least peripherally with reconnection of the mother-daughter bond and with the tentative reconnection of the autonomous new woman with collective green-world sources of matriarchal energy. But at the same time Corinna's primary mode remains one of independence: she lives by "courage" (297) and "without happiness" (298), an alien in a fallen world, representing perhaps the author herself, who wrote in her autobiography that she was born into "a hostile world": "I stood alone. I stood outside."[23]

Barren Ground (1925) effectively synthesizes many of the themes adumbrated in earlier novels into a powerful work that articulates the Persephone-Demeter resurrection myth seen in Cather's great works *O Pioneers!* and *My Ántonia*. In its depiction of this feminine vision *Barren Ground* stands shoulder to shoulder with these masterpieces. Significantly, the writing of the novel was for Glasgow an epiphanal event; describing it as a "vehicle of liberation," she noted years later that it effected a "conversion" for her to a new vision, bringing her to "the other side of the wilderness."[24] The passage was for Glasgow, as for Wharton and Cather, from the wilderness of male-supremacist

ideology toward the "promised land" of woman-identification, affirmation of the values and ethos of the mothers (but nevertheless not
quite reaching it).

Barren Ground is a classic repetition of the Persephone-Demeter
cycle and as such may represent the psychic transformation the author herself was undergoing at the time. The novel opens in the 1890s
("that pre-Freudian age" [13]) in winter, the nadir of the vegetative
cycle. Our first view of twenty-year-old Dorinda Oakley is stark:
"Bare, starved, desolate, the country closed in about her" (3). The
land is infertile: it "took everything and gave back nothing" (39). All
that grows is "broomsedge," scruffy shallow-rooted brush, the title of
the first section. Succeeding sections are entitled "Pine" and "Life-
Everlasting," signifying vegetation with deeper roots that is more permanent. Dorinda lives on a farm with her ineffectual father, her obsessively self-sacrificial mother, and her worthless brothers. She feels
trapped: "No matter how desperately she struggled, she could never
escape. . . . She was held fast by circumstances as by invisible wires of
steel" (57). Her only salvation, she believes, is through romance with
Jason Greylock, a young doctor for whom she has conceived a secret
passion. He, however, abandons her. She is pregnant and moves to
New York City for the duration of her pregnancy. Once again the city
serves as a patriarchal nether world for a fallen woman. While there
Dorinda is hit by a cab, loses the fetus, but gets a job and begins saving
money. In her dark night a transformation occurs within her, a psychic resurrection that is described metaphorically in terms of newborn
vegetation.

> For the first time since she had left home, she felt that earlier
> and deeper associations were reaching out to her, that they
> were groping after her, like tendrils of vines, through the dark-
> ness and violence of her later memories. Earlier and deeper
> associations, rooted there in the earth, were drawing her
> back. . . . Passion stirred again in her heart, but it was passion
> transfigured. . . . With a shock of joy, she realized that she was
> no longer benumbed, that she had come to life again. (244–45)

Thus, attached to the rising aspect of the Demeter-Persephone cycle,
and having learned in the process of her fall how to negotiate the world
of capitalist patriarchy, Dorinda returns home determined to become a
small-business entrepreneur and make a success of their farm. And

while the area still looks desolate and barren upon her return, Dorinda has developed the psychic tools of the new woman necessary for success: she is "the picture of . . . self-reliance" (260); she is "armoured in reason" (282). As in *O Pioneers!* the death of the father signifies Dorinda's rise to power. Her mother, characteristically weak and victimized, is nevertheless intrigued by Dorinda's enterprise and works at her side. But like the early (and unlike the later) Ántonia, Dorinda's identity remains somewhat masculine: she wears her brother's overalls and has a willful, conquering spirit (303). Nevertheless, "Kinship with the land was filtered through her blood into her brain. . . . Dimly, she felt that only through this fresh emotion could she attain permanent liberation of the spirit" (306). But this remains Dorinda's only emotion; since her betrayal by Jason she cannot feel love for other people. She cannot express affection to her mother (318); she realizes she "may have lost feeling" (325). Like Marie Rogers in Agnes Smedley's *Daughter of Earth* (1929) and like other characters seen in this study, Dorinda feels that love leaves one too vulnerable; it is associated in her mind with women's perennial victimhood, and, therefore, she rejects sentiment in order to be invulnerable.

Her mother is different. In fact, she dies sacrificially as the result of lying to protect her son. The exertions of testifying on his behalf in a trial are too much for her and, fatally weakened, she dies shortly thereafter. Dorinda realizes that her mother's gesture is something she could not encompass. The only figure Dorinda does love is a clubfooted boy who loves animals (both Dorinda and her mother exhibit love for their animals throughout). Eventually, she marries the boy's father, but their relationship remains one of passionless companionship.

Meanwhile, Dorinda's old flame, Jason, who still lives in the area, is degenerating visibly. He becomes an alcoholic; his wife commits suicide, and Dorinda takes him in on his way to the poorhouse, shortly before his death, a sign of her ultimate triumph (Gabriella has similarly taken in her dissipated ex-husband just before his death of alcoholism in *Life and Gabriella*).

Dorinda's husband also dies, leaving her a solitary figure, but one who has achieved peace and contentment through her reconnection with the green-world matriarchy of Demeter.

> Turning slowly . . . she could see the white fire of the life-everlasting. The storm and hag-ridden dreams of the night were over, and the land which she had forgotten was waiting to

take her back to its heart. . . . The spirit of the land was flowing into her, and her own spirit, strengthened and freshened, was flowing out again toward life. . . . Yes, the land would stay by her. . . . Again she felt the quickening of that sympathy which was deeper than all other emotions of her heart . . . the living communion with the earth under her feet . . . [W]hile the seasons bloomed and dropped, while the ancient, beneficial ritual of sowing and reaping moved in the fields, she knew that she could never despair of contentment. (525)

She has acceded to the level of Demeter—not the prelapsarian, unconscious, preliterate figure seen in the vision of the nineteenth-century local colorists, but one who has learned to speak patriarchal discourse, who has adopted some patriarchal ways but who has managed a successful synthesis. In this perhaps she represents the daughter-author of the early twentieth century who learned the ways of the fathers, who passed through exile, but who struggled nevertheless to return to the inspiring sources of the mothers' earth, beyond barren ground. In this she resembles Nan Prince (although the underworld cycle in that novel is performed by Nan's mother rather than by Nan herself).

Glasgow's next three novels—*The Romantic Comedians* (1926), *They Stooped to Folly* (1929), and *The Sheltered Life* (1932), classified as urban "comedies" of manners—are a change of pace, though the term *comedy* is appropriate only in the most technical of senses (a novel that deals with social interactions in a drawing-room setting). *The Sheltered Life*, the most interesting of the three, is really a revenge tragedy that brings to culmination the theme of women's revenge in Glasgow's works—seen heretofore principally in the short stories and to a lesser extent in *Barren Ground* (Dorinda tries to shoot Jason after his betrayal but cannot bring herself to pull the trigger).

They Stooped to Folly also merits discussion, however, principally because of the further development of the consciousness of one of the mothers in this novel. Indeed, the influence of Virginia Woolf and the stream-of-consciousness technique is first seen in this novel: Mrs. Littlepage, the archetypal mother figure in the work, bears considerable resemblance to Mrs. Ramsay in *To the Lighthouse* (1927).

The novel plots the rebellions of the new women against their mothers and against conventional standards of morality. Unfortunately, however, the new women—Milly and Mary Victoria—compete ruthlessly with one another over a man, Martin Feldman. Their relationship contrasts markedly with the lifelong friendship Mary Victoria's mother, Mrs. Littlepage, has had with a positively depicted spinster, Louisa. The passage used as epigraph to this chapter describes their bond as surpassing the love of husband and wife and as belonging to a pre-Freudian era when relationships between women had not yet been stigmatized by sexologists' notions of deviance.[25] Another woman of Mrs. Littlepage's generation, Aunt Agatha, by contrast, had been seduced and abandoned in her youth, consigned thereby to "Life Imprisonment, nothing less. A free spirit consigned to perpetual captivity" (125).

But it is the consciousness of Mrs. Littlepage that is of the greatest interest. Characteristically, she deplores hunting, making the woman-animal identification explicit: "It is horrible the way people hunt [foxes] with dogs. And deer too. It is horrible to be hunted, when human beings are civilized, they will stop hunting things to death. . . . And women. They used to hunt fallen women, and witches too, as cruelly as they hunt animals now" (161).

As she was dying, Mrs. Littlepage felt she had "some secret of tremendous significance to divulge—only she did not know how to begin. What was the meaning of it?" (192). Mrs. Littlepage belongs to the preliterate realm of silent mothers; on the margins of patriarchal discourse, she cannot speak. It is for the daughter-authors to articulate their vision, as Jewett's narrator-author does in *The Country of the Pointed Firs,* as Cather's persona Jim Burden does in *My Ántonia;* but in this novel there are no such daughters, only self-centered careerists bent upon assimilation. Milly emphatically rejects her mother: "I don't even like her. She ruined my life" (27). "I . . . want to be free . . . free to go and come when I choose" (237). In a conversation that takes place in a "ruined garden" (238), Mr. Littlepage is shocked at her rejection of mother love.

Meanwhile, Mrs. Littlepage tries vainly to communicate her vision; she struggles to write a letter to her family but ends in mid-sentence: "There is something I wish to say to you—" (193). Later she reflects, "words are not real, thoughts are not real. They are only the folded leaves of something that is hidden" (213; see also 228). "They might wither, these clustering leaves, they might even drop away, and yet she knew that her deeper self, her hidden centre, would remain inviolable" (202).

The Sheltered Life is a powerful novel that also plots a new woman–old woman confrontation. There are also echoes from *To the Lighthouse*—

especially a central section entitled "The Deep Past" that recalls the "Time Passes" section of Woolf's novel. In it an elderly man articulates what is essentially a green-world matriarchal vision: he opposes hunting, expressing empathy with the "bewilderment . . . doubt . . . agony . . . [and] wondering despair" of the hunted deer,[26] and rejecting the empiricist claims of modern science (145).

The "new woman" figure is actually a young girl, Jenny Blair Archebald, who is somewhat rebellious (she finds *Little Women* too "poky" [8]), engages in what she thinks is a harmless flirtation with a neighbor, George Birdsong, and has the ambition of going to New York to become an actress (she is only seventeen when the novel ends).

Meanwhile, George's wife, Eva, who represents the older, repressed generation of women, suffers regular nervous collapses, largely because of George's philandering (much of it with their black laundress Memoria). George is also a hunter, and Jenny realizes "he was never so happy . . . as when he had just killed something beautiful" (382). "He enjoyed killing. He was possessed, she could see, by that strange exultation which comes to the sportsman when he has shot something that was alive" (383). Meanwhile, Jenny's flirtation with George continues despite the fact that she is also fond of Eva. It advances to the point where she and George occasionally engage in passionate kissing.

The finale of the novel occurs when Eva happens upon one of these embraces. It follows directly upon George's return from a duck-hunting venture, laden with bloody ducks. Eva had been repulsed, saying, "I can never understand why men enjoy killing, especially killing beautiful wild creatures" (386). Then she mused about the ducks, showing her empathy: "I suppose . . . ducks are more important to themselves than anything else. Do you imagine they would consider it an honour to be sent round to one's acquaintances with visiting cards tied to their necks?" (387). The latter question was uttered, we are told, "mockingly" (387).

The denouement is predictable. After seeing her husband kissing Jenny, Eva grabs the gun and shoots him, leaving him lying amid the spattered ducks. It is an act of vengeance, of defiance, of return for the years of betrayal and neglect she has endured (she had given up a promising career to marry him), and an act of solidarity with the beautiful woodland creatures perpetually destroyed in the patriarchal ritual of hunting. Her act is a gesture of reconnection with the green world, the "buried forest," but because of the depths of her oppression, it can only come in the form of violence. Jenny had, upon seeing Eva and before the shooting, run away and her grandfather prevents her from returning to the scene for fear her "innocence," ironically, would be destroyed.

Certainly one of Glasgow's greatest works (along with *Virginia, Barren Ground,* and *The Sheltered Life*) is *Vein of Iron* (1935). This novel, set in Appalachian Virginia, brings to culmination the hunter-hunted theme seen in earlier works. It opens with a scene in which an idiot boy is being chased by a group of children. Ada Fincastle, then aged ten, is one of them, but in the course of the chase she suddenly "in a flash of vision . . . [felt] that she and Toby had changed places."[27] It brings to her mind the time "she had seen a rabbit torn to pieces by hounds" (5).

Ada lives with her mother, a benign figure, one of the few positive mothers in Glasgow's repertoire; her father, a somewhat ineffectual but good-hearted philosopher; an aunt, Meggie, a sensitive and generous woman; and her grandmother, who expresses at times the vision of patriarchal (Calvinist) opprobrium. Ada's empathies extend to mice, even to trees and her dolls. "Grandmother thought it was only silliness to pretend that things like trees and dolls had real feelings. But they may have, [Ada] thought; you never can tell" (67).

Ada goes through the seduction and abandonment cycle. At one point she wants to leave the rural area for the city, but "the strong pull of roots in the soil [held] her steadfast" (185). While she is pregnant (although unmarried) she thinks of the forest world: "Oh, but the wilderness! If only she might hide away and have her child on a bed of pine boughs!" (248). She spends much of her time in pastoral meditation: out in the fields the sheep and lamb would butt up against her. "[S]he would lie flat on the earth" (253).

Her grandmother, at first outraged at Ada's unpardonable sin, finally relents as her granddaughter begins to experience labor pains. "She was pressed to a bosom as stout as oak, as sustaining as fortitude" (260)—an image of intergenerational female solidarity. Shortly thereafter, however, Ada goes into town, where she discovers she is still branded. As in the opening scene, a crowd of children collect; they chase after her, throwing mud clods and calling her names. She is saved, ironically, from her pursuers by Toby, the idiot boy now grown up. Ada wonders whether "all life [was] divided . . . between the pursued and the pursuers" (264).

Eventually Ada's lover returns from World War I; they marry and move the entire family to the city because the depression has hit and they must seek work. Through these years of struggle, which is cast as a period of exile and a time of the fall (Ada's father feels the earth has turned to "a vast plain, treeless and dead" [295]), Ada works as a saleswoman. Everyone around them suffers miserably from poverty and hunger. Ada again wonders, "Was she an idiot fleeing over a twisted path? Was she something soft, warm, furry, with eyes like small, terrified hearts?" (396)—an allusion to the rabbit described in the opening scene. In the end, however, Ada, like the other survivors in Glasgow's novels, manages to negotiate among the hunters while retaining the sensibility of the hunted. She does so because like them she is rooted in matriarchal soil. The novel ends on a note of ascendancy. Ada and her family return to their rural farm, ready to begin again. Demeter rising, the land in renewal, Glasgow concludes this great novel with Ada in her garden, her husband leaning against her, repeating the ancient myth's vision of feminine resurrection.

Thus, as in Wharton's final novel, *The Gods Arrive,* published three years earlier, Glasgow presents in her last major novel (she published one further novel, *In This Our Life,* in 1941, but it is not entirely successful) a vision of Demeter triumphant. One suspects that, like Wharton and Woolf, Glasgow may have been responding to her political environment. In this case, the motivating experience seems not so much to have been the rise of fascism as the Great Depression. A central portion of *Vein of Iron* depicts the joblessness and poverty Ada and her family endure during the depression years, significantly lived in the city. Their return to the land clearly expresses repudiation of monopoly capitalism and an endorsement of a precapitalist "use-value" realm—historically the economic world of the mothers.[28]

Conclusion

The Demeter-Persephone myth is the literary means by which Wharton, Cather, and Glasgow chose to mediate the historical shift in ideology—the revaluation of the masculine and denigration of the feminine—described in chapter 1. As such, it has political significance.

The central interpretation offered in this study is a political feminist criticism in that it seeks to locate the writings of women within their historical ideological context. Like certain veins in Marxist criticism, it assumes that ideology impinges upon texts: first, in providing the moral parameters within which writers conceive their characters, plot, and so forth; and, second, in defining a contradictory base against which writers dialectically imagine alternative syntheses. Unlike conventional myth criticism (of the Jungian type, for example), the approach taken here does not assume the mythic pattern to be universal, nor an expression of the writer's individual traumas. Rather, it is seen as an expression of a particular group (in this case, female, white, educated, and middle-class), which is faced with fundamental contradictions and who attempt to resolve those contradictions in their fiction.

The basic contradiction confronted by these women was how, as women, to feel valuable in a world where only the masculine was so held; how as *women* writers to feel legitimate when only male writers were held worthy. One response, which one could call a gesture of false consciousness in that it involved a fundamental betrayal of group identity and solidarity, entailed denying their identity as women, assuming instead male postures and styles. In their early years all three writers followed this tack. We know this from biographical material, but also through the use of male narrators, protagonists, and personae in their fiction. Thematically, this phase of their own psychic estrangement is represented by the Persephone period—the period of patriarchal captivity—in the Demeter-Persephone myth. But each of the writers seems to have come eventually to a reappreciation of the feminine, thus posing a thesis in dialectical opposition to the reigning ideology of their historical moment. In this sense the myth expressed in their later work may be seen in critical counterpoint to its ideological context.[1]

All the writers came to focus upon Demeter rising. *O Pioneers!*, *My Ántonia*, *Barren Ground*, and *Vein of Iron* are the most dramatic examples, but even the characters in Wharton's late novels, *The Gods Arrive* and *Hudson River Bracketed*, come to value the feminine and seek to reconnect with matriarchal sources. However, the writers differ significantly in their "matriarchal" visions; as noted in the preface, Cather's and Glasgow's remain firmly rooted in a rural, agricultural culture, while Wharton's rediscovery of the "mothers" seems connected rather to an urbane literary tradition (its antecedent being Goethe's *Faust*). Also the treatment of the myth's phases in their works is not synchronous. Cather—probably because of Jewett's influence and/or because of her own emotional identification with women—presented her vision of a triumphant Demeter in the early years of the century, while Wharton was focusing on the phase of Persephone in captivity. Cather's final vision (in the mid-forties) was of Demeter in eclipse, while Wharton's and Glasgow's (in the mid-thirties) were celebratory, of Demeter reigning. I have suggested in the conclusions to each chapter that the influence of such political events as the emergence of fascism, the depression, and World War II may help to explain their various responses. All the events impinged, it must be stressed, insofar as they were expressions of the idolatry of the masculine introduced in the male-supremacist ideologies treated in chapter 1. That is, each writer's matriarchal vision was clearly an imaginary alternative counterposed to reigning patriarchal ideologies and practices.

Furthermore, the visions of Demeter seen in the writings of Wharton, Cather, and Glasgow are of a figure who has retrieved the Persephone aspect of the feminine cycle and synthesized it. The vision is of postlapsarian triumph, of reconnection after the fall. Whereas, in the writings of nineteenth-century women, the "female world of love and ritual"—the world of Almira Todd—is prelapsarian in the sense that the matricentric bonds and rituals are primordial and uncompromised.

The synthesis envisaged by the twentieth-century women thus remains in this sense problematic. Wharton's matriarchal vision is had by a male protagonist; Cather's is presented in *My Ántonia* by a male narrator and in *The Professor's House* by male characters; Glasgow's women go through Persephone phases that destroy their happiness. Patriarchal intervention into women's culture seems irremediable.

Nevertheless, these women's vision aims at transcendence. From a feminist and socialist point of view this transcendence may seem false in that it does not incorporate the political wisdom that one might wish. It may seem more an escape into the "feminine" than a renewed commitment to personal and political alliances with women. But this would be too narrow a notion of how the literary imagination responds to political realities. Rather, one must view the thematics of Demeter seen in these women's writings as "allegories of desire," as "imaginary resolutions of a real contradiction."

From this perspective literary creation—the act of inventing imaginary solutions—may itself be seen as ideological, as Fredric Jameson points out in *The Political Unconscious*.[2] The vision of Demeter is therefore a utopian projection, an imagined expression of the authors' wishes: for the emotional fulfillment inherent in the maternal embrace, for respect and appreciation of the feminine, for pacifism, for use-value production, and for ecological holism. Those desires arose in dialectical response to the negative realities, the "social contradictions," of their own social and ideological environment, in which women's bonding, especially the mother-daughter connection, had been ruptured, in which the feminine, and especially women's literary culture, had become devalued, and in which a destructive scientific imperialism (exemplified in abhorrent practices from vivisection to atomic warfare) had gained hegemony.

Jameson suggests further that the literary text may be seen as a "restructuration of a prior historical or ideological *subtext*," which itself must be critically reconstituted (81)—as historians of women's culture such as Carroll Smith-Rosenberg and Nancy Sahli have done for the nineteenth-century women's culture.

While Jameson as a Marxist sees that texts must be identified in the context of the ideological confrontation between classes, in this study I am urging by my practice that women's literary texts must be positioned within the ideological confrontation between another set of dominator and dominated—namely, patriarchy and women—but understood in terms of the complex problems of identity faced by any group that is branded inferior by the master ideology. Feminist criticism necessarily reads texts in terms of patriarchal cultural contexts.

Marxist critics—particularly those most under a Hegelian influence, such as the members of the Frankfurt School or Georg Lukács—have posited two phases in the critical process or dialectic: negative criticism, in which the text's absences, gaps, omissions are noted, as well as the reified, destructive forms that are inscribed therein, and in which the text is critically related to a posited ideological context (in this case that of patriarchy); and positive criticism, in which the liberatory dimension is envisaged, in which an aspired utopian horizon is delineated.[3]

In *One-Dimensional Man,* for example, Herbert Marcuse notes that through the modes of Logos and Eros, "two modes of negation," the human consciousness can "break the hold of established, contingent reality and strive for a truth incompatible with it."[4] Similarly, Ernst Bloch, in *A Philosophy of the Future,* urges that critics must recognize the utopian dimension implied in even the most negative visions: "works of art . . . are not wholly circumscribed by their transient existential basis and its corresponding ideology. . . . [A] 'cultural surplus' is clearly effective: something that moves above and beyond the ideology . . . [remains] as [a] substrate that . . . is essentially utopian."[5] Several years ago in "Critical Re-Vision" I suggested that feminist criticism must follow a similar, dialectical trajectory.[6]

Marcuse, in turning to Eros as a force of liberation, also turns toward Freudian theory, which he sees as "describing the conditions of possibility of a society from which aggression will have been eliminated and in which libidinally satisfying work will be conceivable."[7] In *Eros and Civilization* Marcuse connected the utopian vision of Eros with the preoedipal realm of experience. The "notion of reality," he remarks, "which is predominant in Freud and which is condensed in the reality principle is 'bound up with the father.' " There is, he posits, however, a "maternal libidinal morality" that is represented mentally by the "superid." This voice reflects "traces of a different, lost reality, or lost relation between ego and reality," rooted in the "child's libidinal relation to the mother"—a phase that " 'recalls' the maternal phases in the history of the human race."[8] Thus, the utopian or positive phase of the critical dialectic is connected by Marcuse to the realm of preoedipal Eros, the realm of Demeter.

While critics are enjoined to engage in such a dialectical hermeneutic, it is not too much of an extension to hold that authors are in their way also critical interpreters. While their "text" is often another literary work or reality itself, they too operate in terms of a negative and a positive hermeneutic. In *New England Local Color Literature: A Women's Tradition* (1983) I suggested the term *women's realism* to cover the critical attitude taken by a long tradition of women writers (stretching back to the fourteenth century) toward the romance. Their critical realism toward the form reflected their "negative" realization that it was inimical to their aspirations as free and conscious human beings (because it proposed a circumscribed, stereotypical, or reified view of women's possibilities). On the other side of this negative critique was, however, the positive delineation of women's communities where emotional possibilities were fulfilled, where the Demeter-Persephone bond had not been ruptured. This vision—seen primarily in the works of the New England local colorists of the nineteenth century—to a great extent reflected the communitarian base of nineteenth-century women's culture but, especially as that culture was being threatened—toward the end of the century—expressed a utopian vision of an unalienated world where the mother-daughter libidinal economy remained intact and inviolate (Mrs. Todd and her mother in *The Country of the Pointed Firs*).

Wharton, Cather, and Glasgow began their careers in a climate when that vision had been compromised, and their early works express an ideologically encouraged male identification, a "false consciousness." But it is apparent that much of their imaginative energy went toward the reclamation of their predecessors' matriarchal vision. This struggle, continued heroically in a world "after the fall," informed their greatest works with enduring power.

Appendix I: The Demeter-Persephone Myth in Virginia Woolf and Colette

The Demeter-Persephone myth is also strikingly present in British and Continental women writers of the same generation as Wharton, Cather, and Glasgow—particularly in the writings of Virginia Woolf and French writer Colette.

In her recent study of Woolf, Madeline Moore remarks that "the myth of Demeter and Persephone . . . was central to much of Woolf's work."[1] Jane Marcus urges that Woolf's personal grief over the death of her own mother in 1895 made her especially responsive to the Demeter-Persephone myth.

> The "Hymn to Demeter" and the story of Persephone were especially moving for a writer who always thought of herself as a "motherless daughter." It may help us to understand what she meant by "thinking back through our mothers" [an idea in *A Room of One's Own*]. . . . The Demeter-Persephone myth affirms eternal refuge and redemption, as well as resurrection. The mother will never abandon her daughter. She will weep and wail and search the underworld, bring her out of the darkness of sexual experience, childbirth, madness, back into the world of light and freedom. She will restore her virginity.[2]

Moore similarly estimates that "as a spiritual lesbian, the myth of Demeter and Persephone assured [Woolf] that the mother will search constantly for her abandoned daughter, will deliver her from the darkness of heterosexual rape, and restore her to her natural virginity" or integrity.[3] Both Marcus and Moore note that Woolf was strongly influenced by classical scholar Jane Harrison, especially the Demeter-Persephone section of her *Prolegomena to the Study of Greek Religion,* which Woolf owned.[4]

Woolf's first novel, *The Voyage Out* (1915), deals centrally with the myth through the mother-daughter relationship between Helen Ambrose and Rachel Vinrace. The latter is a young girl, whose mother had died when she was eleven. The two women meet on a sea voyage to South America. When Rachel announces her engagement to Terence Hewet, Helen jumps on Rachel in an apparent fit of jealousy and wrestles her to the ground. "Raising herself and sitting up, [Rachel] too realised Helen's soft body, the strong and hospitable arms, and happiness swelling and breaking in one vast wave."[5] Shortly thereafter Rachel contracts a mysterious disease and dies.

The lesbian connection between Rachel and Helen is much more explicit in the first draft of the novel, which was entitled *Melymbrosia* (completed in 1908). And, according to Louise DeSalvo, the mother-daughter character of their tie is also clearer in that version; the mother is jealous of the daughter's involvement with a man. The wrestling scene is also more developed in earlier drafts: "Helen pursues Rachel, tumbles her to the ground and professes *her* love. During the embrace, Helen tries to force Rachel to admit that she loves Helen better than she loves Terence. Rachel refuses."[6]

Helen thus takes on the threatening, controlling aspects of the maternal seen in Edith Wharton's works. "Helen represents a malicious, life-threatening maternity to Rachel, a maternity which embraces, caresses, and smothers simultaneously. . . . Helen becomes . . . the maternal figure smothering the traitorous child" (57). DeSalvo amplifies, "Helen is both lover and mother-surrogate, a woman smothering her child for the transgression of loving a man. Rachel cannot love or kiss a man without betraying a mother or encountering her wrath" (129). Thus, Helen assumes the mien of the vengeful Demeter.

The novel takes place in part aboard the ship *Euphrosyne.* It is named after a fifth-century saint who disguised herself as a monk to escape her father's marriage designs—thus engaging in a cross-dressing "masquerade" to escape from the traffic in women. The allusion draws attention to the fact that in succeeding versions of the novel Woolf progressively engaged in what Jewett called masquerading. By the 1913 version "all overt references to Rachel's homosexual love for Helen were eradicated" (102). DeSalvo remarks the difference between the "openness of the early draft and the masquerade of the late one" (104).

Thus, like the authors treated in this study, Woolf seems to have become inhibited by changing attitudes toward lesbianism in the early twentieth century. But, as in their works, the mother-daughter tension remains a primary concern. Indeed, Woolf's masterpiece *To the Lighthouse* has as its central script the Demeter-Persephone myth, as Annis Pratt has pointed out.[7] Again, I would suggest, however, that the principal reason for the predominance of this theme was not so much Woolf's personal relationship with her own mother but rather the influence of the historical mother-daughter generational transition occurring in women's culture during this period.

Two other British novels published at this time express in classic terms the tensions of the mother-daughter relationship. In both May Sinclair's *Mary Olivier: A Life* (1919) and Radclyffe Hall's *The Unlit Lamp* (1924), an ambitious daughter who longs for education and a career is tied to a controlling mother who wants her to stay home. In both cases the relationship to the mother has lesbian overtones, and in both cases the daughter remains with the mother, finding a measure of happiness in that course.

Mary Webb's powerful *Gone to Earth* (1917) also repeats the Demeter-Persephone myth. The novel concerns the doom of a woodland figure, Hazel Woodus—a Diana-Persephone, whose mother is dead and who is raped and abducted by a Hades figure. Her main companion is a pet fox. She is killed attempting to rescue him from a fox-hunt.

Before her mother, a gypsy, had died, she had bequeathed to her daughter "an old, dirty, partially illegible manuscript-book of spells and charms."[8] This book seems to represent the lost tradition of women's words, the inaudible sounds of Demeter (see further discussion in appendix 2). In recalling her mother's vision of the forest world, Hazel said,

> You'll hear soft feet running, and you'll see faces look out and hands waving, and gangs of folks come galloping under the leaves. . . . And my mam said the trees get free that night. . . . And last comes the lady . . . riding in a troop of shadows, and sobbing, "Lost—alost! Oh, my green garden!"[9]

The allusion is to the Lady of Wild Things, a form of the Great Goddess, Demeter. And, as suggested throughout this study, the early years of the twentieth century were a historical moment in which Demeter's green garden was gone, her daughter lured and victimized beyond its boundaries. *Gone to Earth* dramatically expresses this loss.

The Demeter-Persephone myth is also central in the writings of Colette. In her autobiographical works her own mother, Sido, takes on the role of Demeter, while she, the daughter, is Persephone. As Jane Lilienfeld points out, Colette's marriage to Willy is presented as a living death in Colette's *My Apprenticeships*. And her return to her mother is seen as a feminine resurrection.[10]

In that work Colette describes the place where she lived after her marriage as having "no light, no air," a realm of "strange gloom" where she gradually lost strength, where her "life was ebbing."[11] But she dreams that "it could be cured miraculously by my death and resurrection, by a shock that would restore me to my mother's house, to the garden, and wipe out everything that marriage had taught me."[12]

Her mother's house is construed as an edenic bower, a place of light filled with animals and plants, while her married abode is an underworld of lifeless gloom. Marriage to Willy is seen as a fall into patriarchal captivity. But as with the writers treated in this study, Colette's return to the mother's bower is problematic and fraught with the conflicting desires for autonomy on the one hand but attraction to the maternal erotic on the other.

Appendix II: Demeter as Absent Referent

Another ancient myth somewhat similar to that of Persephone in that it involves a woman's rape is the story of Philomela and Procne, sisters. Procne was married to Tereus, who developed a passion for Philomela, whom he rapes. When she threatens to tell her sister, he cuts out her tongue. But she manages to communicate with her sister anyway by means of a tapestry on which she weaves her story.[1]

Here as in the Demeter-Persephone myth a rapist-patriarch attempts to destroy communication between women, and here too the women manage to reconnect. Despite enforced silence, the raped woman is able to find nonverbal signifiers to tell her story.

To an extent women writers are in the position of Philomela. Raped by their enforced conscription into patriarchal commerce, robbed of their own tongue by enforced conscription into the patriarchal Symbolic, women writers have had to find compromised means to tell their story.

Insofar as language and literature are products of a patriarchal civilization, all women writers are to a greater or lesser extent Persephones who must consume the pomegranate seed in order to engage in literary production. They travel between the preliterate preoedipal realm of their mothers—Demeter—and the patriarchal realm of the Symbolic, the words of the fathers. To be successful writers they must learn to negotiate the "no man's land" between two realms; they must learn two languages. If they remain in the preliterate world of silence, their production is absent, nonexistent, inaudible, and invisible. But if they lose touch with their mothers' gardens, they risk losing the emotional integrity that is the source of artistic inspiration. This seems to be the message of central women's texts treated in this study—from *The Country of the Pointed Firs* to *My Ántonia, Hudson River Bracketed,* and *Vein of Iron.*

In her recent study of nineteenth-century British women's literature, Margaret Homans explores the ambiguous positioning of the woman writer between the mother's and the father's languages. Taking a Freudian perspective, Homans remarks that "the dominant myth of Western languages . . . [is] structured on a quest romance, based on the boy's postoedipal renunciation of the mother and his quest for substitute objects of desire."[2] She notes further that "virtually all the founding texts of our culture" present versions of the myth "that the death or absence of the mother . . . makes possible the construction of language and of culture" (2).

Homans relies on the Lacanian theory, therefore, that language is a "chain of signifiers that refer . . . to other signifiers" (7). What is missing is the "forbidden mother" (7), the absent referent. Like all women, women writers have a special relationship with the absent referent in that it has a female character and because their own relationship with their mothers is not obstructed by the oedipal maturation processes the male must pass through. (This study suggests, however, that as women become more socially independent their relationships with their mothers become more problematic—thus indicating that historical circumstances rather than a universal oedipal process may condition the parent-child relationship.)

Homans's main point is that there is a kind of "literal" language that women writers (daughters) share with their mothers that is "presymbolic," characterized by a "lack of gaps between signifier and referent" (14). As an example, Homans cites a scene from *To the Lighthouse* in which Mrs. Ramsay is putting her daughter to bed: "the words matter as sounds . . . [it is] a literal language shared between mother and daughter: a language of presence, in which the presence or absence of referents . . . is quite unimportant" (18). Homans sees as a model of relatively literal discourse the journals of Dorothy Wordsworth, who "writes entirely without the thought or hope that she is writing 'literature,' [and] takes unadulterated pleasure in writing in a language that is as literal as possible and that literalizes" (39).

The writers treated in this study—Wharton, Cather, and Glasgow—

were eager to write "literature," to write in "official" modes (to borrow a term from Russian critic Mikhail Bakhtin), and to be accepted as serious (male) authors. Their stylistic practice, therefore, was conventional, inscribed within the traditions of literary realism, using for the most part objective third-person narration—the voice of the alienated daughter—and even occasionally assuming a male persona. Rather than attempting to escape the patriarchal sentence imposed in "The Yellow Wallpaper" (to return to Paula Treichler's analysis), they accepted it—unlike the modernists who attempted experimental modes of disrupting it and of thus transmitting their stories in variant ways.

Nevertheless, the thematics explored in this study—the use of the Demeter-Persephone myth—indicate a discomfort with patriarchal forms—a longing for a more intimate expression of the language of Demeter, a more direct connection with the absent referent. In *The Wheel of Life* Glasgow says that the women's embrace expresses an "intimate knowledge, which is uttered without speech" (462). In *They Stooped to Folly* Mrs. Littlepage struggles to communicate a hidden knowledge—"some secret of tremendous significance" (192). In the end she, like Sylvia in "A White Heron," remains silent; she cannot or will not translate her knowledge into a patriarchal "chain of signifiers." Similarly, women remain silent in *Ethan Frome;* their discourse is hidden in "The Yellow Wallpaper," inscribed in a gypsy woman's "partially illegible manuscript-book of spells and charms" (3) in *Gone to Earth.* Wharton's sensitivity to women's dual stylistics is evident in *Bunner Sisters,* where Evelina uses ambiguous "swelling periods" that obscure communication with her sister Ann Eliza. And in *The Reef* we learn that Sophy became "inexpressive or sentimental" (262) when trying to convey her emotions; she was "really powerless to put her thoughts in writing" (44). Whereas Anna, whose style is remarkable for "the clear structure of its phrases" (45), is cut off from the expression of genuine feeling. In her later works Wharton seems to have rediscovered the importance of maintaining contact with these emotional sources, recognizing the wisdom of Demeter's knowledge expressed in her early playlet "Pomegranate Seed": "I hear the secret whisper of the wheat" (291).

But it is Cather's intuitions about women's creative sphere that are perhaps the most provocative. In particular, her idea of telling *O Pioneers!* to her literary foremother Jewett suggests alternative stylistic possibilities. In addition, Ántonia's "preoedipal" communication with the cricket (seen in numerous other works, such as *Gone to Earth,* where women communicate with animals), Claude's mother's narration of the Joan of Arc legend while baking a pie in *One of Ours*, the Indian women's pottery, and Mahailey's quilt all indicate that Cather was looking to alternative feminine ways of communicating—for an art that was integral with women's lives. Like Philomela, she sought alternative signifiers to communicate women's otherwise silenced world.

The ambivalences and ambiguities of these women writers belong to their moment in history, but their utopian insights point to transcending possibilities.

Notes

Introduction

1. The synopsis that follows and the citations are from "To Demeter," in *Hesiod, the Homeric Hymns and Homerica*, ed. and trans. Hugh G. Evelyn-White (Cambridge: Harvard University Press, 1964), pp. 289–325.

2. C. G. Jung, "Psychological Aspects of the Mother Archetype," in *The Archetypes and the Collective Unconscious*, 2d ed. (Princeton: Princeton University Press, 1969), p. 81.

3. Robert Graves, *The White Goddess: A Historical Grammar of Poetic Myth* (1948; reprint ed., New York: Octagon, 1976), p. 66.

4. Ibid., pp. 422, 481.

5. C. Kerényi, *Eleusis: Archetypal Image of Mother and Daughter* (New York: Pantheon/Bollinger, 1967), p. 70.

6. C. G. Jung, "The Psychological Aspects of the Kore," in *Archetypes*, p. 195.

7. Carroll Smith-Rosenberg, *Disorderly Conduct: Visions of Gender in Victorian America* (New York: Knopf, 1985), p. 32. Further references follow in the text.

8. Sir James Frazer, *The Golden Bough: A Study in Magic and Religion*, abridged ed. (New York: Macmillan, 1951), p. 461.

9. Kerényi, *Eleusis*, p. 28. See also Jane Harrison, *Prolegomena to the Study of Greek Religion* (1903; reprint ed., New York: Meridian, 1957): "Demeter and Kore [Persephone] are two persons through one god" (p. 272).

10. On their relationships with their mothers, see Cynthia Griffin Wolff, *A Feast of Words: The Triumph of Edith Wharton* (New York: Oxford University Press, 1977); Sharon O'Brien, *Willa Cather: The Emerging Voice* (New York: Oxford University Press, 1987); J. R. Roper, *Without Shelter: The Early Career of Ellen Glasgow* (Baton Rouge: Louisiana State University Press, 1971), pp. 29–31.

Chapter 1

1. As cited in William R. Taylor and Christopher Lasch, "Two 'Kindred Spirits': Sorority and Family in New England, 1839–1846," *New England Quarterly* 36, no. 1 (March 1963): 32.

2. H. J. Rose, *A Handbook of Greek Mythology* (New York: Dutton, 1959), pp. 112ff. Artemis appears to have been of Cretan origin, "a goddess of a conquered race" (113) not respected by Homer, who expressed the patriarchal bias of the classical Greek tradition. Artemis was worshiped in the cult of Ephesis, a relic of earlier matriarchal religions. Further references to Rose follow in the text.

3. See Christine Stansell's analysis of Elizabeth Stuart Phelps's *Story of Avis* (1877) in "Elizabeth Stuart Phelps: A Study in Female Rebellion," in *Woman: An Issue*, ed. Lee R. Edwards, Mary Heath, and Lisa Baskin (Boston: Little, Brown, 1972), pp. 239–56.

4. Elizabeth Ammons, "Cool Diana and the Blood-Red Muse: Edith Wharton on Innocence and Art," in *American Novelists Revisited: Essays in Feminist Criticism*, ed. Fritz Fleischmann (Boston: G. K. Hall, 1982), pp. 209–24. See also Wolff, *Feast of Words*, pp. 299, 322.

5. The transition is also particularly evident in the works of Elizabeth Stuart Phelps. See Josephine Donovan, *New England Local Color Literature: A Women's Tradition* (New York: Ungar, 1983), pp. 82–98 (for Phelps) and 119–38 (for Freeman).

6. Alice Walker, "In Search of Our Mothers' Gardens," *Ms.* 2, no. 11. Mary E. Wilkins [Freeman], "Evelina's Garden," *Harper's* 93 (June 1896); reprinted in *Silence and Other Stories* (New York: Harper, 1898).

7. Ola Hansson, *Modern Women*, as cited in Linda Susanne Panill, "The Artist-Heroine in American Fiction, 1890–1920" (Ph.D. diss., University of North Carolina, 1975), p. 34. The original source of the quote appears to be Hansson, *Alltagsfrauen: Ein Stück moderner liebesphysiologie* (1891).

8. As cited in Helen M. Bannan, "Spider Woman's Web: Mothers and Daughters in Southwestern Native American Literature," in *The Lost Tradition: Mothers and Daughters in Literature*, ed. Cathy N. Davidson and E. M. Broner (New York: Ungar, 1980), p. 274.

9. Bannan, p. 275.

10. Madeleine Grumet, "Conception, Contradiction and Curriculum" (1981), as cited in Nel Noddings, *Caring: A Feminine Approach to Ethics and Moral Education* (Berkeley: University of California Press, 1984), p. 200. Further references to Noddings follow in the text.

11. See Nancy Chodorow, *The Reproduction of Mothering: Psychoanalysis and the Sociology of Gender* (Berkeley: University of California Press, 1978).

12. Max Horkheimer and Theodore W. Adorno, *Dialectic of Enlightenment* (New York: Herder and Herder, 1972), p. 23.

13. Sandra Harding, *The Science Question in Feminism* (Ithaca: Cornell University Press, 1986), p. 124.

14. As cited in Colin Gordon, Afterword to *Power/Knowledge: Selected Interviews and Other Writings 1972–1977* by Michel Foucault (New York: Pantheon, 1980), p. 238.

15. Michel Foucault, *Histoire de la sexualité*, vol. 1, *La volonté de savoir* (Paris: Gallimard, 1976), p. 61 (my translation).

16. A point made by Annis Pratt, "Women and Nature in Modern Fiction," *Contemporary Literature* 13 (Autumn 1972): 476–90. See also her discussion of the "green-world archetype" in *Archetypal Patterns in Women's Fiction* (Bloomington: Indiana University Press, 1981).

17. Louise Bernikow, *Among Women* (New York: Harmony, 1981), p. 30.

18. A useful introduction is Jacques Lacan, *The Language of the Self: the Function of Language in Psychoanalysis*, trans. with a commentary by Anthony Wilden (Baltimore: Johns Hopkins University Press, 1968).

19. Hélène Cixous, "Castration or Decapitation?" *Signs* 7, no. 1 (Autumn 1981): 45.

20. Xavière Gauthier, "Is There Such a Thing as Women's Writing?" in *New French Feminisms: An Anthology,* ed. Elaine Marks and Isabelle de Courtivron (New York: Schocken, 1980), pp. 163–64.

21. Sarah Orne Jewett, "A White Heron" (1886), in *The Country of the Pointed Firs and Other Stories* (Garden City, NJ: Anchor, 1956), p. 167.

22. Ibid., p. 171. Portions of the above analysis appeared in Josephine Donovan, "Silence or Capitulation: Prepatriarchal 'Mothers' Gardens' in Jewett and Freeman," *Studies in Short Fiction* 23, no. 1 (Winter 1986): 43–48.

23. Mary E. Wilkins Freeman, "Old Woman Magoun" (1905), in *The Winning Lady and Others* (New York: Harper, 1909), p. 273.

24. Rose, p. 92. In *Eleusis* (p. 179), Kerényi says *mentha pulegium,* "some variety of pennyroyal," was part of Demeter's special drink, *kykeon.* On the Demeter-Persephone pattern in *Pointed Firs,* see Elizabeth Ammons, "Jewett's Witches," in *Critical Essays on Sarah Orne Jewett,* ed. Gwen L. Nagel (Boston: G. K. Hall, 1984), p. 175; and Sarah W. Sherman, "Victorians and the Matriarchal Mythology: A Source for Mrs. Todd," *Colby Library Quarterly* 22, no. 1 (March 1986): 63–74.

25. See Josephine Donovan, "Sarah Orne Jewett's Critical Theory: Notes toward a Feminine Literary Mode," in *Critical Essays on Jewett,* ed. Nagel, pp. 212–25.

26. Marjorie Pryse, "An Uncloistered 'New England Nun,' " *Studies in Short Fiction* 20, no. 4 (Fall 1983): 289–95.

27. Edith Hamilton, *Mythology* (1940; reprint ed., New York: Mentor, 1959), p. 116.

28. Mary E. Wilkins [Freeman], "Arethusa" (1900), in *Understudies* (New York: Harper, 1901), p. 155. It must be acknowledged that the mother in this story behaves atypically in that she encourages her daughter to marry.

29. Ibid., p. 169.

30. Mary E. Wilkins [Freeman], "A Poetess," in *A New England Nun and Other Stories* (New York: Harper, 1891), p. 140. Further references follow in the text. Another Freeman story particularly emblematic of the "fall" theme is "The Tree of Knowledge," in *The Love of Parson Lord and Other Stories* (1900; reprint ed., Freeport, NY: Books for Libraries Press, 1969). See my analysis in *New England Local Color Literature,* pp. 20–21.

31. Ann Romines, "A Place for 'A Poetess,' " *The Markham Review* 12 (Summer 1983): 63.

32. Mary Jacobus, "The Difference of View," in *Women Writing and Writing about Women,* ed. Jacobus (New York: Barnes and Noble, 1979), p. 10.

33. Ibid., p. 12.

34. Jane Marcus, "Virginia Woolf and Her Violin: Mothering, Madness and Music," in *Mothering the Mind: Twelve Studies of Writers and Their Silent Partners,* ed. Ruth Perry and Martine Watson Brownley (New York: Holmes and Meier, 1984), p. 182. Woolf's comment is from "A Sketch of the Past," in *Moments of Being,* ed. Jeanne Schulkind, 2d ed. (San Diego: Harcourt Brace Jovanovich, 1985), p. 95.

35. Jane Marcus, "A Wilderness of One's Own: Feminist Fantasy Novels of the Twenties: Rebecca West and Sylvia Townsend Warner," in *Women Writers and the City: Essays in Feminist Literary Criticism,* ed. Susan Merrill Squier (Knoxville: University of Tennessee Press, 1984), p. 139. Marcus discovers the Dianic/Daphne myth recurring in two novels published in the late 1920s. Such a development may augur the reemergence of cultural feminism, as seen in Woolf's *Three Guineas* (1938), or it may, as Marcus suggests, reflect disillusionment with assimilationist feminism. A brief discussion of the Demeter-

Persephone myth in British and French women's fiction of the early twentieth century appears in Appendix I.

36. Mary Helen Washington, "I Sign My Mother's Name: Alice Walker, Dorothy West, Paule Marshall," in *Mothering the Mind*, pp. 142–63. See also Barbara Christian, *Black Women Novelists: The Development of a Tradition, 1892–1976* (Westport, CT: Greenwood, 1980).

37. Mary Kelley, *Private Woman, Public Stage: Literary Domesticity in Nineteenth-Century America* (New York: Oxford, 1984), pp. 37–55. My thanks to Barbara White for drawing this to my attention.

38. Ellen Moers, *Literary Women* (Garden City, NJ: Anchor, 1977), p. 354.

39. Paula A. Treichler, "Escaping the Sentence: Diagnosis and Discourse in 'The Yellow Wallpaper,' " *Tulsa Studies in Women's Literature* 3, no. 1/2 (Spring/Fall 1984): 62. Further references follow in the text.

40. For a fuller discussion, see Josephine Donovan, *Feminist Theory: The Intellectual Traditions of American Feminism* (New York: Ungar, 1985).

41. This factor is considered by Nancy Sahli, "Smashing: Women's Relationships before the Fall," *Chrysalis* 8 (Summer 1979): 25. Further references to Sahli follow in the text.

42. Estelle Freedman, "Separatism as Strategy: Female Institution Building and American Feminism, 1870–1930," *Feminist Studies* 5, no. 3 (Fall 1979): 514. Further references follow in the text.

43. Ann Douglas, *The Feminization of American Culture* (New York: Avon, 1977), p. 397.

44. Henry James, *The Bostonians* (1886; reprint ed., New York: Penguin, 1966), p. 290.

45. As cited in Theodore Roszak, "The Hard and the Soft: The Force of Feminism in Modern Times," in *Masculine/Feminine: Readings in Sexual Mythology and the Liberation of Women,* ed. Betty and Theodore Roszak (New York: Harper, 1969), p. 91. Further references to Roszak follow in the text.

46. Ellen Glasgow, *They Stooped to Folly: A Comedy of Morals* (Garden City, NY: Doubleday, Moran, 1929), p. 185.

47. Lillian Faderman, "The Morbidification of Love between Women by Nineteenth-Century Sexologists," *Journal of Homosexuality* 4 (1978): 73–90. See also Faderman, *Surpassing the Love of Men: Friendship and Romantic Love between Women from the Renaissance to the Present* (New York: Morrow, 1981).

48. See notes 41, 47.

49. R. v. Krafft-Ebing, *Psychopathia Sexualis, with Especial Reference to the Antipathic Sexual Instinct,* trans. F. J. Rebman (of the 12th German ed.) (New York: Medical Art Agency, 1906), p. 195.

50. Ibid., p. 325.

51. Jonathan Katz, ed., *Gay/Lesbian Almanac: A New Documentary* (New York: Harper, 1983), p. 303.

52. Havelock Ellis, *Sexual Inversion* (1897), pp. 99–100, as cited in Sahli, p. 25.

53. Wanda Fraiken Neff, *We Sing Diana* (1928), as cited in Faderman, *Surpassing,* p. 299.

54. George Chauncey, Jr., "From Sexual Inversion to Homosexuality: Medicine and

the Changing Conceptualization of Female Deviance," *Salmagundi* 58–59 (Fall 1982–Winter 1983): 144–45. Further references follow in the text.

55. Charlotte Perkins Gilman, *His Religion and Hers* (1923; reprint ed., Westport, CT: Hyperion, 1976), p. 54.

56. Ibid., p. 95.

57. Christina Simmons, "Companionate Marriage and the Lesbian Threat," *Frontiers* 4, no. 3 (Fall 1979): 57. Further references follow in the text.

58. Aspects of cultural feminist theory continued into the 1920s and 1930s in some of the social legislation eventually passed in the New Deal. See Donovan, *Feminist Theory*, chap. 2; and Stanley J. Lemons, *The Woman Citizen: Social Feminism in the 1920s* (Urbana: University of Illinois Press, 1975).

59. Jacques Barzun, *Darwin, Marx, Wagner: Critique of a Heritage* (1941; rev. 2d ed. Garden City, NJ: Doubleday, 1958), p. 92.

60. Charles Darwin, *The Descent of Man, and Selection in Relation to Sex* (1871; rev. 2d ed. New York: American Publishers, 1874), p. 18. Further references follow in the text.

61. Herbert Spencer, *Principles of Sociology*, as cited in Carlton J. H. Hayes, *A Generation of Materialism, 1871–1900* (1941; reprint ed., New York: Harper, 1963), p. 11.

62. Charlotte Perkins Gilman, *The Man-Made World, or Our Androcentric Culture* (1911; reprint ed., New York: Johnson Reprint, 1971), p. 215. Jane Addams also refuted this aspect of social Darwinism in *Peace and Bread in Time of War* (1922). See also Olive Schreiner, *Women and Labor* (1911).

63. See Richard Hofstadter, *Social Darwinism in American Thought* (1944; rev. ed. New York: Braziller, 1955).

64. David Parry, *The Scarlet Empire* (1906), as cited in Peter Conn, *The Divided Mind: Ideology and Imagination in America, 1898–1917* (Cambridge: Cambridge University Press, 1983), p. 84. A somewhat parallel study is T. J. Jackson Lears, *No Place of Grace: Antimodernism and the Transformation of American Culture, 1880–1920* (New York: Pantheon, 1981). Neither work focuses enough on the "masculinity crisis" inherent in the cultural history of this period, however.

65. Joe Dibbert, "Progressivism and the Masculinity Crisis," *Psychoanalytic Review* 61, no. 3 (Fall 1974): 444. Further references follow in the text.

66. Eliza Burt Gamble, *The Evolution of Woman, an Inquiry into the Dogma of Her Inferiority to Man* (New York: Putnam's, 1893); and Charlotte Perkins Gilman, *Women and Economics* (1898; reprint ed., New York: Harper, 1966). See also Ruth Hubbard, "Have Only Men Evolved?" in *Discovering Reality*, ed. Sandra Harding and Merrill B. Hintikka (Dordrecht, Holland: Reidel, 1983), pp. 45–69.

67. Ellen Glasgow, *A Certain Measure* (New York: Harcourt, Brace, 1938), p. 58.

68. Willa Cather, *Not Under Forty* (New York: Knopf, 1953), preface.

Chapter 2

1. Sarah Orne Jewett, *A Country Doctor* (Boston: Houghton Mifflin, 1884), p. 12. Further references follow in the text. A slightly different version of this chapter appeared in *Colby Library Quarterly* 22, no. 1 (March 1986): 17–27.

2. According to Raphael Patai, *The Hebrew Goddess* (1971), pp. 13–14, the Hebraic

religion absorbed the notion of the tree of good and evil from the Canaanite religion, where it "symbolized the Canaanite goddess Asherah, whose places of worship were marked by trees." Thus, in Genesis Adam "is forbidden to partake of the goddess symbol" (Peggy Reeves Sanday, *Female Power and Male Preference: On the Origins of Sexual Inequality* [Cambridge: Cambridge University Press, 1981], p. 223). The tree is another emblem of the Great Goddess discussed in the preface, and Nan's connection with it is symbolic of her ties to matriarchal roots.

3. See Donovan, *New England Local Color Literature.*

4. Wilkins [Freeman], "The Tree of Knowledge," p. 139.

5. Rose, *Handbook,* p. 259.

6. Hamilton, *Mythology,* p. 173.

7. Ibid., p. 174.

8. Houghton MS Am1743.7, Miscellaneous Notes for *A Country Doctor.* Cited by permission of the Houghton Library, Harvard University.

9. Jewett wrote this comment on the back of a letter she had received from S. S. McClure, dated 7 June 1889, in which he had asked her for a story that would embody her "ideal young woman." Houghton MS Am1743.7. Cited by permission of the Houghton Library, Harvard University. See also Malinda Snow, " 'That One Talent': The Vocation as Theme in Sarah Orne Jewett's *A Country Doctor," Colby Library Quarterly* 16 (1980): 138–47.

10. Carroll Smith-Rosenberg and Charles Rosenberg, "The Female Animal: Medical and Biological Views of Woman and Her Role in Nineteenth-Century America," *Journal of American History* 60, no. 2 (Sept. 1973): 336.

11. Ann Douglas Wood, " 'The Fashionable Diseases': Women's Complaints and Their Treatments in Nineteenth-Century America," in *Clio's Consciousness Raised,* ed. Mary Hartman and Lois W. Banner (New York: Harper, 1974), p. 8.

12. Alice Rossi, ed., *The Feminist Papers* (1973; reprint ed., New York: Bantam, 1974), p. 305

13. Barbara Welter, "The Cult of True Womanhood: 1820–1860," *American Quarterly* 18, no. 2, pt. 1 (Summer 1966): 173.

14. Houghton MS Am1743.7, Vol. 1, folder 6. Cited by permission of the Houghton Library, Harvard University.

15. Houghton MS Am1743.7, Vol. 1, folder 9. Cited by permission of the Houghton Library, Harvard University.

16. Krafft-Ebing, *Psychopathia Sexualis,* p. 285. Further references follow in the text.

17. Several works of the period featured women physicians: Harriet Beecher Stowe's *My Wife and I* (1871), Mark Twain's *Gilded Age* (1873), Elizabeth Stuart Phelps's *Dr. Zay* (1882), William Dean Howells's *Dr. Breen's Practice* (1881), and Louisa May Alcott's *Jo's Boys* (1886). Two works immediately following *A Country Doctor* are of particular interest. Oliver Wendell Holmes's *A Mortal Antipathy* (1885) recounts a romantic friendship between two women, one of whom wishes to become a physician. The denouement is that each of the women marries, and the potential medical student renounces her ambition. Interestingly, Holmes uses the Atalanta motif consciously in the novel, having the women defeat the men in a canoe race; their boat is the "Atalanta." The work also appears to parody sexologist case studies by noting cases where men developed "antipathies" to spiders and women—which suggests that the notion of "antipathic" instincts was definitely in the air in Boston in the 1880s.

Henry James's *The Bostonians* (1886) also followed on the heels of *A Country Doctor*. It presents a woman physician, Dr. Prance (surely a verbal echo of Prince), relatively positively but deals more critically with the women's rights movement and the "romantic friendship" between Olive Chancellor and Verena Tarrant. At least one scholar has suggested that James had Annie Fields and Jewett specifically in mind in creating these characters (see Helen Howe, *The Gentle Americans, 1864–1960: Biography of a Breed* [New York: Harper, 1965], p. 83), but this remains speculation.

18. Delores Klaitch, *Woman Plus Woman: Attitudes toward Lesbianism* (New York: Simon and Schuster, 1974), p. 56.

19. Manuscript obituary of Theodore Herman Jewett by Sarah Orne Jewett, Houghton MS Am1743.22 (28). Cited by permission of the Houghton Library, Harvard University.

20. Faderman, *Surpassing the Love of Men*, p. 239.

21. Jewett's lesbian tendencies, or engagement in romantic friendships, are documented in Josephine Donovan, "The Unpublished Love Poems of Sarah Orne Jewett," *Frontiers* 4, no. 3 (Fall 1979): 26–31, and Faderman, pp. 197–203.

22. Margaret Fuller, *Woman in the Nineteenth Century* (1845; reprint ed., New York: Norton, 1971), p. 40.

23. See Ammons, "Cool Diana and the Blood-Red Muse," pp. 209–24, and Marcus, "A Wilderness of One's Own."

Chapter 3

1. Edith Wharton, "Life and I," unpublished manuscript, p. 10. The Collection of American Literature, Beinecke Rare Book and Manuscript Library, Yale University. Published by permission. Further references follow in the text.

2. See, for example, "April Showers" (1900), "Copy" (1900), "Expiation" (1903), and "Writing a War Story" (1919). Numerous other stories put down the clubwoman interested in "culture": "The Pelican" (1899), "The Legend" (1910), and "Xingu" (1911). And several see women's sentimentalist taste as corrupting the integrity of "high art": "The Portrait" (1899), "The Rembrandt" (1900), "The Verdict" (1904), and "The Pot-boiler" (1904). All are in *The Collected Short Stories of Edith Wharton*, ed. R. W. B. Lewis (New York: Scribner's, 1968).

3. See especially "The Rembrandt" (1900), "The Moving Finger" (1901), "The Verdict" (1904), "The Daunt Diana" (1909), "The Debt" (1909), "The Eyes" (1910), "Coming Home" (1915), and "Miss Mary Paske" (1925). All are in *Collected Stories*.

4. Edith Wharton, *The Bunner Sisters*, in *Madame de Treymes and Others: Four Novelettes* (New York: Scribner's, 1970), p. 280. *The Bunner Sisters* was first published in 1916, although written by 1891. Further references follow in the text.

5. As cited in Wolff, *Feast of Words*, p. 258. Further references follow in the text.

6. Louis Auchincloss, Introduction to *A Backward Glance*, by Edith Wharton (New York: Scribner's, 1934), p. vii.

7. As cited in Mary Sue Schreiber, "Darwin, Wharton, and 'The Descent of Man': Blueprints of American Society," *Studies in Short Fiction* 17, no. 1 (Winter 1980): 37–38.

8. R. W. B. Lewis, *Edith Wharton: A Biography* (New York: Harper, 1975), pp. 443, 444.

9. Edith Wharton, "The Valley of Childish Things, and Other Emblems," *Collected Stories* 1:58.

10. Donovan, "Sarah Orne Jewett's Critical Theory," pp. 212–25. On the Persephone-Demeter pattern in *Pointed Firs,* see chap. 1, n. 24 above.

11. See Kathryn Allen Rabuzzi, *The Sacred and the Feminine: Towards a Theology of Housework* (New York: Seabury, 1982), pp. 146–47.

12. See Donovan, *Feminist Theory,* chap. 2.

13. Wharton, *A Backward Glance,* pp. 293–94.

14. Donovan, *New England Local Color Literature,* pp. 44, 105.

15. *Backward Glance,* p. 4.

16. Edith Wharton, "Pomegranate Seed," *Scribner's* 51, no. 3 (March 1912): 288. Further references follow in the text.

17. See Nancy K. Miller, *The Heroine's Text* (New York: Columbia University Press, 1980).

18. Edith Wharton, *The Touchstone,* in *Madame de Treymes and Others: Four Novelettes,* p. 32. Further references follow in the text.

19. Edith Wharton, "The Angel at the Grave," *Collected Stories* 1:249. Further references follow in the text.

20. Edith Wharton, *The Valley of Decision,* 2 vols. (New York: Scribner's, 1902), 1:224. Further references follow in the text.

21. See Josephine Donovan, "The Silence Is Broken," in *Women and Language in Literature and Society,* ed. Sally McConnell-Ginet, Ruth Borker, and Nelly Furman (New York: Praeger, 1980), pp. 205–18.

22. Edith Wharton, *Sanctuary,* in *Madame de Treymes and Others: Four Novelettes,* p. 110. Further references follow in the text.

23. See Schreiber, "Darwin, Wharton, and 'The Descent of Man'," pp. 31–38, for a perceptive analysis of this story.

24. Edith Wharton, "The Mission of Jane," *Collected Stories* 1:371. Further references follow in the text.

25. Jung, "Psychological Aspects of the Kore," in *Archetypes,* p. 203.

26. Edith Wharton, "The House of the Dead Hand," *Collected Stories* 1:509. Further references follow in the text.

27. Elaine Showalter, "The Death of the Lady (Novelist): Wharton's *House of Mirth,*" *Representations* 9 (Winter 1985): 134.

28. In this respect she resembles Hedda Gabler, who represents Kierkegaard's "aesthetic" stage of development, as opposed to the ethical stage where humane consideration of others' realities bears weight. See Søren Kierkegaard, *Either/Or* (1843; reprint ed., New York: Doubleday, 1959).

29. Edith Wharton, *The House of Mirth* (1905; reprint ed., New York: New America Library, 1964), p. 15. Further references follow in the text.

30. Showalter, p. 137.

31. Juliet Mitchell, *Feminism and Psychoanalysis: Freud, Reich, Laing, and Women* (New York: Vintage, 1975), p. 413.

32. Ibid., p. 408.

33. Gayle Rubin, "The Traffic in Women: Notes on the 'Political Economy' of Sex," in *Toward an Anthropology of Women,* ed. Rayna R. Reiter (New York: Monthly Review, 1975), pp. 188–89.

34. Elizabeth Ammons, *Edith Wharton's Argument with America* (Athens: University of Georgia Press, 1980), p. 35. Further references follow in the text.

35. Wendy Gimbel, *Edith Wharton: Orphancy and Survival* (New York: Praeger, 1984), p. 45.

36. Ibid., p. 54.

37. Edith Wharton, "The Hermit and the Wild Woman," *Collected Stories* 1:581. Further references follow in the text.

38. Edith Wharton, *The Fruit of the Tree* (New York: Scribner's, 1907), p. 298. Further references follow in the text.

39. Edith Wharton, "All Souls," *Collected Stories* 2:897.

40. Edith Wharton, "Afterward," *Collected Stories* 2:173.

41. Edith Wharton, "The Letters," *Collected Stories* 2:178. Further references follow in the text.

42. Lewis, *Edith Wharton*, p. 309.

43. Pratt, *Archetypal Patterns*, pp. 22–24. Other Wharton stories that involve this figure include "Fullness of Life" (1893), "The Duchess at Prayer" (1900), "The Lady Maid's Bell" (1902), and "The Pretext" (1908).

44. See Rabuzzi, pp. 146–47, and Donovan, "Sarah Orne Jewett's Critical Theory," for a similar interpretation of "Martha's Lady."

45. Edith Wharton, *Ethan Frome* (1911; reprint ed., New York: Scribner's, 1970), pp. 16, 27. Further references follow in the text.

46. Ammons interprets Zeena as a black witch complete with cat in *Edith Wharton's Argument with America*, pp. 63–64.

47. Sandra Gilbert and Susan Gubar, *The Madwoman in the Attic* (New Haven: Yale University Press, 1979), pp. 77–78, 86.

48. See also Gimbel's interpretation of the elm tree as a symbol of the Great Mother in her terrible aspect, *Edith Wharton*, p. 90.

49. Edith Wharton, "Xingu," *Collected Stories* 2:212. Further references follow in the text.

50. Wharton's assumption and repudiation of sentimentalist themes and characters would be the subject of another book. See Barbara A. White, "Edith Wharton's *Summer* and Women's Fiction," *Essays in Literature* 11, no. 2 (Fall 1984): 223–35, for such material in *Summer*.

51. Edith Wharton, *The Reef* (1912; reprint ed., New York: Scribner's, 1965), p. 29. Further references follow in the text.

52. Ammons, *Edith Wharton's Argument with America*, p. 63.

53. Edith Wharton, *The Custom of the Country* (New York: Scribner's, 1913), p. 75. Further references follow in the text.

54. Edith Wharton, "Kerfol," *Collected Stories* 2:292. Further references follow in the text.

55. Edith Wharton, *Summer* (1918; reprint ed., New York: Harper, 1980), p. 14. Further references follow in the text.

56. Wolff, Appendix, pp. 407–15.

57. Edith Wharton, *The Age of Innocence* (New York: D. Appleton, 1920), p. 38. Further references follow in the text.

58. Ammons, "Cool Diana," p. 222.

59. Edith Wharton, "Writing a War Story," *Collected Stories* 2:370.

60. Adeline R. Tintner, "Mothers, Daughters, and Incest in the Late Novels of Edith Wharton," in *The Lost Tradition,* ed. Davidson and Broner, p. 147.

61. Edith Wharton, *The Old Maid* (New York: D. Appleton, 1924), p. 98. Further references follow in the text.

62. See Ammons, *Edith Wharton's Argument with America,* pp. 188–96, for a perceptive analysis of this theme in the final works.

63. Edith Wharton, *Hudson River Bracketed* (New York: D. Appleton, 1929), p. 336. Further references follow in the text.

64. Edith Wharton, "Pomegranate Seed," *Collected Stories* 2:778. Further references follow in the text.

65. Edith Wharton, "Roman Fever," *Collected Stories* 2:841.

66. O'Brien, *Willa Cather,* p. 369.

67. Wolff, *Feast of Words,* pp. 343, 391, similarly senses an artificiality in Wharton's late works and dismisses them as inferior.

68. Ammons, *Edith Wharton's Argument with America,* p. 173, suggests similarly that Wharton was deeply affected by World War I and that she felt civilization needed to be regrounded in a maternal principle.

Chapter 4

1. E. K. Brown, *Willa Cather: A Critical Biography* (New York: Knopf, 1953), pp. 44–45. In *Willa Cather* Sharon O'Brien characterizes Cather's views in the 1890s as "misogynist," "devaluing women and exalting men" (p. 124).

2. Coral Lansbury, *The Old Brown Dog: Women, Workers, and Vivisection in Edwardian England* (Madison: University of Wisconsin Press, 1985); see also Josephine Donovan, "Animal Rights and Feminist Theory," *Signs* 15, no. 1 (Autumn 1989).

3. Willa Cather, "Four Women Writers," *Leader,* 8 July 1899, in *The World and the Parish: Willa Cather's Articles and Reviews, 1893–1902,* ed. William M. Curtin, 2 vols. (Lincoln: University of Nebraska Press, 1970), 2:697–99. See also *World and the Parish* 1:277; 2:694, n. 3; and 2:961–64.

4. According to George Seibel, cited in Phyllis C. Robinson, *Willa: The Life of Willa Cather* (Garden City, NY: Doubleday, 1983), p. 153.

5. ALS, Willa Cather to Sarah Orne Jewett, 10 May 1908, Houghton Library, Harvard University. Cited by permission of the Houghton Library.

6. ALS, Willa Cather to Sarah Orne Jewett, 18 November [1908], Houghton Library, Harvard University. Cited by permission of the Houghton Library.

7. Especially E. K. Brown, James Woodress, Phyllis Robinson, Sharon O'Brien, and Josephine Donovan.

8. Brown, *Willa Cather,* p. 140.

9. Annie Fields, ed., *Letters of Sarah Orne Jewett* (Boston: Houghton Mifflin, 1911), pp. 247–50.

10. Ibid., pp. 246–47.

11. Jonathan Katz, ed., *Gay American History: Lesbians and Gay Men in the U.S.A.* (New York: Avon, 1976), pp. 353–61.

12. Ibid., pp. 365–68.

13. Willa Cather, "On the Gulls' Road," *McClure's,* December 1908, in *Collected Short*

Fiction, 1892–1912, ed. Virginia Faulkner, rev. ed. (Lincoln: University of Nebraska Press, 1970), p. 87. Further references follow in the text.

14. Sharon O'Brien, " 'The Thing Not Named': Willa Cather as a Lesbian Writer," *Signs* 9, no. 4 (Summer 1984): 582.

15. Ibid., p. 586.

16. "Willa Cather Talks of Work," *Philadelphia Record,* 9 August 1913, in *The Kingdom of Art: Willa Cather's First Principles and Critical Statements, 1893–1896,* ed. Bernice Slote (Lincoln: Unversity of Nebraska Press, 1966), p. 448.

17. Ibid., p. 449.

18. On Jewett's "lesbianism" see Josephine Donovan, "The Unpublished Love Poems of Sarah Orne Jewett," *Frontiers* 4, no. 3 (Fall 1979): 26–31; reprinted in *Critical Essays on Sarah Orne Jewett,* ed. Nagel, pp. 107–17. I follow the broad definition offered by Blanche Wiesen Cook ("women who love women, who choose women to nurture and support and to create a living environment . . . are lesbians"), "Female Support Networks and Political Activism: Lillian Wald, Crystal Eastman, Emma Goldman," *Chrysalis* 3 (1977): 48. See also O'Brien, " 'Thing Not Named,' " and Deborah Lambert, "The Defeat of a Hero: Autonomy and Sexuality in *My Ántonia,*" *American Literature* 53, no. 4 (January 1982): 476–90. In *Willa Cather* O'Brien offers the interesting suggestion that Cather's "relationship to the female literary tradition [which means primarily to Jewett] . . . strongly replays the preoedipal issues characterizing the early mother-daughter bond" (p. 165, n. 22).

19. Moers, *Literary Women,* p. 364.

20. See especially Blanche H. Gelfant, "The Forgotten Reaping Hook: Sex in *My Ántonia*" (1971), in *Critical Essays on Willa Cather,* ed. John J. Murphy (Boston: G. K. Hall, 1984), pp. 147–59; and Sharon O'Brien, "Mothers, Daughters, and the 'Art Necessity': Willa Cather and the Creative Process," in *American Novelists Revisited,* ed. Fleischmann, pp. 265–98.

21. W[illa] Cather, "The Clemency of the Court," in *Collected Short Fiction,* p. 517. Further references follow in the text.

22. O'Brien, " 'Thing Not Named,' " p. 595.

23. [Willa Cather], "The Burglar's Christmas," in *Collected Short Fiction,* p. 565.

24. Willa Cather, "The Strategy of the Were-Wolf Dog," in *Collected Short Fiction,* p. 445. Further references follow in the text.

25. Willa Cather, "Tommy, the Unsentimental," in *Collected Short Fiction,* p. 474. Further references follow in the text. See also Robinson's discussion of this story in *Willa,* pp. 77–78.

26. See Donovan, *New England Local Color Literature,* pp. 20–22, 36, for a discussion of the "female quixote" in American women's fiction.

27. Willa Cather, "A Resurrection," in *Collected Short Fiction,* p. 426. Further references follow in the text.

28. As cited in *Gay American History,* pp. 785–86.

29. Sarah Orne Jewett, *The Country of the Pointed Firs* (Boston: Houghton Mifflin, 1896), p. 174.

30. Willa Cather, "The Way of the World," in *Collected Short Fiction,* p. 401. Further references follow in the text.

31. Willa Sibert Cather, "Eric Hermannson's Soul," in *Collected Short Fiction,* p. 363. Further references follow in the text.

32. Willa Sibert Cather, "El Dorado: A Kansas Recessional," in *Collected Short Fiction*, p. 294. Further references follow in the text. O'Brien suggests that the sense of exile apparent in Cather's view of the plains stems from the fact that Cather's move (as a child) from Virginia to Nebraska "recapitulated the child's separation from the mother" (*Willa Cather*, p. 64). This may explain why East is Eden for Cather.

33. Willa Sibert Cather, "The Professor's Commencement," in *Collected Short Fiction*, p. 286. Further references follow in the text.

34. Willa Sibert Cather, "The Treasure of the Far Island," in *Collected Short Fiction*, p. 268. Further references follow in the text.

35. Rabuzzi has characterized aspects of the traditional female life-style as being in the waiting mode, in *The Sacred and the Feminine*, pp. 143–53. See Donovan, "Sarah Orne Jewett's Critical Theory," pp. 121–25, for an application of this idea to Jewett.

36. Willa Sibert Cather, "A Death in the Desert," in *Collected Short Fiction*, p. 200. Further references follow in the text.

37. *Letters of Sarah Orne Jewett*, pp. 247–48.

38. Willa Sibert Cather, "The Sculptor's Funeral," in *Collected Short Fiction*, p. 179. Further references follow in the text.

39. Moers, *Literary Women*, p. 391.

40. Willa Sibert Cather, "The Joy of Nelly Deane," in *Collected Short Fiction*, p. 60. Further references follow in the text. In *Willa Cather* O'Brien sees this story as a pivotal text, showing Cather's movement "from male to female identification" (p. 376).

41. Elizabeth Sargeant, as cited in O'Brien, "Mothers," p. 278; James Woodress, *Willa Cather: Her Life and Art* (New York: Pegasus, 1970), p. 139.

42. Willa Cather, *Not Under Forty* (New York: Knopf, 1936).

43. Bernice Slote, Introduction to *Alexander's Bridge* (1977), in *Critical Essays on Willa Cather*, p. 98.

44. Ibid., p. 102. Sharon O'Brien, *Willa Cather*, has an interesting discussion of Annie Fields's influence on Cather (pp. 311–325). It was "compelling, authoritative" (311); Cather saw her as a "Beacon Hill Demeter" (319), but she proved too domineering. Jewett's influence, according to O'Brien, proved more nourishing in the end (332).

45. Willa Cather, *Alexander's Bridge & April Twilights* (Boston: Houghton Mifflin, 1937), p. 113. Further references follow in the text.

46. Willa Cather, *O Pioneers!* (1913; reprint ed., Boston: Houghton Mifflin, 1937), p. 13. Further references follow in the text.

47. See Pratt, *Archetypal Patterns*, pp. 16–24.

48. Evelyn Helmick, "The Mysteries of Ántonia," *Midwest Quarterly* 17, no. 2 (January 1976): 176. Further references follow in the text.

49. Willa Cather, *My Ántonia* (1918; reprint ed., Boston: Houghton Mifflin, 1954), pp. 30–32.

50. As cited in Helmick, "Mysteries," pp. 178–79.

51. Willa Cather, *The Song of the Lark* (1915; reprint ed., Lincoln: University of Nebraska Press, 1978), p. 102. Further references follow in the text.

52. The first passage is from O'Brien, "Mothers," p. 284; the second from O'Brien, *Willa Cather*, p. 416.

53. David Stouck, "Willa Cather's Last Four Books" (1973), in *Critical Essays on Willa Cather*, p. 295.

54. Ibid., p. 299.

55. As cited in O'Brien, "Mothers," p. 268. For a further discussion of Cather's growing inclination toward women's folk art, see Josephine Donovan, "Willa Cather and Women's Art" (forthcoming).

56. Cather, *Not Under Forty*, preface.

57. Leon Edel interprets it this way in "A Cave of One's Own" (1959), in *Critical Essays on Willa Cather*, p. 214.

58. See Slote, Introduction, p. 108, and Susan J. Rosowski, "The Pattern of Willa Cather's Novels," *Western American Literature* 15, no. 4 (February 1981): 243–63.

59. Willa Cather, *One of Ours* (New York: Knopf, 1922), p. 207. Further references follow in the text.

60. Willa Cather, *A Lost Lady* (New York: Knopf, 1923), p. 169.

61. Evelyn Thomas Helmick, "The Broken World: Medievalism in *A Lost Lady*" (1975), in *Critical Essays on Willa Cather*, p. 185.

62. Leon Edel sees the professor as in a state of infantile regression, "A Cave of One's Own," p. 207; Blanche Gelfant views him as an example of childish narcissism, "The Forgotten Reaping Hook," p. 151.

63. Hélène Cixous, "The Laugh of the Medusa" (1976), in *New French Feminisms*, p. 252.

64. Willa Cather, *The Professor's House* (New York: Knopf, 1925), pp. 22–23. Further references follow in the text.

65. See chap. 3, pp. 58–62 (discussion of *House of Mirth*); see also Donovan, *Feminist Theory*, pp. 107–9.

66. See Jane Lilienfeld, "Reentering Paradise: Cather, Colette, Woolf and Their Mothers," in *The Lost Tradition*, ed. Davidson and Broner, pp. 163–64; and O'Brien, "Mothers," pp. 293–95.

67. As cited in Brown, *Willa Cather*, p. 277.

68. Willa Cather, "Old Mrs. Harris," in *Obscure Destinies* (New York: Knopf, 1932), p. 190.

69. Willa Cather, *Lucy Gayheart* (New York: Knopf, 1935), p. 225. Further references follow in the text.

70. Edel, "A Cave of One's Own," p. 207.

71. Willa Cather, "The Best Years," in *The Old Beauty and Others* (New York: Knopf, 1948), p. 97. Further references follow in the text.

Chapter 5

1. J. R. Roper, *Without Shelter: The Early Career of Ellen Glasgow* (Baton Rouge: Louisiana State University Press, 1971), identifies the garden/jungle dichotomy in Glasgow, but he sees it in the context of southern American history.

2. Ellen Glasgow, *One Man in His Time* (Garden City, NY: Doubleday, Page, 1922), p. 282. Further references follow in the text.

3. Ellen Glasgow, *A Certain Measure: An Interpretation of Prose Fiction* (1938; reprint ed., New York: Harcourt, Brace, 1943), p. 14.

4. Ellen Glasgow, " 'Evasive Idealism' in Literature," in *Literature in the Making by Some of Its Makers*, ed. Joyce Kilmer (New York: Harper, 1917), p. 238.

5. Linda W. Wagner, *Ellen Glasgow: Beyond Convention* (Austin: University of Texas Press, 1982), p. ix.

6. Ellen Glasgow, *The Descendant* (1897; reprint ed., New York: Arno, 1977), p. 92. Further references follow in the text.

7. Ellen Glasgow, *Phases of an Inferior Planet* (New York: Harper, 1898), p. 48. Further references follow in the text.

8. In *A Certain Measure*, p. 29, Glasgow indicates that her publishers were encouraging her to write the then popular historical romances. Even Jewett succumbed to this fad with her *Tory Lover* in 1901.

9. In *The Deliverance* (New York: Doubleday, Page, 1904) there is an interesting female resurrection pattern, which anticipates that seen in later works: Maria Fletcher says of her first marriage: "I went down into hell" (435). Renewed appreciation of the natural world effects her resurrection (345–46).

10. Ellen Glasgow, *The Wheel of Life* (New York: Doubleday, Page, 1906), p. 78. Further references follow in the text.

11. Ellen Glasgow, *The Ancient Law* (New York: Doubleday, Page, 1908), p. 105. Further references follow in the text.

12. Ellen Glasgow, *Barren Ground* (1925; reprint ed., New York: Random, 1933), p. 46. Further references follow in the text.

13. Ellen Glasgow, *The Romance of a Plain Man* (New York: Macmillan, 1909), p. 32. Further references follow in the text.

14. See Pratt, *Archetypal Patterns*, pp. 22–24.

15. Ellen Glasgow, *The Miller of the Old Church* (Garden City, NY: Doubleday, Page, 1911), p. 361. Further references follow in the text.

16. Ellen Glasgow, *Virginia* (1913; reprint ed., Garden City, NY: Doubleday, Doran, 1938), p. 13. Further references follow in the text.

17. Ellen Glasgow, *The Woman Within* (New York: Harcourt, 1954), p. 9. Other women writers of the period also used the fox hunt in similarly symbolic terms with the woman identified with the fox, most notably and explicitly in Mary Webb's *Gone to Earth* (1917) but also in Radclyffe Hall's *Well of Loneliness* (1928). See also Harriette Arnow, *Hunter's Horn* (1949).

18. Glasgow, *Woman Within*, p. 39.

19. See chap. 3, n. 27.

20. See chap. 4, pp. 86–87.

21. Ellen Glasgow, *Life and Gabriella: The Story of a Woman's Courage* (Garden City, NY: Doubleday, Page, 1916), p. 5. Further references follow in the text.

22. Ellen Glasgow, "Whispering Leaves," in *The Collected Stories of Ellen Glasgow*, ed. Richard K. Meeker ([Baton Rouge]: Louisiana State University Press, 1963), p. 146. "The Shadowy Third" and "Dare's Gift" are also in this collection.

23. Glasgow, *Woman Within*, pp. 19, 144.

24. Ellen Glasgow, preface to *Barren Ground* (1933), p. v. I might mention here that *Barren Ground*, more than other Glasgow novels, contains racist passages. While these do not intrude upon my thesis, they do mar the novel. One can, of course, argue that Glasgow was merely mimetically reflecting the prejudices of her day, and this does seem to be the case—given her generally liberal outlook. Nevertheless, in *Barren Ground* an

ironic critical context is not clearly enough presented for one to be sure. Many of the blacks in the work come across as at best quaint local decor and at worst stereotypically inferior beings. To what extent Glasgow's Darwinism infected her views of race is not clear to me, but I fear it may have.

25. Ellen Glasgow, *They Stooped to Folly: A Comedy of Morals* (Garden City, NY: Doubleday, Doran, 1929), p. 185. Further references follow in the text.

26. Ellen Glasgow, *The Sheltered Life* (Garden City, NY: Doubleday, Doran, 1932), p. 142. Further references follow in the text.

27. Ellen Glasgow, *Vein of Iron* (1935; reprint ed., New York: Harcourt Brace Jovanovich, 1963), p. 4. Further references follow in the text.

28. See Donovan, *Feminist Theory*, pp. 72, 89.

Conclusion

1. Here the work of Pierre Macherey seems relevant: "the work is certainly determined by its relation to ideology, but this relation . . . is always more or less contradictory. A work is established against an ideology as much as it is from an ideology" (*A Theory of Literary Production* [London: Routledge and Kegan Paul, 1978], p. 133).

2. Fredric Jameson, *The Political Unconscious: Narrative as a Socially Symbolic Act* (Ithaca: Cornell University Press, 1981), p. 79. This discussion owes much to Jameson, especially pp. 67–102.

3. See ibid., pp. 235–36; also Georg Lukács's *History and Class Consciousness* (1922).

4. Herbert Marcuse, *One-Dimensional Man* (Boston: Beacon, 1964), p. 127.

5. Ernst Bloch, *A Philosophy of the Future* (1970), in *Marxism and Art: Essays Classic and Contemporary*, ed. Maynard Solomon (1973; reprint ed., Detroit: Wayne State University Press, 1979), pp. 584–85.

6. Josephine Donovan, "Afterword: Critical Re-Vision," in *Feminist Literary Criticism: Explorations in Theory*, ed. Donovan (Lexington: University Press of Kentucky, 1975), p. 75. See also Josephine Donovan, "Radical Feminist Criticism," in *Feminist Literary Criticism: Explorations in Theory*, 2d ed. (Lexington: University Press of Kentucky, 1989) for an elaboration of the ideas presented in this conclusion.

7. Fredric Jameson, *Marxism and Form: Twentieth-Century Dialectical Theories of Literature* (Princeton: Princeton University Press, 1971), p. 115.

8. Herbert Marcuse, *Eros and Civilization* (1955; reprint ed., New York: Vintage, 1962), pp. 209–10. Freud made this connection himself in "Female Sexuality" (1931), where he compared the preoedipal period with Minoan civilization, a connection further developed by Juliet Mitchell in *Feminism and Psychoanalysis*, pp. 56, 109–12, 366 (see also Donovan, *Feminist Theory*, chap. 4).

Marx's vision of a classless society is really that of a "primitive matriarchal communism," as noted by Maynard Solomon; its primary description obtains in Engels's *Origin of the Family* (1884), which relies heavily on nineteenth-century matriarchal theory, in particular Lewis Morgan's *Ancient Society* (1877). Solomon notes: "The first alienation in biology is the separation of the child from the mother; class society begins with matricide. Prehistory will end with the restoration of subject and object, with the smashing of the instrumentalities of the state (which are the historical-symbolical projections of father-right), and by the ultimate 'withering away' of the state itself. It is the revolutionary restoration . . . of primitive communism and of the primal mother-child harmony which is the Marxist Utopia" (*Marxism and Art,* p. 470).

Appendix I

1. Madeline Moore, *The Short Season between Two Silences: The Mystical and the Political in the Novels of Virginia Woolf* (Boston: Allen and Unwin, 1984), p. 25.

2. Jane Marcus, "Thinking Back through Our Mothers," in *New Feminist Essays on Virginia Woolf,* ed. Jane Marcus (Lincoln: University of Nebraska Press, 1981), p. 13.

3. Moore, p. 155.

4. Ibid., p. 42; Marcus, "Thinking Back," p. 13.

5. Virginia Woolf, *The Voyage Out* (1915; reprint ed., London: Hogarth Press, 1957), p. 347.

6. Louise DeSalvo, *Virginia Woolf's First Voyage: A Novel in the Making* (Totowa, NJ: Rowman and Littlefield, 1980), p. 33. Further references follow in the text.

7. Pratt, *Archetypal Patterns,* p. 171.

8. Mary Webb, *Gone to Earth* (1917; reprint ed., New York: E. P. Dutton, 1934), p. 3.

9. Ibid., p. 75.

10. Jane Lilienfeld, "The Magic Spinning Wheel: Straw to Gold—Colette, Willy, and Sido," in *Mothering the Mind,* ed. Perry and Brownley, p. 167.

11. Colette, *My Apprenticeships* (New York: Farrar, Straus and Giroux, 1978), pp. 21–23.

12. Ibid., p. 23.

Appendix II

1. See Rose, pp. 262–63, and Hamilton, pp. 270–71, for summaries of this myth.

2. Margaret Homans, *Bearing the Word: Language and Female Experience in Nineteenth-Century Women's Writing* (Chicago: University of Chicago Press, 1986), p. 41. Further references follow in the text.

Selected Bibliography

Ammons, Elizabeth. *Edith Wharton's Argument with America*. Athens: University of Georgia Press, 1980.

Brown, E. K. *Willa Cather: A Critical Biography*. New York: Knopf, 1953.

Cather, Willa. *Alexander's Bridge & April Twilights*. Boston: Houghton Mifflin, 1937.

———. *Collected Short Fiction, 1892–1912*. Ed. Virginia Faulkner. Rev. ed. Lincoln: University of Nebraska Press, 1970.

———. *A Lost Lady*. New York: Knopf, 1923.

———. *Lucy Gayheart*. New York: Knopf. 1935.

———. *My Ántonia*. 1918. Reprint. New York: Houghton Mifflin, 1954.

———. *Not Under Forty*. New York: Knopf, 1936.

———. *O Pioneers!* 1913. Reprint. Boston: Houghton Mifflin, 1937.

———. *Obscure Destinies*. New York: Knopf, 1932.

———. *The Old Beauty and Others*. New York: Knopf, 1948.

———. *One of Ours*. New York: Knopf, 1922.

———. *The Professor's House*. New York: Knopf, 1925.

———. *The Song of the Lark*. 1915. Reprint. Lincoln: University of Nebraska Press, 1978.

Curtin, William M., ed. *The World and the Parish: Willa Cather's Articles and Reviews, 1893–1902*. 2 vols. Lincoln: University of Nebraska Press, 1970.

Darwin, Charles. *The Descent of Man, and Selection in Relation to Sex*. 1871. Rev. 2d ed. New York: American Publishers, 1874.

Davidson, Cathy N., and E. M. Broner, eds. *The Lost Tradition: Mothers and Daughters in Literature*. New York: Ungar, 1980.

Donovan, Josephine. *Feminist Theory: The Intellectual Traditions of American Feminism*. New York: Ungar, 1985.

———. *New England Local Color Literature: A Women's Tradition*. New York: Ungar, 1983.

———, ed. *Feminist Literary Criticism: Explorations in Theory*. 2d ed. Lexington: University Press of Kentucky, 1989.

Evelyn-White, Hugh G., ed. and trans. *Hesiod, the Homeric Hymns and Homerica*. Cambridge: Harvard University Press, 1964.

Faderman, Lillian. *Surpassing the Love of Men: Friendship and Romantic Love between Women from the Renaissance to the Present.* New York: Morrow, 1981.

Fields, Annie, ed. *Letters of Sarah Orne Jewett.* Boston: Houghton Mifflin, 1911.

Fleischmann, Fritz, ed. *American Novelists Revisited: Essays in Feminist Criticism.* Boston: G. K. Hall, 1982.

Foucault, Michel. *Power/Knowledge: Selected Interviews and Other Writings 1972–1977.* Ed. Colin Gordon. New York: Pantheon, 1980.

———. *La volonté de savoir. Histoire de la sexualité.* Vol. 1. Paris: Gallimard, 1976.

Frazer, Sir James. *The Golden Bough: A Study in Magic and Religion.* Abridged ed. New York: Macmillan, 1951.

Freeman, Mary E. Wilkins. *The Love of Parson Lord and Other Stories.* 1900. Reprint. Freeport, NY: Books for Libraries Press, 1969.

———. *A New England Nun and Other Stories.* New York: Harper, 1891.

———. *Silence and Other Stories.* New York: Harper, 1898.

———. *Understudies.* New York: Harper, 1901.

———. *The Winning Lady and Others.* New York: Harper, 1909.

Gimbel, Wendy. *Edith Wharton: Orphancy and Survival.* New York: Praeger, 1984.

Glasgow, Ellen. *The Ancient Law.* New York: Doubleday, Page, 1908.

———. *Barren Ground.* 1925. Reprint. New York: Random, 1933.

———. *A Certain Measure: An Interpretation of Prose Fiction.* 1938. Reprint. New York: Harcourt, Brace, 1943.

———. *The Collected Stories of Ellen Glasgow.* Ed. Richard K. Meeker. [Baton Rouge]: Louisiana State University Press, 1963.

———. *The Deliverance.* New York: Doubleday, Page, 1904.

———. *The Descendant.* 1897. Reprint. New York: Arno, 1977.

———. *Life and Gabriella: The Story of a Woman's Courage.* Garden City, NY: Doubleday, Page, 1916.

———. *The Miller of the Old Church.* Garden City, NY: Doubleday, Page, 1911.

———. *One Man in His Time.* Garden City, NY: Doubleday, Page, 1922.

———. *Phases of an Inferior Planet.* New York: Harper, 1898.

———. *The Romance of a Plain Man.* New York: Macmillan, 1909.

———. *The Sheltered Life.* Garden City, NY: Doubleday, Doran, 1932.

———. *They Stooped to Folly: A Comedy of Morals.* Garden City, NY: Doubleday, Doran, 1929.

———. *Vein of Iron.* 1935. Reprint. New York: Harcourt Brace Jovanovich, 1963.

———. *Virginia.* 1913. Reprint. Garden City, NY: Doubleday, Doran, 1938.

———. *The Wheel of Life.* New York: Doubleday, Page, 1906.

———. *The Woman Within.* New York: Harcourt, 1954.

Graves, Robert. *The White Goddess: A Historical Grammar of Poetic Myth.* 1948. Reprint. New York: Octagon, 1976.

Hamilton, Edith. *Mythology.* 1940. Reprint. New York: Mentor, 1959.

Harrison, Jane. *Prolegomena to the Study of Greek Religion.* 1903. Reprint. New York: Meridian, 1957.

Jameson, Fredric. *The Political Unconscious: Narrative as a Socially Symbolic Art.* Ithaca: Cornell University Press, 1981.

Jewett, Sarah Orne. *A Country Doctor.* Boston: Houghton Mifflin, 1884.

———. *The Country of the Pointed Firs and Other Stories.* Garden City, NY: Anchor, 1956.

Jung, C. G. *The Archetypes and the Collective Unconscious.* 2d ed. Princeton: Princeton University Press, 1969.

Katz, Jonathan, ed. *Gay American History: Lesbians and Gay Men in the U.S.A.* New York: Avon, 1976.

———. *Gay/Lesbian Almanac: A New Documentary.* New York: Harper, 1983.

Kerényi, C. *Eleusis: Archetypal Image of Mother and Daughter.* New York: Pantheon/ Bollinger, 1967.

Krafft-Ebing, R. v. *Psychopathia Sexualis, with Especial Reference to the Antipathic Sexual Instinct.* Trans. F. J. Rebman (of the 12th German ed.). New York: Medical Art Agency, 1906.

Lacan, Jacques. *The Language of the Self: The Function of Language in Psychoanalysis.* Trans. Anthony Wilden. Baltimore: Johns Hopkins University Press, 1968.

Lewis, R. W. B. *Edith Wharton: A Biography.* New York: Harper, 1975.

Marcuse, Herbert. *Eros and Civilization.* 1955. Reprint. New York: Vintage, 1962.

———. *One-Dimensional Man.* Boston: Beacon, 1964.

Mitchell, Juliet. *Psychoanalysis and Feminism: Freud, Reich, Laing and Women.* 1974. Reprint. New York: Vintage, 1975.

Murphy, John J., ed. *Critical Essays on Willa Cather.* Boston: G. K. Hall, 1984.

O'Brien, Sharon. *Willa Cather: The Emerging Voice.* New York: Oxford University Press, 1987.

Perry, Ruth, and Martine Watson Brownley. *Mothering the Mind: Twelve Studies of Writers and Their Silent Partners.* New York: Holmes and Meier, 1984.

Pratt, Annis. *Archetypal Patterns in Women's Fiction.* Bloomington: Indiana University Press, 1981.

Rabuzzi, Kathryn Allen. *The Sacred and the Feminine: Toward a Theology of Housework.* New York: Seabury, 1982.

Robinson, Phyllis C. *Willa: The Life of Willa Cather.* Garden City, NY: Doubleday, 1983.

Roper, J. R. *Without Shelter: The Early Career of Ellen Glasgow.* Baton Rouge: Louisiana State University Press, 1971.

Rose, H. J. *A Handbook of Greek Mythology.* New York: Dutton, 1959.

Sahli, Nancy. "Smashing: Women's Relationships before the Fall." *Chrysalis* 8 (Summer 1979): 17–27.

Slote, Bernice, ed. *The Kingdom of Art: Willa Cather's First Principles and Critical Statements, 1893–1896.* Lincoln: University of Nebraska Press, 1966.

Smith-Rosenberg, Carroll. *Disorderly Conduct: Visions of Gender in Victorian America.* New York: Knopf, 1985.

Solomon, Maynard, ed. *Marxism and Art: Essays Classic and Contemporary.* 1973. Reprint. Detroit: Wayne State University Press, 1979.

Squier, Susan Merrill, ed. *Women Writers and the City: Essays in Feminist Literary Criticism.* Knoxville: University of Tennessee Press, 1984.

Wagner, Linda W. *Ellen Glasgow: Beyond Convention.* Austin: University of Texas Press, 1982.

Wharton, Edith. *The Age of Innocence.* New York: D. Appleton, 1920.

———. *A Backward Glance.* New York: Scribner's, 1934.

———. *The Collected Short Stories of Edith Wharton.* Ed. R. W. B. Lewis. 2 vols. New York: Scribner's, 1968.

———. *The Custom of the Country.* New York: Scribner's, 1913.

——. *Ethan Frome*. 1911. Reprint. New York: Scribner's, 1970.

——. *The Fruit of the Tree*. New York: Scribner's, 1907.

——. *The Gods Arrive*. New York: D. Appleton, 1932.

——. *The House of Mirth*. 1905. Reprint. New York: New America Library, 1964.

——. *Hudson River Bracketed*. New York: D. Appleton, 1929.

——. *Madame de Treymes and Others: Four Novelettes*. New York: Scribner's, 1970.

——. *The Old Maid*. New York: D. Appleton, 1924.

——. *The Reef*. 1912. Reprint. New York: Scribner's, 1965.

——. *Summer*. 1918. Reprint. New York: Harper, 1980.

——. *The Valley of Decision*. 2 vols. New York: Scribner's, 1902.

Wolff, Cynthia Griffin. *A Feast of Words: The Triumph of Edith Wharton*. New York: Oxford University Press, 1977.

Woodress, James. *Willa Cather: Her Life and Art*. New York: Pegasus, 1970.

Woolf, Virginia. *Moments of Being*. Ed. Jeanne Schulkind. 2d ed. San Diego: Harcourt Brace Jovanovich, 1985.

Index